SAVING FACE

Faces are all around us and fundamentally shape both everyday experience and our understanding of people. To lose face is to be alienated and experience shame, to be enfaced is to enjoy the fullness of life. In theology, as in many other disciplines, faces, as both physical phenomena and symbols, have not received the critical, appreciative attention they deserve.

This pioneering book explores the nature of face and enfacement, both human and divine. Pattison discusses questions concerning what face is, how important face is in human life and relationships, and how we might understand face, both as a physical phenomenon and as a series of socially-inflected symbols and metaphors about the self and the body. Examining what face means in terms of inclusion and exclusion in contemporary human society and how it is related to shame, Pattison reveals what the experiences of people who have difficulties with faces tell us about our society, our understandings of, and our reactions to face.

Exploring this ubiquitous yet ignored area of both contemporary human experience and of the Christian theological tradition, Pattison explains how Christian theology understands face, both human and divine, and the insights it might offer to understanding face and enfacement. Does God in any sense have a physically visible face? What is the significance of having an enfaced or faceless God for Christian life and practice? What does the vision of God mean now? If we want to take face and defacing shame seriously, and to get them properly into perspective, we may need to change our theology, thought and practice – changing our ways of thinking about God and about theology.

Explorations in Practical, Pastoral and Empirical Theology

Series Editors

Leslie J. Francis, University of Warwick, UK
Jeff Astley, St Chad's College, Durham University, UK
Martyn Percy, Ripon College Cuddesdon and The Oxford
Ministry Course, Oxford, UK

Theological reflection on the church's practice is now recognized as a significant element in theological studies in the academy and seminary. Ashgate's series in practical, pastoral and empirical theology seeks to foster this resurgence of interest and encourage new developments in practical and applied aspects of theology worldwide. This timely series draws together a wide range of disciplinary approaches and empirical studies to embrace contemporary developments including: the expansion of research in empirical theology, psychological theology, ministry studies, public theology, Christian education and faith development; key issues of contemporary society such as health, ethics and the environment; and more traditional areas of concern such as pastoral care and counselling.

Other titles in the series include:

Using the Bible in Practical Theology
Historical and Contemporary Perspectives
Zoe Bennett

Military Chaplaincy in Contention
Chaplains, Churches and the Morality of Conflict
Andrew Todd

Exploring Ordinary Theology
Everyday Christian Believing and the Church
Edited by Jeff Astley and Leslie J. Francis

Asylum-Seeking, Migration and Church
Susanna Snyder

How Survivors of Abuse Relate to God
The Authentic Spirituality of the Annihilated Soul
Susan Shooter

Saving Face
Enfacement, Shame, Theology

STEPHEN PATTISON
University of Birmingham, UK

ASHGATE

Published by
Ashgate Publishing Limited
Wey Court East
Union Road
Farnham
Surrey, GU9 7PT
England

Ashgate Publishing Company
110 Cherry Street
Suite 3-1
Burlington, VT 05401-3818
USA

www.ashgate.com

British Library Cataloguing in Publication Data
A catalogue record for this book is available from the British Library

The Library of Congress has cataloged the printed edition as follows:
Pattison, Stephen.
  Saving face : enfacement, shame, theology / by Stephen Pattison.
     pages cm. -- (Explorations in practical, pastoral, and empirical theology)
  Includes bibliographical references and index.
  ISBN 978-1-4094-3691-1 (hardcover) -- ISBN 978-1-4094-3692-8 (pbk.) -- ISBN 978-1-4094-3693-5 (ebook) -- ISBN 978-1-4724-0419-0 (epub) 1. Interpersonal relations. 2. Dignity. 3. Appearance (Philosophy) 4. Social psychology. I. Title.
  HM1106.P38 2013
  302--dc23

                                                                                    2013002711

ISBN 9781409436911 (hbk)
ISBN 9781409436928 (pbk)
ISBN 9781409436935 (ebk – PDF)
ISBN 9781472404190 (ebk – ePUB)

Printed in the United Kingdom by Henry Ling Limited, at the Dorset Press, Dorchester, DT1 1HD

Contents

This book is dedicated to the memory of
Philip Cadbury
(1953–1982)
whose face continues to live in my heart and mind

Preface

I have been very lucky to have had a great deal of help in putting the text of this book together.

The first bit of luck came with the invitation to be a visiting scholar at the Centre for Medical Humanities in Durham in autumn 2010, a position generously supported by the Wellcome Trust. I am very grateful to the members of the Centre, academic and administrative, who made me so welcome: particular thanks to the Directors, Martyn Evans and Jane Macnaughton, and to Sarah Atkinson and Corinne Saunders, the Associate Directors. I would also like to thank Angela Woods and Polly De Giorgi who helped me a lot in theoretical and very practical ways while I was trying to get the outline of the book in order and to undertake basic research. Two academics from Durham's stellar theology department were kind enough to spare me some time; Andrew Louth and Mark McIntosh stimulated my thoughts and saved me a lot of wasted effort. I would like to pay tribute to the interdisciplinary imagination of the Centre, and of Durham University in general. I could not have had a better place in which to begin a project of this kind. I am also very grateful to the staff and residents of Trevelyan College where I spent a very happy term, partly and memorably snowed in!

A number of people have commented on, or provided stimulus for, aspects of the book, often in response to talks and presentations. In this connection I would like to thank, in no particular order, Drew Gibson, Chris Hughes, Manon Ceridwen Parry, Sally Nash, Cecelia Clegg, Alan Boyd, Chris Rowland, Jolyon Mitchell, Nicola Slee and James Poling.

Daniel Louw, Frances Young and Robert Jewett made fundamental contributions to the basic thinking underpinning this work, and I thank them deeply for their interest, trouble and stimulus. I would also like to express my gratitude to Charles Strietelmeier for allowing me to use one of his poems here.

Chris Shannahan picked up my work for a term which allowed me to finish this book, and I am very grateful to him for his very safe pair of hands. Charmian Beer very kindly read and straightened out parts, and also shared the journey of turning swirling ideas into linear prose. Thank you both, very much indeed.

Sarah Lloyd and her team at Ashgate have been wonderfully engaged, efficient, responsive, patient, helpful and kind as publishers. What higher tribute can I pay them?

This book is dedicated to the memory of a person whose face I have not seen for 30 years, and will never see alive again. Philip Cadbury was a close school friend who died accidentally when we were both 29. A courageous, committed social activist and peace worker, I continue to grieve his loss and unfulfilled potential: 'Blessed are the peacemakers, for they will be called children of God' (Matt. 5:9).

Stephen Pattison
Birmingham
Advent 2012

Introduction
Lost Faces

Blessed are the pure in heart,
they shall see God.

(Matt. 5:8 NJB)

So long thy power has blest me, sure it still will lead me on,
Oe'r moor and fen, o'er crag and torrent, till the night is gone,
And with the morn those angel faces smile,
Which I have loved long since, and lost a while.

(John Henry Newman, 'Lead, kindly Light')

One of the least-noted, but most human, poignant passages in the New Testament (NT), is to be found in Acts 20. There, the apostle Paul tells the elders of the church at Ephesus that they will not see his face again because he is going to Jerusalem; he does not know what will happen to him there. He prays with them, and then, the author records, 'By now they were all in tears; they put their arms round Paul's neck and kissed him; what saddened them most was his saying they would never see his face again' (Acts 20:27 NJB). It seems really to have mattered to the elders, as it might to anyone, that they were not going to see Paul's physical face. It was going to be lost to them.

Passages like the one from Acts, and the last two lines of Cardinal Newman's hymn, 'Lead, kindly light', where finding faces is mentioned, have haunted me since childhood. In the case of the latter, I am unable to hear them without a mixture of sadness and joy. I think this is probably because I see the angel faces in my mind's eye as a sign of coming home, a mediation of the shining, smiling face of God, enjoying and accepting humanity in mutual joy.

This vision of God is what is promised to the pure in heart in the beatitudes (Matt. 5:8). Indeed, for centuries, the aim and end of Christian life was the direct, face-to-face vision of the face of God, the *visio dei*. This idea is also implicit in the Aaronic blessing in the Old Testament (OT):

May Yahweh bless you and keep you.
May Yahweh let his face shine on you
and be gracious to you.
May Yahweh show you his face
and bring you his peace. (Num. 6:24–6 NJB)

This is a beatific vision, indeed! The sight of God's face is reflected in the face of the humans created in his image and all shine, and are changed, by the vision of God's glory (2 Cor. 3:18–4:6).

For many of us 'normally' sighted and enfaced humans, it is in the face of another that we find ourselves recognised and reflected. So seeing the face of God or that of another person is an apposite, profound metaphor for having a close and intimate encounter, for experiencing full presence in which we are recognised, known and seen for what we are, with love.

It is curious, then, that both human and divine faces seem to have been almost wholly absent in recent Christian theology and practice. Theology, especially post-Enlightenment Western Protestant theology, has emphasised hearing and obeying the word of God, rather than seeing God or the face of the divine (Pattison 2007b, 91–103). At best, the face of God is regarded as a thin metaphor for the presence of a firmly invisible divinity. And in ecclesial and pastoral practice, there has been a similar emphasis on words and hearing (Morris 2008). Following Freud and other modern intellectuals and therapists, Christian pastoral practice, while often a matter of direct face-to-face encounter, has tended to emphasise the oral and the aural, what is said and heard, not the visual (Searles 1984). In a sense, people become narratives or texts, and their faces, along with their bodies, become taken-for-granted, even invisible (Elkins 1997, 165–70).

In contemporary Christian life and thought, then, face, whether human or divine, is largely absent or invisible, except as a metaphor for presence. Face, particularly physical face, is lost or missing. It is as if, for those of us who see faces, they are too common to be worth thinking about. They are so glaringly obvious that we seem to become unaware to them, or at least unconscious of them, so we do not regard them as being worthy of particular note or consideration.

In this book, I hope to do something to restore face to a more central, conscious place in Christian theology and practice. Saving face is redeeming face. Redemption is a complex, multifaceted theological concept. I am going to take redemption and saving here simply to denote bringing face back into awareness, attention and consciousness, this for the benefit of individuals and of humankind as a whole. There are three main categories of face that I want to suggest need this kind of redemption or bringing back: human faces generally; problematic faces that seem to raise difficulties for self, others and society; and the face of God.

This is not just a matter of finding a neglected concept or phenomenon and then trying to exaggerate its importance for the sake of general interest. Rather, I see this as a vital and important pastoral imperative. For the loss of face as a category not only denotes disinterest in face, it also serves as an important sign and accompaniment for shame and exclusion.

Those who have lost face, whose faces are not seen or recognised or who are seen by others with expressions of disgust on their faces, may experience shame. Shame as a social and psychological phenomenon is often understood in visual terms: the personally shamed person will often physically lower their eyes, slump and avoid the gaze of others, failing to engage with them facially (Hollander 2003).

And it is often possible to be shamed and excluded by being facially disfigured or damaged in some way, or by physically having difficulty in recognising and responding to the faces of others; people whose faces do not work properly because they have had strokes or Parkinson's disease, for example, can experience a kind of exclusion from the visual, enfaced world that dehumanises them.

On the other hand, to be given face, to be enfaced, is to have a recognised, honoured and respected place in the community. The person who belongs and is wanted feels the faces of others shining upon them. They take their place in a community of metaphorically, and sometimes literally, smiling, shining faces. To be possessed of face, literally and metaphorically, is to have the potential for a full, rich personal and social life. To have lost face, in whatever sense, may be to live an excluded, diminished existence.

This book explores some aspects of the phenomenon of face in all its many different senses. But in some ways, of course, it is arbitrary to think about face on its own. Where does 'face' begin and end? Does it include the hair and the throat, or are we just talking about the visible skin from the chin up to the forehead and round to the ears? When we meet people, we encounter them in social and material contexts with artefacts; we see them as whole bodies, capable of different postures movements and gestures, not just as Cheshire cat-like faces cut off from the rest of themselves.

Nonetheless, face is often identified as a separate category for both academic study and everyday appreciation or denigration; thus, it seems reasonable to follow the contemporary trend to focus on face almost as an isolated entity. It must be remembered, however, that it is constantly being drawn back into the whole body and socio-physical context of life.

Reifying and separating face off for purposes of close consideration has the advantage of bringing into focus this complex, protean organ that moves so quickly and is so important in human relationships and understandings of what it is to be human. Face and faces are seen through metaphors and socially constructed meanings, but they are also themselves the source of many signs, metaphors and metonyms. Thus, they can easily be seen as the centre of the self, the entrance to the person. Face therefore deserves some particular attention as we try to establish something of both the 'facts' and the meanings surrounding it.

Having suggested what these might be for contemporary humans, it will then be expedient to consider what the theological tradition and notions of the face of God might add to the understanding of both God and humanity before asking some questions about how we might better respond to faces, shamed and shining, in the world today. If the pastoral task is to help to include those who are rejected and marginalised within God's loving gaze – to help them find face before God's face and so to find face ourselves and maybe together to have the possibility of seeing God face-to-face – then we need to think much more carefully about faces of all kinds and to take them, whether metaphorically or physically, more seriously. It is my instinct that there is a sense in which, somehow, God and humans together create and reflect each other's faces; in some way, they must enface each other

(Pattison 2000, 315). Exploring what this might or might not mean in theory and practice is the main substance of this critical, but constructive, exercise in practical theological endeavour.

Many people, particularly those who are blind, would maintain that face is overrated and preoccupation with it reinforces the unthinking hegemony of able-bodied normativity in life, thought and theology (Hull 1991, 2000; Kleege 1999; Magee and Milligan 1998). While I think this view is extremely important, perversely, perhaps, I will be arguing that those who live in the sighted world and think with its categories do not take physical faces and their implications seriously enough. Nonetheless, it is important to recognise the critique from the perspective of disablement, and to affirm that it is normal to have a full, integrated emotional, personal and social life without being unduly concerned about face. It is my view that face is, paradoxically, both over- and under-estimated in our understandings of what it is to be human (Abe 2006, 32).

The Approach of Practical Theology

The approach I adopt here embodies a particular version of practical theology. Modern practical theology, broadly conceived, is concerned with critically considering the implications of belief and thought for practice, and the implications of practice for belief and thought (Woodward and Pattison 2000). Practical theologians are students of action-influencing worldviews – undergirding beliefs and assumptions – that structure life and practice. They work from the perspective of being committed inhabitants of a particular worldview, in my case, Christianity. Practical theologians are concerned with what people do, why they do it, and the implications of this for their faith, thought and practice. They then relate this in a critical way to faith traditions which are taken to contain insight, truth and validity.

Practical theology asks, from a standpoint of faith commitment:

- What do people do?
- Why do people do what they do?
- What do they think and believe about what they are doing?
- How do the ways in which people act affect what they think and believe, and vice versa?

And, finally:

- Should they change their ways of acting, thinking or believing?

The most important question in practical theology is, 'So what?' Thinking, analysis, understanding and faith must be correlated with concrete ways of acting, or this kind of theology is not actually practical.

Practical theology tends to proceed from *description* – what is the case – through *understanding* – why is it this way – to *prescription* – what might be done and considered differently – and then to *action*. This broadly characterises the movement of this book. It starts here by considering the issue that face, apparently such an important part of human life and experience, is so relatively ignored in Christian theology and practice. It then moves on to try to understand how face can be analysed and understood using the insights of a variety of different disciplines from evolutionary biology and art history to philosophy. Thereafter, it engages in conversation with aspects of the theological tradition to a point where some suggestions can be made as to how face should be understood and responded to.

An easy way of understanding this process is as a searching, critical, interdisciplinary conversation between contemporary human experience, the insights of modern non-theological disciplines and practices and aspects of the theological tradition (Pattison and Woodward 2000). We want to know more about face and how to understand and respond to it in the light of the Christian theological tradition so we draw in various theological and non-theological partners for a metaphorical 'conversation' in which we can discover new ways of thinking and acting.

The Structure of Book

The structure of this volume roughly reflects the 'moments' in the process of practical theological critical conversation, just outlined.

To 'give face' or to promote enfacement, it is necessary to find face. So the first part of the book is devoted to finding and understanding face, human and divine. In the first four chapters, I engage with the human face and try to understand what face is, what it does, how it is understood and how it generates meanings and understandings. I draw largely on perspectives drawn from non-theological arts and science disciplines such as psychology, biology, philosophy and art.

In Chapter 1, I try to get a 'fix' on face so that it is clear what we are trying to see and understand. It may seem obvious what face is and where it is to be found. Both literally and metaphorically, however, face is difficult to pin down and define. It is in constant movement, both physically and intellectually. I explore the ways in which face might be understood, paying particular attention to the way in which it has been differently conceived in different historical periods and cultures. I then consider the ways in which face is constantly bound up with and refracted through different metaphors and systems of understanding.

In Chapter 2, I consider the biological, physical and social 'facts' and functions of face as it is presently understood within a range of disciplines. What is it that face does? Why is it important to embodied humans, and do we really properly understand and see face? Do we place too much or too little importance upon it? How does physical face relate to inner identity, and how is the human capacity to play with face/identity by means of masking, veiling and acting to be understood?

Having explored approaches, meanings and facts about face in the first two chapters, I then move on to consider the loss of face and the implications this has for shame in Chapter 3. Many people have difficulties with face, either in terms of their own appearance, or in perceiving that of others. I consider the importance of face for acceptance and flourishing in society and also the shame that surrounds those who have physically or metaphorically lost face. Shame and the estrangement and alienation it denotes are often enemies of human flourishing. They must therefore be of direct concern to Christians aspiring to respect and enhance the image of God in their fellow human beings.

In Chapter 4, which serves as a hinge to the more theological part of the book, I briefly explore ideas of presence, absence and the 'face behind face'. While face is often thought to be an obvious, physical entity in the world, it can also figure mystery and the unknown, acting at least as much as a barrier as door to the desired 'other'. Gaining a sense of this fundamental ambivalence is important in approaching ideas about the presence and absence which seems to characterise the theology and experience of the divine in Jewish and Christian experience.

At this point, it becomes important to consider the theological tradition concerning face and the face of God. So the next few chapters are devoted to finding the face of God. In the modern Western world, God is mostly taken to be entirely invisible: great is God's facelessness, to parody the hymn. However, God has not always been regarded as entirely invisible. In this part of the book, then, I explore aspects of Christian teaching and experience about face and about God so that these can be used to raise critical questions both about God, theology and Christian practice. These can then be brought into dialogue with the contemporary human experience explored previously in the practical theological 'conversation'.

Chapter 5, 'Seeing the Face of God in the Bible', considers the biblical and early theological evidence for thinking about the face of God. Aspects of the OT tradition bear witness to the partial visibility of the divine. The glory of God is figured in visible terms in both Old and New Testaments. It can be argued that a more holistic, thicker kind of perceiving in the ancient world meant that seeing God's face was not simply a metaphor for invisible presence. The visible presence of God is to be found in the NT in aspects of the life and work of Jesus who can himself be seen as the living Temple, the locus of God's visible glory. The tradition of present visible glory clearly also influenced St Paul and other NT writers. This kind of thinking is discussed in relation to issues of justice, inclusion and shame distribution. I argue that early Christian seeing was linked to the inversion and redistribution of shame in the kingdom community which was a new Temple on earth where God's glory shone forth and was to be found partly in the faces of Christians themselves.

The tradition of thick seeing of the divine continues into the life of the early church, and beyond that into medieval times, where the vision of God as the end of Christian life remains constant. Chapter 6, then, examines the theological tradition of the *visio dei* up till the time of Thomas Aquinas when it reached its zenith. Chapter 7 goes on to consider why the vision of God, and of the face of God, became so neglected and lost in the Middle Ages, suggesting that the decline in the possibility of seeing God may have contributed to a lack of theological interest in human faces that has continued largely unbroken to the present day. I then outline some modern theological resources for taking both the face of God and the faces of humans more seriously, more materially and less metaphorically.

In Chapter 8, then, I am in a position to outline some theological horizons and questions that might allow for the emergence of a more positive practical theological approach to faces, human and divine. This can be encapsulated in the image of 'shining up the face of God' that denotes the mutual creation and recognition of faces shared between humans and God. While the practical theological insights and principles that emerge here are loose, forming an 'imaginary' rather than a set of tight theological norms, they are intended to provide the basis for more creative approaches to face in everyday contemporary life (Jantzen 1999; Taylor 2004). These are then developed in Chapter 9 where the practical theological journey concludes with some suggestions about changed practices and attitudes to face that may be more sensitive and inclusive. Just seeing, acknowledging and validating the appearance of the faces of others, is not necessarily easy to accomplish. It is, however, essential if some kinds of face-related shame and alienation are to be overcome. Thus my progression from problem (neglect and alienation of faces), through description, to analysis, to theological reflection, to new perceptions and practices (acceptance and inclusion of faces, human and divine) concludes.

How this Book Came to be Written

It may help to understand this work better if I say a little bit about how I became interested in this general topic area and began to link face to shame and visuality.

I was researching the topic of shame – a profoundly visually understood condition – when I came across Jonathan Cole's excellent book, *About Face* (1998). Cole, a medical practitioner, was himself puzzled that not much had been written about face. His own explorations began with an old lady who had had a stroke so could not respond facially to others. He noticed that, tragically, this woman gradually faded away as a person.

This led to Cole's thinking about other people who had problems with face, either in dealing with the faces of others, or with aspects of their own faces. In the latter category he found people who had had facial injuries, strokes, Parkinson's disease and people with temporary or permanent paralysis of the face through Bell's palsy or Moebius syndrome (total immobility of the face which can be a condition from birth). These categories actually include many members of the human race, either temporarily or permanently. In the former category, he identified blind people and those who have problems with recognising or coping with faces, for example those with Capgras Syndrome (in which people cannot put a name to familiar faces, even though they can relate emotionally to the people behind them, so clearly, in some sense, recognise them) or those with Asperger's syndrome who seem to find the complexity of the human face very difficult to deal with. From these sometimes extreme and rare examples of people who have various kinds of difficulties with face, Cole explored the evolution, nature and function of face with a view to asking how clinicians and others might understand and take face more seriously.

What struck me most forcibly about Cole's book in the context of my work on shame was how often difficulties and problems with the physical reality of face became entangled with the psycho-socio-political realities of normativity, marginalisation and depersonalisation represented by shame. People whose faces do not 'fit' because of disfigurement, or because they do not have the same kind of facial expressions as others or who cannot facially interact in the same way as cultural 'normals' can easily find themselves living on the edge of social relations, even becoming non-persons.

A particularly telling example of this in Cole's book was that of a man with Moebius syndrome who had never been able to move his facial muscles.[1] This man had become a clergy person in the hope of being acceptable and useful to others, but had found that it was only by leaving the ministry that he could actually accept and be himself. While he does not describe his life as being shame-bound, the rejection and stigma he experienced were typical of those who live shamed lives with damaged identities. Cole's work, and this particular example in it, indicated to me that there might be an important intrinsic relationship between shame and face, both literally and metaphorically, and it was that relationship that I resolved to explore at some point.

This desire was underlined by reading a second very important book, theologian David Ford's *Self and Salvation* (Ford 1999). Ford explores salvation and atonement with God in this book using the metaphors of facing and enfacement, pointing towards many of the themes I explore here about acceptance, community and shame dissolution. However, unlike Cole, Ford actually paid very little attention to the physical reality of face and the interdisciplinary literatures that illuminate it, a point made forcibly by blind theologian John Hull (2000). I thought, too, that he had not given enough space to visual aspects of faith experience and to the concept of the face of God. Ford moved too quickly away from the reality of face towards theology. I thought that a slower, in some ways more critical, journey might be needed to do full justice to face and faces in approaching theology and ideas about God and redemption which I, too, wanted to relate to enfacement, alienation and reconciliation.

Having published *Shame: Theory, Therapy, Theology*, I took my explorations into shame as a starting point for exploring visuality generally, and my next major publication was about human relations with humanly created objects and artefacts, *Seeing Things: Deepening Relations with Visual Artefacts* (Pattison 2000, 2007b). The realm of humanly manufactured 'stuff', like face, is always with us; it shapes

---

[1]   Cole has subsequently written a whole book about people with Moebius syndrome (Cole with Spalding 2009).

and forms us, forming an important part of our 'cultural DNA'. However, it, too, is often treated as though it did not matter – as marginal and somehow shameful to the religious, who should have their minds on more heavenly or transcendent things, perhaps. The book was an attempt to reintegrate artefacts into the gaze of human recognition and acceptability.

If artefacts are to be accepted within the theological and human purview, how much more the faces of humans themselves and the identities, spoiled or otherwise, that they are taken primarily to represent? So in the work before you, drawing on my research into shame and subsequently into perception and seeing, I attempt to explore face (physical, metaphorical, symbolic) and face-related shame to see how this might be critically related to Christian theology and practice. My aim is to explore how taking face and the shame that often accompanies it seriously might be responded to from within Christianity – but might also raise critical questions for this tradition. This seems very important in a world that takes human faces with enormous, perhaps over-exaggerated seriousness, including and excluding, rewarding and punishing people often just on the basis of their looks or the way they that they look at others.

I conclude this introduction with a poem, 'Saving Face', kindly sent to me by Pastor Charles Strietelmeier in response to my work on shame. It makes clear the relation between face and shame that I hope to explore herein after in this book. It is used, gratefully, and with the author's permission:

Saving Face

When you're so poor
you only have one face
to wear out in the world,
you hope yours pleases.
(Looks like I slept in mine
last night – see all the creases!)
And though we rinse it in
the morning light,
who has the time
to scrub off the remains
of each disgrace,
or mend the tears?
With face uplifted,
we wear it with its stains
and face our fears.

Chapter 1
Fixing Face

There is in God (some say)
A deep, but dazzling darkness ...

(Henry Vaughan, *The Night*)

Part six-million-year old display rule predictor, part emotion readout, part cultural, part innate, part conscious, part not, the face is, in Duchenne's words, a "divine fantasy" and we will remain fascinated and enraptured by its movements as long as we remain interested in one another as individuals.

(Cole 1998, 200)[1]

We live in an age of the face. Mass media of all kinds confirm this. The newspaper *The Times* of London, even in its contemporary tabloid form, is not known for its lavish illustrations. However, on the 48 double-spread pages of the main paper for 1 December 2010 there were to be found at least 353 discrete, discernible faces or part faces in photographs, line drawings and cartoons. The front page main photograph was of three smiling African boys' faces, peering at the viewer through a hole – this was associated with an appeal, as was the photograph of an African baby with an anguished expression on her face which appeared later in the paper. Most of the faces were human, though some were animal.

Within living memory, *The Times* had no photographs or illustrations at all. Now, in common with most other media, it is full of faces of all shapes and sizes, illustrating stories, selling consumables, guaranteeing brand quality, engaged in action, embodying evil, expressing emotions, demanding compassion, summoning to imitation, even just revealing what the article author looks like. *The Times* offers its readers 353 faces before breakfast. These are all individual, all recognisable to someone, all unique.

Faces have multiplied and proliferated in modern society. There are nearly seven billion living sets of eyes, ears, noses and mouths on the planet now, with more on the way. There are also infinite numbers of reproductions and representations of these faces in newspapers, photographs, portraits, cartoons and on the internet –

---

[1]   Cole is here quoting and slightly bending Duchenne's meaning. Duchenne refers to facial expressions rather than face as a whole: 'In the face, our Creator was not concerned with mechanical necessity. He was able, in his wisdom ... or in pursuing a divine fantasy, to put any particular muscles into action, one alone, or several muscles together, when he wished the characteristic signs of the emotions, even the most fleeting, to be written on man's face' (Duchenne de Boulogne 1990, 19).

you do not have to be important or famous for your face to go around the world in seconds. Websites and magazines with titles like Facebook and *The Face* simply emphasise the importance attached to this bodily feature.

Most Westerners, unlike their medieval, village-inhabiting forebears, see hundreds of new faces every day. Furthermore, to enter a country, or to register for a library card or driving license, you have to hand over a copy of your face; this then becomes the guarantor of your identity. If you conceal your face under a veil you may be thought to be hiding something, or to be oppressed. If someone wants to take your photograph, you are supposed to be pleased or flattered. If you want to demonstrate how honest and genuine you are, you call a face-to-face meeting or agree to appear on TV so other faces can scrutinise yours and see that what you are saying is true and that you can really be trusted. If your face is disfigured, ugly or in some other way unsatisfactory, you can have it surgically altered. Apparently, the thing that most worries lay people about 'face transplants' in which the skin of a donor is transplanted onto the head of another is that they will acquire the identity of the donor and so no longer be themselves (Royal College of Surgeons 2003).[2] In fact, the transplanted 'face' would look neither like that of the donor nor the recipient, but different from both. This fear again witnesses to the close association in popular belief between personal identity and facial appearance. Face, identity, authenticity and well-being are, it seems, inextricably bound up together.

We have an almost infinite fascination with faces, as well as a huge capacity to recognise and respond to them. It is strange, then, how difficult it is to get a fix on face, to really see and understand it.

Towards the conclusion of one his most famous passages, the meditation on love in 1 Cor. 13, Paul refers to seeing the face of God: 'For now we see indistinctly [as in] a mirror, then we will see [God] face-to-face. Now I know in parts, then I will know [wholly] as I am known' (1 Cor. 13:12. My translation). I cite this well-known passage here to draw attention to Paul's use of the image of the mirror, and the indistinct or dim vision of face, whether human or divine, that is gained with it. Face, and the study of face, is obscured or illuminated by a myriad metaphors of this kind. This reflects the experience of face of which all we ever have is partial knowledge and understanding. The living physical organ itself is constantly in motion and it is seen from many different angles. Marcel Proust compared individual faces to those of Oriental gods whose faces are presented as a whole group of faces juxtaposed on different planes so it is impossible to see them all simultaneously (http://www.scholarisland.org/face.htm.

---

[2]   There is some doubt as to whether, and how many, full facial transplants have taken place thus far. The first full transplant may have taken place in Spain in 2010. See http://www.bbc.co.uk/news/magazine-20493572. Accessed 28 November 2012. Partial transplants are more common and extensive facial replanting or transplanting is very important in cases of facial cancers and accidents. See http://www.savingfaces.co.uk/about-us-mainmenu-26.html. Accessed 28 November 2012.

Accessed 7 November 2012). This is an image well illustrated by some of Picasso's Cubist portraits of women's faces (Sousslof 2006, 110–14).

It is almost impossible to catch any living face completely in all its aspects – expressions flit across it momentarily. It is only with difficulty, and perhaps in death, that face can actually be fixed.[3] Many people have lamented their incapacity to see or remember faces, even dead faces, whole, rather than just in parts. Barthes, for example, grieving for his mother, laments the fact that he can never summon up the totality of her features (Barthes 2000, 63).

It is not possible even to see one's own face properly: 'Of all the faces we come across, our own is the one that we know the least' (Melchior-Bonnet 2002, 248). In a mirror, the face that looks back at you will only be part of your face. Can you see under your chin? If so, some of your forehead will be missing. You can only see parts of your face in any one glance. The face that you see will, in any case, be less bright and so a bit deader in the mirror than it seems to other people. It will be about a third of the size of your actual face (trace the circumference of it on a steamed mirror) and the wrong way round. Worst of all, as you gaze at your image, you will probably have composed your features into some version of 'me as I see myself'; your face will therefore not contain the expressions that it does when you are involved in unreflective action. The face you consciously compose and see in the mirror is not your 'real' face (McNeill 1998 110–17). You may not even recognise your real, moving face when you catch it by accident in a window reflection or in the eye of another.

Freud recounts the following events from his own life, and from that of the philosopher Ernst Mach, seeing himself reflected in a mirror or window on a bus:

> [Mach] formed a very unfavourable opinion about the shabby stranger who entered the omnibus, and thought "What a shabby-looking school-master that man is who is getting in!" – I can report a similar adventure. I was sitting alone in my *wagon-lit* compartment when a more than usually violent jolt of the train swung back the door of the adjoining washing-cabinet and an elderly gentleman in a dressing gown and a travelling cap came in. I assumed that in leaving the washing-cabinet, which lay between the two compartments, he had taken the wrong direction and come into my compartment by mistake. Jumping up with the intention of putting him right, I at once realised to my dismay that the intruder was nothing but my own reflection in the looking-glass on the open door. I can still recollect that I thoroughly disliked his appearance. (Freud 1985, 371n1)

---

3   Dead faces in some ways do not look like live ones at all. Damien Hirst, the artist, beside one of his exhibits in Tate Modern, London, noted that 'to see something you have to kill it'. The implication of this is that one can never see a living thing wholly while it lives. Paradoxically, when it is dead, there is another way in which it cannot fully be seen as the life and movement is no longer in it.

Commenting on this kind of experience, Cumming writes:

> Nobody really knows quite what ... she looks like ... All we have are the
> camera's partial images and the intangible reflections of mirrors. And mirrors
> can only give ... whatever we choose to give them: a face arranged to fit the
> mood of the moment, perhaps, to make us look as we feel, or would like to feel.
> A face marked by the effort of looking or pretending not to look, or the effort of
> keeping still. A fact-checking face, paying close attention to detail but missing
> the bigger picture – which can't be seen all at once, alas, and which never stays
> still for a second; the eye moves, its reflection shifts: we are altered by our
> viewing conditions. (Cumming 2009, 138)[4]

Human face, let alone the divine face, is, at best, a partially perceived and
understood mystery. It is a 'divine fantasy' perhaps, or maybe a 'deep, but
dazzling darkness'. Defying total knowledge and understanding, it then unfolds
and recursively dissipates in coronas of countless meanings and metaphors. Face
is so overwhelming and complex that we cannot really see it. It is as if, like the
after-effects of looking at the sun, all we can really see is darkness in the midst of
dazzling light.

With this metaphor or image of imperfect, partial vision of face as something that
defies comprehension or total vision, I come to the study of face and faces. Face is
an elusive phenomenon that has physical, social, psychological, representational,
metaphorical and many other aspects. It is seen and unseen, veiled and hidden,
partially understood and a mystery.

When I first approached this topic, I expected to be overwhelmed with relevant
academic literature. Strangely, it is oddly selective and sporadic. In academic
study, as well as in everyday experience, it is difficult to get a full picture of face.
Scholars and researchers segment face and study aspects of it, for example its
evolution, its communicative function, its visible representation, its metaphorical
importance. But there is no comprehensive synthesis of ideas and understandings
of face. Disciplines such as philosophy, art history, evolutionary biology,
sociology and experimental psychology provide only partial understandings.
These often exist in complete isolation from other perspectives. Those who focus
on facial expression seldom refer to the insights about face provided by novelists
or sociologists, while the latter mostly ignore the former, repaying the insult.
Different disciplinary approaches thus provide relatively discrete glimpses, rather
than integrated understandings, of face. Intellectual theories and understandings of
face are uneven, sometimes very narrow and segmented and full of holes and gaps.
They do not combine to provide integrated understandings for engaging with face.

Having recognised in a preliminary way the complexity of face and its
meanings, together with the difficulties of apprehending and understanding it, the

---

[4]   For more on mirrors and facial reflection, see for example Gregory (1997), Burt and
Kline (2008), McNeill (1989).

rest of this chapter is devoted to providing background understandings of this multivalent phenomenon.

First, I will provide some historical background to the present 'age of face' or 'faciality'. Face has not always had the same significance that it has in contemporary Western culture. It is important to understand something of how meanings and perceptions have changed to relativise what might seem 'obvious', and so to begin to develop a more critical perspective. Having outlined some changing understandings and significances of face, I will speculate on why individual human faces have become such important objects and symbols today. Finally, turning to the corona of culturally generated meanings and metaphors that surround and refract the physical object, face, I will consider some of the ways in which these affect understandings and perceptions of face and its significance in society. Face generates rich, varied, sometimes contradictory, understandings, representations and metaphors. These representations are often then the lenses through which face and actual faces are seen and understood in an infinite regression and recursiveness that is often difficult to recognise, yet alone to follow, in everyday life. Developing critical awareness and sensitivity to their nature and effects is therefore an important preliminary task here.

Face in Historical Perspective

Face, faces and faciality are ubiquitous in contemporary Western society. It was not ever thus. To get their contemporary prominence in perspective, it may be helpful to cast an eye over the recent history of understanding the face.

There is no single history of the importance and understanding of face as category or phenomenon over the last few centuries. However, something of the changing understandings and views of face over time can be apprehended through the work of sociologists, and of historians of science, photography and portraiture. These trace a broad trajectory from face as that which conceals essence and identity in public life to the present situation where face is seen as the guarantor of identity, authenticity and sincerity. This trajectory is generally towards giving far greater importance to the psychology and individuality of persons as apprehended through their faces. It reflects significant changes in attitudes to self, body, society and God that end in the individual face being seen as the most important emblem and symbol of the person. Unfortunately, there seem to be few direct accounts of how people have felt about, understood and managed their faces in the past. And there are none from the non-literate, the majority of the enfaced across time.

In pre- and early-modern societies where individuality was not important, naked faces were generally of little significance (Berger, Berger and Kellner 1974). It was role, marked by outward garb, accoutrements and deportment that was important for identifying who and what people were, what group they belonged to and how they should be related to: hence the importance of the scholar's gown or the coat of arms for knowing the identity of the person who was being related to. Individual portraits were rare in this period, often stereotyped and formal; they mostly did not attempt to index the inner reality or psychology of the subject through careful attention to their facial expressions (Woodall 1997).

This kind of respect for the external signs and status markers of the person survived well into the eighteenth century. People in public life adopted clothes, complexions and roles that said nothing about their psychology or inner essence; they dealt with each other, as it were, impersonally. So, for example, the shape of the head was deliberately disguised by elaborate wigs or coiffure. As to the face:

> Nowhere was the attempt to blot out the individual character of a person more evident than in the treatment of the face. Both men and women used face paint, either red or white, to conceal the natural colour of the skin and any blemishes it might have. Masks came back into fashion, worn by both men and women. (Sennett 1986, 70)

It was only in the nineteenth century, and with the advent of industrial urbanisation, that individual faces and expressions came to have more significance. People stopped trying to conceal the skin and its blemishes (many people would have had the marks of diseases on their skins) and became interested in reading the 'natural being' within (Benthien 2002). Skin, including facial skin, became a kind of display area for what were to become two very important kinds of study: physiognomy, the technique and art of discovering temperament and character from outward appearance of the fixed physical features of the face; and pathogony, the study or recognition of emotions through their outward signs and expressions on the face (Benthien 2002, 103).[5]

Physiognomy has a long history (Pearl 2010; Porter 2005). Aristotle wrote a treatise on the relationship of facial features to moral character. It was, however, systematised and popularised in the late eighteenth century by the work of a Swiss pastor, Johann Caspar Lavater (1878). Lavater's *Essays on Physiognomy* became a popular standard work for reading off the characters of individuals from their facial features (Jordanova 1993; Pearl 2010; Rivers 1994; Sobieszek 1999). Like some other physiognomists, Lavater believed that the study of the face was a way of finding the image of the creator God within the soul of the individual, so he saw it as a kind of worship (Hartley 2001; Pearl 2010, 11). But whether theologically

---

[5] Lavater (1878, 12) distinguished physiognomy and pathognomy thus: 'Physiognomy, therefore, teaches the knowledge of character at rest; and pathognomy of character in motion. Character at rest is displayed by the form of the solid and the appearance of the moveable parts, while at rest. Character impassioned is manifested by the moveable parts, in motion. ... Pathognomy has to combat the arts of dissimulation; physiognomy has not.' This distinction implies that over time the expressions that reflect and communicate emotions might contribute to the basic structure of the face which then reflects, as it were, solid character, as might be deduced, for example, from the persistence of 'laughter lines' around someone's eyes.

motivated or not, ordinary nineteenth-century urban dwellers, living amidst a mass of strangers, found it a useful way of categorising people and groups in the streets. It allowed instant judgements to be made on the nature and character of strangers simply on the basis of sight. This eased the confusion and sensory overstimulation of the city streets without intimate contact or relationship being necessary (Pearl 2010, 27).

In the nineteenth century, gas lights began to appear in homes and streets, as well as in the theatre. This meant that people's faces could generally be seen more clearly, even in darkness. It is no accident, then, that with the rise of physiognomy and lighting, theatrical realism was born. For the first time, the faces and facial movements of actors became important: 'creative and innovative actors used the combination of powerful lighting and physiognomic ideas to challenge audience members to be more critical viewers and participants' in the theatre (Pearl 2010, 73). To act well was to have the right face, and to match facial appearance and expression to role to be physiognomically, and therefore psychologically, convincing.

Physiognomy was based on the premise that the fundamental character and identity of a person could be read from their facial features. The deep conviction that faces, emotions and identity in some way relate and correspond was widely influential in the nineteenth century (and survives to this day). As well as engendering theatrical realism, it also influenced portrait-painting. This employed physiognomic ideas and conventions to convey character and biographical depth that transcended mimetic accuracy (Pearl 2010, 88ff.). Cartoons and caricatures that played on physiognomic stereotypes of race also became common, outward facial features being used to indicate inner essence. Born in the mid-nineteenth century, photography, too, was used physiognomically, often to classify and order human conditions such as mental illness and criminality (Gilman 1988; Hamilton and Hargreaves 2001). Within the scientific sphere, physiognomy was an important root for the experimental exploration of human expression and its meanings as scientists tried to systematise the meaning and character of external facial appearances and relate them to particular states and conditions, working from individuals to types (Darwin 1998; Duchenne de Boulogne 1990; Sobieszek 1999). The photographic 'mug shot' of criminals was born and used, ultimately futilely, to try systematically to classify and identify 'bad characters' (Hamilton and Hargreaves 2001; Pearl 2010; Sobieszek 1999). Using some of the same photographic techniques and assumptions, Darwin's cousin Sir Francis Galton began to apply physiognomic typing to races within the context of anthropology (Sturken and Cartwright 2001, 279–85).

The underlying premises, and much of the technology, of physiognomy, have disappeared or have been scientifically discredited. However, one of the interesting features of social history is that different ideas, myths and mindsets can continue to co-exist alongside each other (Otter 2008). Thus, in early twenty-first-century society, many people believe that facial features and expressions reflect the essence, character and identity of the person. We are still inclined 'to read distinction and value' into the faces of others: True or false, right or wrong, physiognomy remains a powerful technology of communication and decision making, a marker of selfhood, and a way of building identity (Pearl 2010, 213).

The evolution and co-existence of ideas about the significance of face can perhaps best be seen in the history of attitudes to portraiture and portrait photography. Photographs and facial portraits act as barometers of formal ideas about the nature and representation of face and its relation to the person (Brilliant 1991; Freeland 2010; West 2004). Until about 1900, these artefacts, which proliferated in middle class and popular culture in the nineteenth century, were seen along physiognomic lines as expressions of inner character and spirit, and almost iconically as bearers of presence (Soussloff 2006, 8ff.).

In the modernist phase of the early twentieth century, this view was challenged. Now it was believed that faces in portraits and photographs could contain no direct presentation of inner personal essence or character. Any expression or emotion inhered, not in the subject or in the artefact, but in the intentions of the painter or photographer – thus Picasso famously painted Gertrude Stein's face as an African-like mask rather than trying to represent it 'realistically' (Freeland 2010, 91). Photos and paintings were then to be regarded as no more than projective surfaces, as raw material for artistic, not subjective, expression.

Moving into more recent, postmodern times, the notion of the expression of essence in portraits and photographs of face has become more playful, dramatic and theatrical. It is not necessary for face and facial representation to convey or reflect a single, unchanging essence. They can convey any number of appearances and essences, according to the whim and mood of the artist or subject. Thus, a number of artists, for example Orlan and Cindy Sherman, have played with self-portraiture and facial alteration to make the point that character is not captured within the physical confines of the face (Sobieszek 1999, 273ff.). Like God, we can have the faces and be the people we want, sporting different faces and being different people on different days: 'These days, we can have almost any face we would like, whenever we want, provided we can afford it' (Kemp 2004, 91).[6] What you see in the face is not, then, what you get in terms of personal identity and essence.

This theme is echoed in attitudes to cosmetic surgery. This is not now only about restoring or disguising the face, but also about performing face (Synnott 1990). Face, like skin, is not so much an empty body-house container for the soul as a dress or mask that can be manipulated within the gaze of self and others (Benthien 2002, chapter 2; Brilliant 1991). The mask is as near as you can get to the essence of self, if, indeed, such essence can be held to exist. Face therefore becomes a matrix of multiple identities, 'at once true and false, assumed and genuine, feigned and sincere' (Sobieszek 1999, 179). The contemporary

---

[6]   Kemp goes on to note that in the UK there were 25,000 plastic surgery procedures in 2002, one in twelve for men. The bill for these was £25,000,000. (The number and cost of procedures increases each year.)

example of the changing face of the late Michael Jackson perhaps bears witness to engagement with the unending multiplicity of possible faces and identities.

Looking back over nearly 200 years of portraits of faces it may be concluded that the human face is a dark glass that is alternately transparent, reflective and fractured (Sobieszek 1999). The physiognomist, modernist and postmodernist views identified above rub along in cheerful, but mostly tacit, contradiction to each other in Western culture to this day. In the course of writing this book, for example, I had a conversation with a practising portrait-painter who expounded the classic naturalist realist position on portraits, stating that it was his job to bring out the essence and character of his subjects in the pictures he was commissioned to paint. And in everyday life, many of us continue to believe that we can make reliable judgments about the essence and character of other people on the basis of brief facial encounters.

We have seen now something of the way in which ideas about face and representation of face and their relations to persons have both changed and remained constant over the last two centuries. For the most part, the individual face with its assumed individual identity, essence and capacity to communicate emotions has become more important as an object of interest and analysis. The time has therefore come to try to ask why face is such an important part of contemporary interests and concerns.

The Contemporary Importance of Face

The prominence and meaning given to face has changed over time, as have ways of understanding faces. In early twenty-first-century society, Westerners seem to be particularly preoccupied with, and intrigued by, face. One reason for this is probably that we are surrounded by more living faces than have ever existed before on earth, many of them now living closely together in mass urban spaces. We are also deluged with reproductions and representations of faces. However, it has to be asked why, in these circumstances, we have not become face blind and indifferent, face-sated? Why have faces become so prominent and important as physical realities and fundamental representations of the person?

It is not easy to give a clear answer to these questions. I have yet to read a good account of the rise and dominance of face and its representation in contemporary culture. Probably a number of factors and trends combine in somewhat underdetermined, and in some ways haphazard patterns, to support a preoccupation with face and faces. Here I discuss just four of them: individualism; issues of identity and authenticity in a changing world; visuality and representation of the self; and scientific developments and understandings.

Individualism

Individualism, even hyper-individualism, is very important feature of contemporary Western society. Western culture is organised around amassing people with very similar-looking bodies and needs in cities. Paradoxically, however, this has been accompanied by an increasing individualisation of the self. Thus, people understand themselves to be wholly unique and ultimately important atomised, psychological individuals in whom rights, choices and potential inhere (Campbell 1987; Giddens 1991, 1992; Lasch 1991; Taylor 1989, 1991). Many, more traditional, cultures are more communally oriented. They foster a more socially porous and responsible self, concerned with corporate, rather than individual, well-being (Malina 1983; Strathern 1988). However, Western society has moved towards emphasising the uniqueness and significance of the autonomous, emotional, hedonic individual, perhaps so that they are free of social bonds and more able to participate freely as producers and consumers in the market economy (Campbell 1987). If people see themselves as autonomous, atomised selves, they are more flexible as workers and more goods can be sold to them.

Western societies exalt the individual and take individuals to be the basic unit of society. This individualism was reflected in the development of the new discipline of psychology in the nineteenth century (Danziger 1997). Psychology evolved to understand the interiority of the individual which had previously been of much less direct interest. The growing importance of the individual was also reflected in the contemporaneous growth of realistic, naturalistic portraits and photographs. These were crucial to the formation of individualism, whereby individual humans are conceived of as having independence, uniqueness, depth and so great significance and value (Hamilton and Hargreaves 2001, 115; Woodall 1997, xiii). Previously, only the wealthy and privileged could have had a portrait representations made of themselves. However, in the nineteenth century, a growing number of middle-class people could afford to have images of themselves created and reproduced freely and cheaply. Felicitously, improvements in health meant that faces and mouths in particular became much healthier looking. So at this point, it was even possible for people for the first time to be represented as openly smiling (Trumble 2004).

Nineteenth century physiognomically- and pathognomically-inspired science and photography revealed and confirmed that each individual has a unique face (Brilliant 1991; Hamilton and Hargreaves 2001). The burgeoning emphasis on the sovereign autonomy, importance and depth of the atomised psychological individual was, then, perfectly symbolised in the living face, unique to each person: 'The face, as unique, physical, malleable and public is the prime symbol of the self' (Synnott 1989, 607).

The face is not just a prime symbol of the self, it is also the prime living expression or manifestation of self, the place where it is widely thought that the precious human individual presents to the world in a unique and authentic way, as a monarch appears on a balcony (Scruton 2012, 78). Face, then, is taken to be the epitome and unique expression of the individual, the guarantor of identity and authenticity in mass, but individualised, society.

More than this, it is perhaps the sacramental appearance of personhood, taken to be sacred in the contemporary world (Goffman 2005, 31, 47; Lynch 2012):

> A face is a centre of human expression, the transparent envelope of the attitudes and desires of others, the place of manifestation, the barely material support for a multitude of intentions. This is why it seems impossible for us to treat a face or a body, even a dead body, like a thing. They are sacred entities, not "the givens of sight". (Merleau-Ponty 1983, 167)

If individual persons are sacred objects, their faces become hallowed objects and icons of precious presence, too; hence the power of defacement that has the force of sacrilege, an assault on the sacred, as witnessed, for example, by the treatment of detainees in Guantanamo Bay (Butler 2006, 73; Scruton 2012, 108–9; Taussig 1999).

Personal Identity and Depth

Closely related to the matter of individualism is the issue of identity. Rapidly changing, multicultural, pluralist capitalist culture problematises the notion of a stable, unchanging personal essence and selfhood in favour of flexibility, flux and experimentation (du Gay, Evans and Redman 2000). Contemporary individuals in an unstable context have, then, regularly to reinvent themselves during a lifetime conceived as a project in self-realisation (Giddens 1991, 1992). They may have many different jobs, a number of different families, a range of friends and relationships and they might move around to live in a large number of cultures and contexts. In this anxiety-provoking context, face serves both as a medium and a metaphor for engaging with continuity and change.

If identity is problematic, then face becomes one of the places where this anxiety is worked out. We take our faces with us through life. And however sophisticated we may think we are, our views of face may be haunted by a desire to find the essence or continuity of the self within the features or expressions of the face. We look at someone's face, perhaps even our own face, hoping to find there something of the real, continuing essence of self, something reliable. 'Facism' is the physiognomically-derived belief that face reliably reflects or reveals the character of the individual so we know whether or not we can trust them (Synnott 1989, 608). Even in a context where it is known that faces can be infinitely manipulated and deceptive, we continue to hold fast to facism, and to its close companion, the 'beauty mystique'. This is the belief that 'the beautiful is good, and the ugly is evil … that the morally good is physically beautiful (or "good looking") and the evil is ugly' (Synnott 1989, 611). In an age of mass communication and mass exposure to faces and people, it is perhaps unsurprising that we want to have a quick visual way of deciding who is and who is not trustworthy and desirable.

Because we are anxious about continuity and authenticity of inner identity, and so about possibilities for reliable relationship, we harken after the idea that we can know something definite about persons through their faces: thus, if we see politicians close-up on TV, we can really evaluate their characters and intentions and know whether or not they are authentic and so trustworthy. This kind of individualised, personality- and face-focused politics may be based on illusion. But it exemplifies a general need in mass society, characterised by ongoing social and individual change, to find something solid to cleave to. And in that context, what can be more reassuring than a face in which, perhaps, one might find the reliable care and trust that one found in the face of the carer into whose face one gazed as an infant?

Face guarantees who it is we are dealing with. If we are uncertain about who and what we and others are, we may look anxiously into the mirrors of others' faces in the hope of eventually discovering ourselves, resolving the enigma of identity and gaining some stability. Face may be all we are left with when all other certainties about society, self and identity have been called into question. For the sake of stable living and relationships, where face is concerned, we desperately want to believe that what we think we see is what we will certainly get.

Visuality and Appearance

In addition to inhabiting a culture of individualism and uncertain identity, this is an age of visuality, image and appearances. Powered by the availability of mass-image producing technologies like photography, television, cinema and computing, visually mediated communication is immediate, accessible, available to all, understandable and assimilable, enjoyable, sensually gratifying, emotionally stimulating, transculturally legible and concise (Stephens 1998).

Pictures and images are valued in an age of rapid communication and short attention spans. Images, especially moving images, connect directly with the emotional, pre- and a-linguistic parts of human consciousness. They convey a lot of information very quickly without requiring much acquired skill or effort on the viewer's part (Pattison 2007b, 85–6). The smiling little boys in the picture on the front of *The Times* newspaper are happy. Without knowing their language or context, their faces immediately engage me in some kind of personal relationship more rapidly and firmly than any text might. The most mobile and communicative, as well as the most unique and distinctive visible part of the human body is the face; thus a facial image is one of the best, most efficient ways of gaining the attention and interest of viewers.

A picture of a face, laughing, grieving or simply static may save a thousand words. However, it should not be forgotten that images, including facial images, are situated within a grammar or language of representation (Mitchell 1986). Thus, Saddam Hussein's face can be used to represent evil, while the face of an

African child is taken to equate with innocent suffering. Facial images form part of an implicit visual rhetoric. Thus, some faces and expressions, for example those of dead UK soldiers or civilians in Afghanistan, are excluded from public mass media, while others, like those of Prince William, are freely viewed and normalised. Butler (2006, xviii) notes:

> Those who remain faceless or whose faces are presented to us as so many symbols of evil, authorise us to become senseless before those lives we have eradicated, and whose grievability is indefinitely postponed. Certain faces must be admitted into public view, must be seen and heard for some keener sense of the value of life, all life, to take hold.

Faces, then, exercise considerable influence in a mass media age. Image producers, editors and consumers all know their power. Whether they are aware of it or not, faces are used to convey powerful social messages and values, helping to define the good, the valuable, the normal, the deviant and the evil.

Faces are commodities and are used to sell commodities in a society where the consuming, enfaced individual is all important (Scruton 2012). They are used to sell, commend and authenticate products and ideas. There was a time when advertisements and newspapers consisted largely or only of text. *The Times* famously resisted having a photograph on its front page long after its competitors. Now, however, advertisements are largely structured round pictures, often of humans. Even *The Times* is lavishly illustrated with faces that extend, contradict, hide and complexify the words of the text – an average of around ten faces per page. Images are slippery and ambivalent, and faces are mercurial. But where they can be aptly situated, they can have an enormous, if indeterminate, effect on viewers.

Curiosity, Social Control and Other Factors

The humanitarian impulse, mediated through the development of science and the Enlightenment, is that the proper study of humanity is humanity. Thus, curiosity about all aspects of the human condition, social, biological and cultural, is taken to be both desirable and essential. In this context, the human face has, since Darwin (1998), come under fairly intense scientific scrutiny.

But curiosity about face is not necessarily innocent or conducted without social purpose. In the contemporary world, there may be several motives for understanding face more adequately. If face, with its structure, movements and expressions can be understood, then it may be possible to use, control, or even to change it. There are many people, from spies and poker players to businessmen, who are interested in disguising their knowledge and feelings by understanding and controlling facial movements. Others want to use their faces to gain advantage, for example by playing on physical attractiveness. Some find it helpful to be able to predict the behaviour of their fellows by being able to read their intentions and emotions facially.

Equally, there are people who are dissatisfied with their faces and identity who would like to know how to ameliorate their dysphoria so they can 'pass' in 'normal' society (Gilman 1998, 1999; Goffman 1968; Haiken 1999). The norms of facial beauty and expression can be tyrannical and exclusive, so knowing how to manipulate and change face, psychologically or physically, for example by cosmetic surgery, is a powerful incentive to gaining scientific knowledge. While once faces would often have borne the indelible marks of illness and disease, and could therefore only have been covered up, there is now the possibility of curing 'problems' with faces to bring them in line with social norms of beauty and acceptability. In a 'plastic age', face, like every other aspect of human existence, is changeable and, at least theoretically, perfectible (Sobieszek 1999, 279).

Outside the field of self-presentation, there has been considerable scientific interest in understanding how autistic people and those with physical and mental health problems and diseases relate to faces and why, so that they can, if possible, be normalised and healed of their supposed 'afflictions' (Frith 2008; Hole and Bourne 2010).

Beyond this, understanding how faces work and what they betoken can help in the control of peoples and populations. Galton and others in the nineteenth century were inspired to work on facial types to see if they could pre-identify criminals by classifying types of faces – this led to the birth of the 'mug shot' (Brilliant 1999; Hamilton and Hargreaves 2001). Work on identification of faces by mechanical means, and on understanding the nature and meanings of expressions, can be an important part of risk management in relation, for example, to crime and terrorism. In a fearful, threatened society, understanding faces can lead to better monitoring of the population. Much research into CCTV is concerned with how cameras can become better at creating recognisable images of suspects; passports now use face recognition as a uniquely reliable way of identifying individuals on entry into a different state (Hole and Bourne 2010). Understanding face, then, provides important opportunities for increased risk management and control, as well as for facilitating acceptance and greater happiness.

There is no one clear reason why face has assumed such prominence in our contemporary social life and imagination. The factors I have considered here are speculative and partial. However, it seems reasonable to assume that individualism, issues of identity and authenticity in a changing world, visuality and representation of the self and scientific developments and understandings have all contributed to the foregrounding of face as a symbol and expression of who and what we are as a society.

Problems with Understanding and Fixing Face

Thus far, I have suggested that faces, their meanings and their relations with persons, have been differently understood as they have moved through time. I have also considered why faces have such prominence and importance in the contemporary world. Faces, literally and metaphorically, are constantly changing physical and social realities. It is difficult to fix exactly what the face is doing and communicating; faces physically move and change all the time. More problematically, the socio-psychological lenses through which we look at and understand face also change and are in constant dialogue with the physical reality of face. Face very quickly becomes something much more complex than a physical reality as sign, symbol and metaphor. Face is always giving off, and being seen through, socially-constructed concepts, metaphors, symbols and meanings, mostly implicit, and often unconscious. These are often as powerful as they are difficult to separate out and detect.

In this section of the chapter, I explore the reflection and refraction of face in signs, symbols and metaphors, paying particular attention to the types of metaphors that face both generates and attracts. This illustrates the richness and complexity of meaning-making and expression-seeking that surrounds, and in some ways obscures, 'face'. First, however, it will be useful to say something about the social construction of meanings around bodies of which faces form a part.

Bodies are not just 'there' and obviously self-disclosing. They are perceived with, and through, a web of meanings and interpretations. Those bodies, and faces in particular, then add to and modify the web of meanings. There is a basic physical reality of body or face. But because faces and bodies are situated in a social context and surrounded with social values and meanings, they cannot be perceived in a direct, 'objective' way. Bodies and faces are used in Western society to determine, age, gender and race, for example. All of these categories carry enormous social meaning and weight, not just in general terms, but for the ways in which individuals understand their own selves and worth. Beyond this, the body, and parts of the body, become major symbols and representations of, and for, the self.

The body (face), then, carries a 'wide range of ever-changing meanings. It is the prime constituent of personal and social identity'. With all its organs, attributes, functions, states and senses, the body (face) 'is not so much a biological given as a social creation of immense complexity, and almost limitless variability, richness and power' (Synnott 1993, 3–4). This implies that the creation of understandings and meanings surrounding the body and its parts may be very different from time to time, and from culture to culture; we have already seen that face can be very differently understood, even in modern Western culture.

Recognising the socially constructed, symbolic and metaphorical richness and ambivalence of the body Synnott (1993, 4) suggests that:

> The body [face] social is many things: the prime symbol of the self, but also of society; it is something we have, yet also what we are; it is both subject and object at the same time; it is individual and personal, as unique as a fingerprint or odour-plume, yet it is also common to all humanity with all its systems, and taught in schools. The body [face] is both an individual creation, physically and phenomenologically, and a cultural product; it is personal, and also state property.

Face is placed in parenthesis in this quote because everything that applies to body generally applies also, and perhaps particularly, to face; this is often seen as a symbolic substitute for the self and the body as a whole, being the body's most expressive exposed organ.

Having introduced the notion of the social construction and mediation of body and face, I will move on to look at face as symbol and sign, and then at the corona of metaphorical meanings surrounding, illuminating, obscuring and refracting the physical reality of face.

Face as Sign and Symbol of Self

It is easy to see why face can easily be taken to be a symbol of the whole self. Prominently displayed on one side of the head, near the brain, the seat of the self in Western culture, the face is one of the most visible and expressive bits of the body. It reflects and enacts the continuity and movement that characterises life. Each face is unique, and most faces are very communicative. To know someone is mostly to have a face-to-face relationship with them; when you see their face, you think, 'That's X', without a moment's hesitation. Similarly, if someone's name is mentioned, or you think about X, their face is likely to come to your mind. If they go missing and you have to give a description of them to the police, you may well say quite a lot about their face. The face then serves as a kind of universal 'natural symbol' for the person or the self (Douglas 1973).

This sounds quite straightforward and commonsensical. But there are many assumptions built into this identification of selves with faces. And symbolisation quickly complexifies further. Because of the continual elision and confusion of meaning and experience between face, body and identity, it is possible for the body as a whole, or for some other part of the body, to represent the face. Levinas finds face in the bent backs of people (Danchev 2011, 40; Davies 1993; Levinas 2006, 201). And even inanimate objects can come to represent face or be seen as portraits. Van Gogh's paintings of his chair or his shoes are sometimes taken to be self-portraits and found, as such, to be moving. While the artist's physiognomy and body are absent, somehow the inanimate conjures up face and presence by a kind of metonymy or indirect mimesis which may make face and person more real in their absence than they might be in straight physical portrayal. Even a fingerprint can come to represent a face and a person in a portrait, as can a brain scan (Gombrich 1977, 202–3). Similarly, to conjure face by drawing a circle and placing two dots at the top, a vertical line in the middle and horizontal line at the bottom is to produce some kind of face. This elementary face quickly acquires expression which attracts interest. In a very basic way, a 'person' seems to be born. What lies behind the face? Who inhabits this face and what are they like?

A similar kind of elision takes place in face itself. So, for example, it can be psychoanalytically argued that for the infant, face becomes a symbolic substitute for the breast. And beyond that, the gleaming eye of the mother becomes the symbol and sign of the face (Ayers 2003). The whole of the embodied, multi-sensorial experience of the infant being with, and experiencing, another person is summarised in the symbol of the eye which, like a Russian doll, contains the symbols of face, breast, body and, by implication, person.

This intriguing capacity of body-face symbols to both contain and extend physical realities, creating the potential for the proliferation of meanings, does not need extensive exploration here. It is, however, important to be aware that this process easily, and often unconsciously, occurs whenever we talk about face. The question needs then to be asked: what is face being used to symbolise or signify? And what are the primary and secondary meanings through which the physical realities are being refracted when we do something as simple as talking about persons and faces? When we talk about, or experience, faces, are we encountering a person's physical features and movements, identities, selves or even their souls? These questions are often not susceptible to clear answers because these different elements are unendingly and recursively enfolded in each other, both in theory and in everyday experience.

Face as Generator and Recipient of Images and Metaphors

Face is endlessly imbricated with symbol and sign that make 'seeing' face a matter of social construction and interpretation as much as actual physical vision. It is also constantly involved in the generation of powerful metaphors and images (Johnson 1990). These are taken from face and applied to other realities (for example, the face of the moon or of my watch). They can also be drawn from other phenomena and then attached to face as ways of understanding and catching the richness and significance of faciality. To more adequately understand how we see and respond to face it will be helpful to acquire a critical awareness of how it gives and receives itself in metaphor.

Face is remarkable in attracting vivid metaphorical judgements and understandings. Being metaphorical, these understandings are polyvalent and capable of conveying many different meanings and connotations (Lakoff and Johnson 1980; Ortony 1993). They are not stable or straightforwardly descriptive. Often, these metaphors and images fit into groups that provide a wider ecology for understanding face, not least because they inflect and carry with them tacit secondary meanings that influence the sense of the primary metaphor that they surround. I will come to some of these families or groups soon.

First, I want to note the fact that face often seems to produce vivid one-line or one-paragraph images and metaphors that are then not extended, connected with others or critically considered. Here, for example, is Wittgenstein: 'The face is the soul of the body' (Wittgenstein 1998, 26e). This beautiful, poetic, intriguing judgement is couched as a single aphorism amidst a number of other, apparently completely unconnected, aphorisms on other topics.

Wittgenstein's metaphor stands in contrast to those physiognomists and others who equally poetically and most equally aphoristically characterise face as a 'mirror of the soul' (Synnott 1989, 614). Here, for example, 1,500 years before Wittgenstein, is St Jerome: 'The face is the mirror of the mind, and eyes without speaking confess the secrets of the heart' (Synnott 1989, 619).

By asserting that face is the soul of the body, Wittgenstein appears to be trying to contest the notion that face merely mirrors some kind of inner essence. This implicitly adds considerable value to physical face. But as with many of the common metaphors and images I will consider here, it is not clear exactly what is intended and the meaning is very underdetermined. Single metaphors or images for face are often thus used in isolation, or perhaps as part of a group of compatible or contrasting metaphors, without any attempt being made by their propagators to provided systematic modelling or thought about the nature of face. It is as if face defeats systematic thought and analysis and simply spawns metaphors. It seems, then, to refract analysis and understanding within a dazzling cloud of metaphors and images, many of them contradictory or incompatible.

Bearing in mind the uncritical and unsystematic, if creative and interesting, metaphorisation of face, I will now go on to outline some of the common individual metaphors and images used for face, situating them, where possible, within their ecologies or families.

Inside/outside

As the quotes from Wittgenstein and Jerome indicate, a popular locus from which metaphors about face are drawn is that of the container, with an inside and outside. For many centuries, the human body was viewed as a kind of house or container for the divinely created soul (Benthien 2002). This particular theological underpinning has diminished in importance in its explicit form. However, physiognomical and pathognomical thinking, presupposing some idea of inner and outer self that are related, still often informs contemporary attitudes to the self.

The idea that the face somehow conceals or gives access to an inner essence, depth or self continues to be a popular metaphor applied to the face as a whole, and to the eyes in particular. Sobieszek (1999, 288), for example, amongst other moderns, seems to accept this when he writes: 'Faces suture together inner and outer, projection and reflection.' And this kind of metaphorical assumption is frequently found in everyday parlance where it seems to be assumed that seeing someone's face will somehow open them up to us – note the container/splitting language – in a way that would not be possible if we merely saw their writing or heard their voice on the phone. The metaphors of inside, within and depth behind face continue to live in our time, even though there is now considerable scepticism as to whether there really is an essence or inner depth to the person.

Architectural metaphors

Alongside the basic metaphorical understanding of inside/outside, it is not surprising to find a family of metaphors for face that are essentially architectural. They are based on the loose understanding that the face is a kind of building, with external and internal architecture and fittings. From external structural architecture, then, are drawn metaphors such as facade (a protective, possibly deceptive or decorated exterior), wall (an impermeable structural barrier that may be evident if people's faces are 'blank'), window (a place where you can see the interior and from which perhaps an interior self 'looks out') and door (face as a place of entry into the self, the brain, the character).

From the language of internal household fittings come metaphors for face like mirror (face as a surface that reflects the self or others), picture (face as a representation of the self), veil (face as something that partly reveals and partly conceals the self), curtain (something that conceals the self), screen (face understood as something upon which others project their feelings) and lamp (face as something that illuminates self and others, perhaps when it smiles). Turning to art, faces can be seen as icons (that allow us to see beyond surface and to engage relationally with a hidden, transcendent world or person) or as idols (object of reverence and worship in and of themselves).

Geography and spatiality

Quite closely related to architectural metaphors as a family for glimpsing or grasping face are what might broadly be described as geographical or spatial metaphors.

Unsurprisingly, face has often been seen as a landscape of mountains (nose, cheeks, forehead) and lakes (the eyes and mouth) in which shadows can be found. Some people have even characterised these features as a kind of desolation with deep, mine-like holes. Deleuze and Guattari (2004, 211), for example, write:

> The face, what a horror. It is naturally a lunar landscape with its pores, plains, bright colours, whiteness and holes: there is no need for a close up to make it inhuman; it is naturally a close-up, and naturally inhuman, a monstrous hood.

Some interpreters of face, fortune tellers or physiognomists would see it as a kind of external map of an interior world. The face has also been compared with stars and planets like the moon and the sun in its beauty, tranquillity, coldness, ferocity or radiance. Again, it has been characterised in terms of meteorology and weather conditions such as storms, clouds and sunshine. This kind of metaphor catches the sense of rapidly changing different moods and expressions. Staying within this broadly geographical/meteorological ecology, the face has been compared with the sea (a powerful and underdetermined mass which reflects strong and mysterious undercurrents), or more pacifically, as a pool or bowl registering ripples of emotion that pass between people on opposite sides.

Turning more towards figures and human activity within the landscape, face has been likened to a lure or trap that is used to attract, hunt or capture others.

The world of human activity
Moving away from metaphors drawn from the natural world, there are a further groups of metaphors emerging from human and technological realms. The theatre produces metaphors of face as itself a kind of dramatic space or stage on which character and emotions are enacted and performed. It also provides the metaphor of mask, habitually used in ancient drama to present the self or persona. Mask has the ambivalent quality of both revealing and concealing self, deceiving and showing the truth.

A set of more modern, perhaps less obvious and congenial metaphors for face has emerged from the worlds of technology, capitalist exploitation and colonialism. Face can be seen as a kind of devouring capitalist and colonising machine that devours and exploits others, particularly non-white faces, excluding them from power (Deleuze and Guattari 2004; Fanon 2008). John Updike uses a similar metaphor to describe the effect of face on much-photographed celebrities: 'Celebrity is a mask that eats into the face' (Kemp 2004, 119).

Staying with this kind of thought in mass society, novelist Milan Kundera (1991) suggests that, far from being unique and distinctive, face functions as a kind of serial number or badge of belonging that makes people the same rather than different from others. And many readers will be familiar with notion of face in Orwell's novel, *1984*, where face is seen as the guiding metaphor both for total domination of the population and also for resistance to totalitarian power (Orwell 1983).

Less pessimistically, from the world of science, metaphors of face as a communications control centre and as a signal station emerge that suggest further extensions of complex modern technological life into understandings of face. From the literary world emerges the understanding of face as a kind of text that can be read and parsed. And from the criminological context comes the very sobering metaphor of face as prison, sometimes applied to people who have problems with facial appearance and expression.

Philosophy and human relations
A final group of metaphors, which shade into sign and symbol, can be loosely characterised as philosophical. Within this ecological group, face can be understood as person (the identity that it is taken to correspond to face), presence (the experience of being with a person), absence (the sense that is evoked when a person is absent but their image is in some way present, for example in a photograph or portrait, even in a mental image), acceptance (face denotes the possibility of relationship), essence (your face is your self) and home (the face as the place where a person finds their place and lives).

In this brief survey, I have only considered a few of the metaphors and metaphorical families that pertain to face. For the most part, I have not explored extended and secondary meanings. However, it will be noted that while some of the metaphors considered may be consonant with each other, some of them clash and contradict one another. Face as a prison contrasts sharply with face as a door to the self, or as a performance of the self.

My purpose has not been to align and arrive at definitive metaphorical understandings of face, but rather to point to their variety and the polyvalent metaphorical meanings of face. Face is perhaps all of these metaphors and more besides. It generates a superfluity of meanings and cannot be confined within any one metaphorical ecology or family. Understanding the nature and variety of the kinds of metaphors that may be applied to face is useful here because it encourages critical awareness of the use of metaphors and their implications, and also of the fact that it is almost impossible to think about and understand face without using them. We see face through, and with, symbol and metaphor, and face itself generates symbols and metaphors. This interestingly complicates the ways in which we approach understanding and viewing face.

Conclusion

Faces are everywhere in this modern era of faciality. In this chapter, I have argued that, despite the ubiquity and obviousness of faces in mass urban society, it is very difficult to get a fix on face. The significance, meanings and understanding of face and its relation to persons changes as face moves through different times and cultures. Even in the contemporary Western world, there are many different understandings of face and its significance; it is difficult to analyse out exactly why it has so much importance when faces are so common. It is difficult to fix face historically and socially because of its varied and ambiguous meanings and significance. Further complexity is added once it is acknowledged that face is fundamentally implicated in, and refracted through social meanings, values, understandings and metaphors. Physical face is lost, sought and found, insofar as it can be, within a corona of meanings and understandings that fundamentally inform our vision. So the first step in trying to save face, to bring it into the world of conscious concern, is to recognise its mobility and complex relationships with humans, and with social and cultural contexts. In many ways it is not possible to gain a steady view and understanding of face, either physically or intellectually. Face must be glimpsed as it continues to move and ramify in terms of both sight and understanding. However, having acknowledged the uncertainty and complexity of seeing and understanding face in general terms thus, it is now appropriate to turn more directly to what can be known of the 'facts' of physical faces and their functions.

Chapter 2
The 'Facts' of Face

The living face is the most important and mysterious surface we deal with. It is the centre of our flesh. We eat, drink, breathe, and talk with it, and it houses four of the five classic senses. It is a showcase of the self, instantly displaying our age, sex and race, our health and mood. It marks us as individuals. It can send messages too elusive for science, so far, and it bewitches us with its beauty. The Trobriand Islanders deemed the face sacred, and well they might, for it is our social identity, compass, and lure, our social universe.

(McNeill 1998, 4)

The meanings and nuances of face may be unfathomable. However, some of the 'facts' about its evolution, features and functions are relatively easy to outline. This chapter looks at the biological and physical 'facts' and evolution of face. It also enquires into what face does within the context of the overall human existence and relational encounters.

I have put 'facts' in inverted commas because the way in which we understand face and faces is refracted through what culture counts as useful knowledge. The last chapter showed that understandings and 'facts' about faces and bodies are endlessly refracted through the lenses of metaphor. 'Facta', as their Latin derivation implies, are things that are made, not found lying around (Brown 1989, 35). So the discussion in the last chapter should not be forgotten in favour of what might look like a simple, plausible, empirical account here. This account is an interpretative construction informed by basic cultural assumptions, for example the belief in biological evolution, belief in the fundamental importance of communication.

A further complicating factor is that not only are faces seen and understood through invisible, but active, metaphorical lenses, they perform many functions simultaneously and very quickly. It is literally and metaphorically hard to grasp the facts of face in a simple, direct way. McNeill (1998, 8) rightly observes, 'Many mysteries of the face don't lie in the face at all. They lie in the mind, in the ways we respond to the face, represent it, hide it, adorn it, and try to remake it'. However, the face has physical complexities that in themselves make it a difficult organ to comprehend. Humans have uniquely well-developed faces that allow us to understand ourselves and each other and which have probably helped us to develop complex inner states and consciousness itself (Cole 1998, 6).

That being acknowledged, here are some of the facts about face as mediated mainly through the discourses of biology and experimental psychology. I will start with looking at the evolution, then the structure and functions of face. Faces are complex organs that accomplish many different things simultaneously, adding to the sense of undetermined 'dazzling darkness' and inappropriability explored

in the last chapter. The discussion of the simultaneous functions of face leads
to further consideration of how far faces can reveal the persons and characters
that lie 'behind' them. The underdetermined, but popularly assumed and enacted
close relationship between face and personality is therefore examined. The
often unacknowledged gap between character and face allows the possibility of
deception and manipulation in activities such as masking, veiling and acting;
these are explored at the end of the chapter. I conclude by asking, whose face is
it anyway?

The Evolution of Face

Non-vegans who say that they don't eat animals that have faces may be
inadvertently disingenuous. Most fish, insects and animals have faces if a face is
basically understood as being composed of two eyes, something like a nose that
separates the eyes and, beneath the eyes, a mouth. It is difficult to know where face
begins and ends (is the side of your head part of your face, or your neck or your
hair?), but this basic pattern constructed round the eyes and mouth is widely found
throughout nature. Human infants will respond to a very basic representational
pattern of the two eyes, the nose that divides and the mouth beneath, even if these
things are only figured by simply lines and dots (Hole and Bourne 2010).

Faces, then, are very common, and they generally follow a common pattern.
Humpty Dumpty is right in his comments to Alice concerning whether they will
recognise each other if they meet again:

> "Your face is the same as everyone else has – the two eyes, so –" (marking
> their places in the air with his thumb) "nose in the middle, mouth under. It's
> always the same. Now if you had the two eyes on the same side of the nose,
> for instance – or the mouth at the top – that would be *some* help". (Carroll
> 1970, 276)

So there is nothing particularly original or unusual about having a face. Faces are
all around us. Millions of our fellow creatures share the same basic facial pattern
of eyes, nose, mouth and ears.

The evolution of the face probably started about 520 million years ago in the
sea. Human faces started as 'fish faces'; indeed there is a stage in embryological
development where foetuses do actually look very like fish (Perrett 2010,
chapter 1; Bates and Cleese 2001). The most important feature of the face was,
and remains, the mouth, the first facial feature to develop embryonically. This is
a salutary reminder that essentially the face is a door – to the gut! The mouth is
the most mobile part of the face and is heavily involved in making and changing
expressions (yawning, laughing, smiling), as well as in the main work of the face

which in terms of physical survival is to do with feeding – sucking, chewing and biting.[1]

Another fundamental, basic function it has is to do with sensing danger or advantage; near the brain in humans, the face is the focus of four of the five senses – seeing, hearing, tasting and smelling, and an important locus for the fifth, touch.

While possessing common properties and features, each human face is unique. Our ears are as unique and individual as fingerprints and the relative spacing of our features – hence the possibility of identifying people through measuring distances between the features in identity photographs.

Human faces share many of the features of other animals, particularly monkeys and apes. However, they do not closely resemble the faces of other species. This has probably contributed to the self-understanding that humans are different from and 'higher' than other animals (McNeill 1998, 18).

There are some distinctive variations and differences that should be noted as we look at the different features that comprise the average human face. In general terms, human faces are distinguished by their flatness and bareness (McNeill 1998, 18ff.). This means that they are very good for communicating and signalling over distances to other species members. Communicative potential is enhanced by the irises of the human eye having a clearly different colour from the pupil. The iris is also ringed by a white sclera. This allows others easily to see where we are looking, following our gaze. The eyes are the psychological centre of face (McNeill 1998, 21). They are little bright, shiny pools of being that subtly change and alter. They attract and give information to others, signalling purpose, interest and desire, amongst many other things.

Human faces also have large, prominent foreheads, and noses that jut out over the mouth and are separated from them. The mouth itself has well-developed lips, tongue and white teeth; this is the feature of the face which is easiest to read from a distance. Eyebrows are another important and prominent feature, enhancing the signalling potential of the face as well as its distinctive recognisability (Perrett 2010, 20). The skin of the cheeks is also a locus for communication of, for example, excitement and fear.

The only species-unique feature of the human face is the small, separated out chin, the effect of the diminished jaw that may be the evolutionary product of not having to chew so much because of the possibility of cooking food. A final feature that should be mentioned here is hair. Hair frames the bare face. Being the largest and most easily changeable part of it, it can be used to change or highlight aspects of its appearance, and so to enhance or conceal expression.

---

[1] So powerful and dominant is the mouth in terms of movement that when it opens, it basically splits the face open. Very few artists or photographers ever portray subjects with open or laughing mouths, so distorting are they (Brilliant 1991, 9ff.). This is just one of the common conventions that dominates and distorts perceptions of face in art and representation.

McNeill (1998, 37) sums up the features of the human face in geographical terms: 'If we view the face as geography, it has two long forests, a pair of multicoloured sunken lakes, a Gibraltar-like peak, and an abysmal pit.'

In structural terms, human faces are composed of solid bone, which gives basic structure in the skull, cheeks and jaw; cartilage, which forms the end of the nose and the ears and continues to grow throughout life; a very large number of muscles – there are twenty-two main groups of these on each side of the face – that allow the face to move so it can signal, suck, bite and chew; fat, which helps to give the face its distinctive shape; and skin (Perrett 2010, chapter 1). Skin is the largest of the body's organs. In cold climates it is most openly, and often most prominently, displayed on the face and hands (Benthien 2002; Connor 2004). Skin colour and tone are also part of communicating with others. Thus it is the facial skin that blushes or turns white in response to embarrassment or threat. A face without skin colour and tone looks very strange; white wax or plaster death masks often look ungendered, even inhuman.

If the face in some ways has the solidity and continuity of a landscape undergirded by the substrate solidity of bone, perhaps its most distinctive and characteristic feature is its malleability and plasticity based on muscle and jaw movement. This means that the face is constantly changing, both from moment to moment and throughout life. The landscape moves and changes radically as we age and react to life around us. This adds to the complexity and perplexity of human face.

The Functions of Face

The face is a very prominent and visible organ of the human body, along with the hands, often the most prominent and visible. It performs many different functions simultaneously, adding both to its intriguing attractiveness and to the difficulty in discerning its importance. Here, then, in no particular order of importance, are some main understandings of the functions of face.

Identity

Faces are used by humans to identify who we are. Humans are born 'face hungry' and they are drawn to faces from birth (McNeill 1998, 180; Perrett 2010, chapter 3). Almost immediately, babies orient to all faces. They can quickly distinguish their mother's faces from those of others within a few days of birth, and within three months, become focused on the faces of those who belong to the same race (Hole and Bourne 2010, chapters 5, 12). This is quite remarkable when it is remembered that faces are constantly moving and are also seen from many different angles (one of the reasons why machines find it difficult to recognise faces accurately).

The ability to recognise faces develops throughout childhood and adolescence; it is thought that we have the ability to distinguish and remember thousands of faces. However, we are not good at identifying unfamiliar faces, which makes eyewitness evidence in court problematic, or at identifying people from two-dimensional photographs where moving light and shade cannot be used to help clarify the exact nature of the face being looked at (Hole and Bourne 2010, chapter 13).

This human hunger for the face, married with the unique constellation of features on individual faces, means that face is a major source of identifying people. Indeed, the face is treated as an instant, self-authorising and unchallengeable way of authenticating the self and its identity. To show my face is to put beyond any doubt the fact that I am who I say I am: 'The face is a signature in flesh and bone, and it remains our frontline against imposture ... Our singularity is our security, and our restraint' (McNeill 1998, 78). Hole and Bourne (2010, 310) argue, similarly, 'Your face is unique, and it's almost always on public display. As such, it is the most important guide to your identity that other people can use, and modern surveillance-obsessed societies rely heavily on this fact'.

Information

Faces don't just tell us *who* people are, they also tell us a lot about *what* people are, what their main salient characteristics are. From looking at the faces of others, humans can tell a great deal about them. The quality and tone of skin and hair, together with the size of a face, particularly the chin and forehead, will probably reveal the gender of a person. The lustre and tone of their facial skin and eyes will indicate whether or not they are healthy, as will the amount of subcutaneous fat that helps to shape the face. People with more yellow and red pigments in the skin look healthier; this reflects a better blood supply (Perrett 2010, chapter 7). Hair colour, wrinkles and the state of teeth, amongst other features, can be used to make a judgement as to someone's age. Another important piece of information that a face can reveal to us is whether or not we are closely related to the person we are looking at; this may be a very important factor in deciding whether or not to mate with them.

Communication

A major function of face is communication with other members of the human race. A facial gesture, a movement of the eyes or even of one eyebrow can communicate an enormous amount to others as to what we are attending to, thinking or feeling. Clear, bare faces with their well-defined mouths and eyebrows and their clearly demarcated eyes maximise the possibilities of non-verbal or supplementary verbal communication. With particular regard to gaze, not only is the face itself a sign of the self that communicates presence, it is also a channel of signs and communication (Argyle and Cook 1976). Gaze, for example, can be used to regulate turn-taking, to express intimacy, to dominate others, to attract their attention, to direct their attention elsewhere, to seduce them and to communicate a variety of emotions and moods, all without words (Argyle and Cook 1976; Bruce and Young 1998, 213–14).

The visual part of the brain in humans develops long before words are acquired, so all infants are brought up initially communicating non-verbally through sight and touch (Gerhardt 2004). This skill in communicating through the face that develops for most sighted people out of early infant gaze shared with the mother or caregiver is of enormous significance, even when words have been acquired. In adult life, a glance, like a picture, can be worth a thousand words, and it takes but a moment, not the seconds that verbal communication might take. Clearly, both words and facial and bodily gestures, at best, complement each other as ways of communicating fully and effectively. But the importance of non-verbal facial communication is often radically underestimated in a word-centred world where verbal cognition is taken to be primary (Cole 1998, 193).

Display and Expression of Emotions and Moods

Closely related to the communicative functions of face are its functions as displayer, expresser and receiver of emotions and moods.

The face is very well suited to communicating with other species members. Among the main things that it communicates are individuals' moods and emotions. This is important in a social species where members need to understand the states and intentions of their potential collaborators or antagonists. The face is a subtle instrument for doing this. With its enormous powers of minute movement, powered by no less than 80 mimetic muscles, a face is capable of anything from 6,000 to 10,000 expressions (McNeill 1989, 180; Synnott 1989, 607). Some theorists believe that humans can manifest anything up to 180 different kinds of smile alone (Bruce and Young 1998, 43). Emotional expressions normally last only a maximum of four seconds, and most are much briefer and often almost undetectable, their duration reflecting their intensity (Ekman 2004, 143).

There is a complex and inconclusive debate about whether or not facial and bodily expressions of emotions are biologically innate and universal or whether they are culturally learned and determined like a sort of language (Russell 1994, 2003). Darwin (1998) and his successors like Ekman (2004) have argued that there are universal emotions which express themselves in ways that are interpretable across times and cultures, even if they are to some extent governed by local rules of display. They adduce evidence such as the fact that blind and sighted children both have the same facial expressions to suggest that at least major emotions such as sadness, anger, surprise, fear, disgust and happiness are highly recognisable, with happiness being the most easily legible of these. Others question this essentialist, substantive view of emotions, querying whether emotions exist in any absolute sense. They point out that many emotions, for example nostalgia, pride, have no necessary outward bodily manifestation at all, that some conditions labelled as emotions like 'surprise' hardly seem to have any lasting emotional content so do not really count as emotions and that even the six or seven 'universal' emotions are not necessarily universally recognised by all. Shame, for example, by its very nature is often hidden and invisible (McNeill 1989, 182; Pattison 2000, chapter 1; Russell 1994, 2003). However, it is unnecessary to get into a detailed debate about the nature and visibility of emotions to assert that, whether biologically implanted or culturally constructed, we and others reveal at least some of our feelings and emotions in our faces.

One interesting aspect of this emotional revealing is that expression is not necessarily under the conscious control of the person displaying the emotion. Someone else may see, or think they see, a look of rage, fear or joy on my face, and I may be inwardly unaware of it. Whether I like it or not, my face is then giving me away to others who may then respond to my expression, not my own perceived state. Their own response, including their facial response, to my displayed, but unconscious expression, may then give me feedback about how I am coming across, and even how I am feeling. Someone may indicate that they think I am angry even though I may not feel this consciously. Having had this kind of response, I then know something about myself that I could not have articulated, or been aware of, before.

This kind of feedback is very important as there is some evidence to suggest that when people cease to manifest emotional expressions, for example because they have no or limited facial movement, others withdraw from them (Cole 1998; Cole with Spalding 2009). They then do not get this kind of powerful information/ reinforcement that helps to maintain them as persons and members of the social world. As social selves who need to live in the minds and faces of others to understand ourselves and others, the continued giving and receiving of emotions via facial expression helps us to understand ourselves, as well as others. The spontaneous and uncontrolled expression of what we take to be innate emotional conditions on the face is thus a very important part of making and keeping human persons human in infinitely varied, often subtle, reciprocal relations of display, recognition and feedback. Perhaps we cannot fully understand ourselves, let alone others, if we do not enter into the facial communication of emotions (Cole 1998; Merleau-Ponty 1964).

Some facial emotional expression is beyond conscious control and so thought to be innate, spontaneous and unavoidable. Thus it is difficult to feign or avoid the furrowed brow that comes with deep grief or the movement around the eyes that accompanies the 'Duchenne' smile (Ekman 2004). However, faces can also be used consciously or semi-consciously wilfully to display emotions. Actors train themselves to be able to adapt different expressions and movements, but even in everyday life, people can use expressions such as smiles to steer themselves through social life. There are many different kinds of smile, perhaps more than 180, ranging from the nervous and placatory through to the full 'Duchenne' smile that involves the muscles round the eyes and indicates real joy (Bruce and

Young 1998, 43; Ekman 2004, 204ff.; Perrett 2010, 22ff.).[2] These smiles may be deliberately deployed to produce certain results in relationships. This raises the question of whether or not you can tell what someone is feeling or thinking from looking at their face as is often, and often quite rightly, assumed. Can you really judge a person's emotions, mood and intentions by the expression on their face? This is an issue to which I will return in a moment. But first a word about the final function of face to be considered here, attraction.

Attraction

It is perhaps not surprising that much work has been done on what makes faces attractive over the last few decades as the physical appearance of face has become so important in all parts of Western culture and people's faces can literally become a key to fame, fortune and advantage – and the reverse if their faces somehow don't appeal: 'Prejudice and discrimination against the ugly are virtually a cultural norm' (Synnnott 1990, 56).

Summarising the empirical 'attractiveness' research that has been done by psychologists recently, Perrett (2010, chapter 3) suggests that humans are hard-wired to pay attention to faces, particularly attractive faces; this starts in infancy. Babies' faces are particularly alluring with their large eyes and foreheads and their small noses and mouths. Thus, most people are at their most attractive to others in infancy, around the age of eight months, but those who continue to have such faces may also be especially attractive (Perrett 2010, chapter 8).

This has continuing effects in the real world. Facially attractive, 'cute looking' babies get more attention and advantage, even in acute care units where they thrive better than less attractive babies (Perrett 2010, 162–3). If you have attractive children, they will live longer, be wealthier and have more self-esteem and descendants (Perrett 2010, chapter 6). Economists have calculated that there are considerable lifelong financial and social gains for facially attractive people that mean in effect that 'ugly' or unattractive people suffer measurable disadvantage and discrimination (Baker 2010; Etcoff 1999; Hamermesh 2011).

Generally, and, it seems, universally, while types, colours and shapes of face differ enormously round the world, people are attracted to faces that are characterised by symmetry and seem to be average within our cultural and tribal setting – we like people who look 'normal' and like us. We tend to be particularly attracted to people who have faces like our opposite sex parent. However, paradoxically, highly attractive people do not conform to the norm (Perrett 2010, chapter 4). Men are said to prefer more feminine-looking women's faces, but

---

[2]   Wittgenstein (2009, #583) contends that smiling is a uniquely human expression: 'A smiling mouth *smiles* only in a human face' (emphasis original). Whether or not Wittgenstein is right about this, smiling and happiness are the most recognisable of human emotional expressions from a distance and are also the most interculturally accurately interpreted facial expressions (Ekman 2004).

women are not necessarily attracted to masculinity in men's faces – the kinds of men's faces they are attracted to may change during ovulation, for example. Although facial attraction is very important in creating relations and making one's way in the world, other factors such as genes, experience, parents, culture, social group, religious beliefs and so on all play a part in creating and cementing relationships. Apparently, we tend to grow to think people are more attractive the longer we are with them. So face, detached from the rest of body, society and culture, is not determinative of destiny, though it does have a significant role to play (Perrett 2010, chapter 11).

The value of the kind of research into attractiveness and facial responsiveness undertaken by Perrett and other psychologists seems problematic (Bruce and Young 1998, chapter 4). In some ways, it seems trivial and unilluminative, possibly even misleading, based as it is on removing people from their everyday cultural and social settings and then simply getting them to react to photographed faces that are manipulated to achieve certain effects. However, it does forcibly underline the danger of stereotyping and responding to faces in particular ways that might be detrimental to relationships. It is certainly disconcerting to discover that by the end of our first 12 months, infants concentrate their facial interest on members of their own tribe and race, and are no longer interested in all faces, as they are when they are first born (Hole and Bourne 2010, chapter 12). This may go some way to explaining why we may initially think that people of different races 'all look just the same'; we then perhaps make the mistake of treating them as if they are, in fact, all the same and quite different from the people 'like us' whose faces we are more interested in, and attracted by.

Having dealt with some of the main functions of face that are all being carried out simultaneously as we identify people, assess their age and health, judge the state of their emotions and character and react to them as more or less attractive to us, it is time to examine at greater length the relationship between inner character and feeling and the outward appearance and performance of faces. Can we really read faces and find a character and emotions beneath or within? Can we trust what we see in people's faces, or is this just an illusion? And what are the implications of activities like acting and masking for the ways in which we might understand the significance of faces and facial interactions? These are some of the issues to which I now turn.

Face and Personality: Exploring Superficiality, Depth and Identity

Some years ago, John Bowden (1988) noted that we probably know a lot about the historical Jesus, but we cannot be clear about what is certainly known by way of facts because they are so mixed in with myths, legends, misunderstandings and ideological assumptions that they cannot really be distinguished from them. It is rather the same with trying to understand the relationship between the notion of face as a physical reality and the inner self or world that it is deemed to reflect. It is often taken to be the case that there is a fundamental relationship between face and person in terms of identity, character, emotional knowledge and so on – but that relationship is a problematic, and possibly variable and unstable one, that does not permit constant, direct correlation. Face is a fluid matrix of forces, not a guide to the soul. It is at one and the same time 'an opaque surface seen and dominated from without and an abysmal depth loaded with subjectivities that can shift and mutate at any moment' (Sobieszek 1999, 75). Amidst this unstable, underdetermined seethe, however, face is still treated as 'suturing' together the 'inner' and 'outer' aspects of the person, its skin-deep surface confusingly acting as the medium for both projection and reflection (Sobieszek 1999, 288). At a trivial level, most people have probably been surprised at least once in their lives to find that the person who had the 'honest, open, nice face' was a bit of a crook, not quite what they appeared to be.

It seems to me that we mostly cannot help acting as if face really does reflect and give access to the inner depth of people. Whether people have had a good sense of the inwardly aware, individuated expressive psychological self or not over history, the tendency to read character, morals and moods off the faces of others goes back into ancient times. A 'reliable' (but as we have seen, deeply flawed and questionable) association between face, character and identity is one of the assumptions upon which our culture has been built. Plato talked of the man who was both good in character and beautiful in form, the two things being taken to be inseparable, and Aristotle wrote a treatise on reading character off facial form (Porter 2005). While formally and scientifically, physiognomy and pathognomy are dismissed as pseudo-science, this does not stop ordinary people from continuing to equate face with character, soul or inner essence. This ideology of 'facism' is often accompanied by the notion of a 'beauty mystique' whereby beauty is equated with goodness and ugliness with evil (hence the many ugly faces of Satan (Eco 2007)) (Synnott 1989, 608). Gilman (1998, 1999) has argued not only that racial and other stigmatised minority groups, such as the Jews and the Irish, have been discriminated against on the grounds of their facial 'ugliness' (= badness), but also that even so sophisticated a technique as cosmetic surgery is legitimated on the basic premise that making a defective face more acceptable to its owner actually accomplishes a kind of psychotherapeutic, inward change so they feel more acceptable to themselves.

The representational traffic between facial appearance and the psyche or soul continues to flow here, as it does in the case of portrait-painting and photography. Here, many producers and consumers still firmly believe that inner essence can somehow accurately be represented or evoked in external appearance (Freeland 2010; Gombrich 1972). A portrait can catch the 'air' of someone and manifest their presence and being, even if it is in reality a flat, two-dimensional reproduction consisting of paper or canvas and chemicals. Our belief in the correspondence between face and interiority is, then, fairly universal and absolute even if it is not rationally based on compelling evidence. Seventy-five per cent of the population believe it is possible to know a person's true personality from looking at their face (Perrett 2010, 183). What accounts for its continuing plausibility?

One reason that this belief is plausible is because it is, in fact, possible to read off some aspects of people's personalities and characteristics in their faces with quite a high degree of accuracy (Perrett 2010, 189). Characteristics like introversion and extroversion, warmth and generosity and attitudes to sexual relations can be discerned; like learning a language, we can come accurately to associate certain character traits and behaviours with particular looks. More attractive people often display traits of extroversion and conscientiousness, for example, and these can be discerned by watchers. It could be that, when we see people with certain facial characteristics, we then treat them as if they have particular qualities, so they then learn to behave in ways that fulfil the expectations of others. Or maybe the habitual set of their face reflects their characteristic moods and emotions and shapes them with lines that are legible as reflecting those characteristics. Perhaps there is a biological or genetic linkage with character traits and facial expressions or features, so that emotions, traits and expressions go together in some way not yet understood. Or again, it is possible that people having certain qualities such as facial attractiveness have easy, privileged lives so it is easy for them to look relaxed, while those born with 'ugly' faces tend to be treated badly, learn to behave badly and develop expressions to match (Perrett 2010, 191). There is no definitive causal explanation here.

Most of us are (over-)confident, unrepentant readers of faces in our eagerness to discern the character, morals, expressions and moods of others. However, the capacity to do this is variable and blotchy; mostly we do not know for a certainty whether our reading is accurate or not. This means that face reading is sometimes a useful, sometimes a terribly misleading mechanism for understanding others. The fact that blind people can get through life satisfactorily without having this highly visible aid to help them in understanding others warns against the infallible usefulness of facial appearance and expression in evaluating people: 'If a face were indispensable, a blind man couldn't know such things as human characteristics, could he?' (Abe 2006, 31). They, and others, have suggested that voice is a more accurate indicator of emotion, truthfulness and authenticity.

However, it is the very fact that reading character and emotions of faces can be such an ambivalent, confusing, misleading, even dangerous experience that lends fascination to various kinds of veiling, masking and deception, both in fiction and in real life. If everyone were just as they appeared or seemed outwardly, so that face functioned infallibly as a kind of brand or meter of character, mood and intention, then many relationships might lack interest and subtlety. It is the fact that face does not always reflect essence or identity, indeed, may mislead concerning both these things, that allows people to play with their faces, and so play with ideas and perceptions of identity, their own and others.

I am, and am not, my face. But maybe you do not know when I am identified with it and when I am trying to deceive you. This might be a subversive or a delightful thought, depending on the circumstances and the context of our relationship. The idea that someone's facial appearance might change, so that their identity, too, might alter, is a worrying one. It potentially subverts trusting relationship based on continuity of character and personal recognition. And if my face changes involuntarily, the thought that other people might then mistake my identity and emotional intentions is equally anxiety provoking. Hence many small children do not like their parents changing their appearances and may be terrified of clowns with their misleading and fixed caricature emotional expressions. Make-up artists in creating new faces, God-like, then create new identities that are not 'real' (Morawetz 2001, 7).

This would seem a good point, then, to discuss the nature and some of the implications of phenomena like masking, veiling and acting. These activities can be seen as actively trying to hide the self, or to deceive and mislead the observer's eye and interpretation. As we will see, however, they are often more ambiguous both in their intentions and their effects.

Masking

Masking, veiling and acting have many things in common. All involve, in one way or another, disguising or manipulating facial appearance. A broad and fairly arbitrary distinction can be made between masking and acting on the one hand and veiling on the other. While veiling is merely a matter of hiding or obscuring the face in whole or in part, masking and acting involve taking on the face of another which then necessarily obscures the 'real' face beneath.

Masks and masking provide a very interesting commentary on face. They play with the notions of continuity and essential identity to which we appear to have in everyday life an apparently unswerving, uncritical commitment. Masking and masks have played an important part in many cultures through history, though their origins and purposes are obscure (Johnson 2011; Mack 1996; Mauss 1990; Napier 1986; Nunley and McCarty 1999). The uses and meanings of masking are, like those of face itself, ambivalent and contextually inflected (Johnson 2011). Usually associated with men rather than women in traditional societies, they have been used as tools of otherworldly power, to represent the dead, to confer ghosthood on the deceased, as homes or manifestations of the gods, and to clean the environment (McNeill 1998, 147ff.). A main function of traditional masks has been to effect some kind of transformation and boundary breaking so that feared things like death and the dead can be identified with, therefore feared no longer (Wurmser 1995, 303ff.). In Greek theatre, masks were used as ways of adopting a particular dramatic character, *prosopon* meaning the face, the mask and the person portrayed in the role.

In contemporary Western society, masks and masking do not have such positive connotations. Perhaps drawing on deep associations of mask and masking with the devil and evil in Christianity, masking is synonymous with falsity, the adoption of a *persona* and the hiding of personality – therefore it is associated with inauthenticity and untrustworthiness (Johnson 2011, chapter 8). Deception, falsity and superficiality are all attributed to masks and masking in contemporary everyday life and parlance, making them rather negative. A mask then is a kind of false front, and it is unmasking rather than masking that is valued, for example when politicians are confronted on television.

Masks, whether material or enfleshed, disguise or manipulate identity: thus, their wearers are not recognised and can avoid moral responsibilities and even behave badly without being identifiable. It is Dorian Gray's mask-like, beautiful, but false, face that allows him to be act like a psychopathic monster (Wilde 2003).

However, masks can have a much more positive role. A mask can allow a person to be present while at the same time being absent. It can permit its wearer to take a rest from themselves and their everyday identity. It can preserve honour and reputation. More than that, a mask can actually allow individuals to express themselves and their real identity. They may be able to be more truthful, authentic and honest than when unmasked. Oscar Wilde typically pithily notes, 'Man is least himself when he talks in his own person. Give him a mask and he will tell the truth' (Kemp 2004, 77). Indeed, a mask, a changed face, might allow the positive transformation of life and identity in a desired direction (Morawetz 2001, 23–43). This is presumably one of the main impulses lying behind facial aesthetic surgery and the extensive use of make-up in our society.

Depending on context and intentions, facial masking might liberate and transform as much as it deceives and misleads. Venetian nobles wore masks in the eighteenth century as much to avoid everyday conventions of deference as to allow themselves license without accountability (Johnson 2011). Perhaps it is this kind of positive role that is indicated by Nietzsche when he writes that 'Everything that is profound loves the mask' (Wurmser 1995, 1).

Whatever the veracity of that speculation, it is undoubtedly true that masking, whether the assuming of a physical object or of certain kinds of expression designed to inform and manipulate others, is an important facility for humans. Arguably, it is not far removed from the necessity of having a visible, socially acceptable and predictable self that can engage with others and this needs to be consistent and if necessary to some extent feigned to protect the privacy and feelings of the self (Velleman 2006, chapter 3). The capacity to play with facial appearance, to don masks, raises fundamental issues about what it is to have a stable, consistent identity and to be human (Morawetz 2001, 202ff.). These disconcerting and fundamental issues lie only skin-deep beneath the use and adoption of masks for the face. Masks breed mystique and mystery (McNeill 1998, 155). A large part of this is the mystery of being humans who can both conceal and reveal their identities by the use of the face. And in the modern world, it should be noted, masks are seldom physical artefacts. They are more likely to be the naked faces of individuals; this puts enormous pressure on individuals to create and perform their own personal mask.

Veiling

Many of the same ambivalent attitudes and assumptions that apply to masks and masking apply also to veils and veiling in contemporary Western society (Butler 2006; El Guindi 1999; Joppke 2009). The honest, open person who is willing to share his or her identity and feelings with others will not want to veil his or her face. If you are proud of our identity and want to show that you are not afraid of others, then you will want others to be able to see your face just as it is as a badge and guarantee of your authenticity. This is perhaps why some secularised Western men find it very difficult to accept that many Islamic women want to keep their faces completely covered, except perhaps for the eyes. This wish for facial hiddenness is then seen as a rejection of facial contact, and thus a rejection of personal honesty. The person who hides their face must have something to hide about themselves that is shameful or harmful to others, the logic seems to run. Or perhaps they are oppressed in some way and not allowed to be themselves, having a full and valued public identity. Thus, veiling represents the occlusion and obscurity of their lives, not just their faces.

Contrary arguments and interpretations can, however, be put alongside this. For some Muslim women, the veil can represent solidarity, belonging to family, community and religion. It provides protection against shame and a place of privacy within which female agency is respected and preserved. It can therefore be worn with modesty and pride and its wearer deserves respect. Seen thus, forcing the removal of the veil and the sight of the female face might in fact represent a violent, dehumanising defacement (Butler 2006, 141–2).

At a rather different level of critique of the ambivalence of veils and veiling, McNeill (1998, 150) notes that veils are semi-masks: 'They hide discretely and partially, and thus enhance beauty and aid dalliance. In Victorian and Edwardian times, women often wore veils to call attention to the face, yet to gauze it in mystery.'

Veils and veiling the face partake in the general ambivalence about facial perception, surface and depth, truth and falsehood, which is enhanced by the ambivalence of revealing and concealing and all the possibilities which that produces in facial display (Lewis 1956). This ambivalence is fully and consciously exploited to its greatest extent in the acting profession, to which we now turn.

Acting

In the light of the foregoing, and of the tradition of using actual physical masks in the Greek and other kinds of theatre, it is not surprising that, historically, actors have been much distrusted in society. If you cannot see a person's 'real' face and associate it directly with the substance of their identity, then relationships of openness and trust can become very problematic.

Contemporary actors, shaped by the naturalistic realist tradition of acting that arose in the nineteenth century, rather than donning standard masks, use their faces and facial expressions to convey the essence and identity of dramatic characters (Pearl 2010). To the extent that they succeed in making audiences believe in the inner identity of their character, they are applauded as performers. Members of the public are, however, less delighted by conmen and spies who use exactly the same techniques to misrepresent and fool them. Theatrical deception is taken to be a playful pleasure. However, wilful manipulation of face/identity in everyday life is somehow seen as illegitimate and wrong.

This, then, is yet another example of the ambivalence of attitudes to the issue of hiding and revealing associated with face and its relationship to the inner essence and authentic depth of the person. Playing with the dynamics of concealment versus revelation (even concealment in order to reveal), consistency versus transformation and recreation versus unfamiliarity underlies all conscious facial change strategies. It seems a profoundly human thing to play around with appearance, and so with identity, in this way. And this obliquely exposes much about our views of relations between face, character and identity. These can be profoundly ambivalent, drawing attention once again to the fundamental complexity and ambiguities of face and its significance.

Whose Face is It, Anyway?

Masking, veiling and acting raise profound questions about the relationship between self and facial appearance. An implication of the assumption of the integral relationship between face and fundamental identity is that we take ourselves to be the owners of our faces, as of the clothes that we wear. Edward Stanton states that 'a man of 50 is responsible for his face' (Cole 1998, 49). Many of us feel instinctively strangely responsible in an ongoing way for our faces in photos, however long ago they may have been taken. It is as if there is some kind of part or skin of presence that has been exuded from our features onto the photograph that is still somehow attached to us (Batchen 2004, 40; Gell 1999, 104). This colludes with the idea that the face is our own unique possession, a kind of space that we can shape and control for our own benefit and which reflects exactly who and what we are inwardly.

A moment's reflection, however, will reveal yet another set of ambiguities about face and its relation to the self. Other people can imitate my face and so, it seems, appropriate my identity. I may have had a facial injury, in which case my face may misleadingly suggest an identity to others that I do not want them to believe in because they attribute to me certain deliberate intentions and attributes that I never wanted to have (Partridge 1990). In this sort of situation, perhaps my face and the ways that people react to it may subtly actually change, rather than reflecting, what I take to be my identity. This is what seems to happen to some celebrities like Princess Diana who died fleeing those who needed her face.

Faces go out into the world and live in public, interacting with other people's faces, going in and out of their eyes and minds. My face can go around the world before lunchtime on the internet, consorting with all sorts of other faces, and I have no influence over it. It can be sucked and chewed by many faces I have never met. Am I, in fact, its responsible owner and controller, or is there a sense in which my face actually belongs to others as much as to me? Was it not they who helped to etch the lines on it by their responses to me? Novelist Milan Kundera (1991, 30) notes of one his characters that 'looks were needles which etched the wrinkles in her face'; every day we are stabbed and affected by thousands of looks from others. And it is others who have in their minds versions and images, *idolata* or skins, of my face that I have lost through ageing, just as I am the guardian of their youthful, even dead, faces (Gell 1999, 104).

Most disconcertingly of all, many of us discover as we grow older that we have met what we thought was uniquely our own face before – in the real or reproduced faces of relatives, or those of our ageing parents perhaps (Burt and Kline 2008). Is my face my own? Is it me? Am I alone responsible for it and how it looks? Or is it a kind of negotiated, part-owned aspect of me that I can only have some influence over as it enters the public realm and interfaces with others. Our faces give us away, perhaps, but they are also given away, even taken from us, as they venture out into the social world.[3]

Conclusion

In the chapter I have surveyed some of the physical 'facts' of face, looking at the evolution, composition and functions of face. Faces are complex, plastic organs, often in perpetual motion. They perform many functions simultaneously, such as establishing identity, information giving and emotional expression. This adds to the difficulties of fixing face identified in the last chapter. Faces are popularly deemed to be accurate indicators of inner personality, character and emotion. However, there is a problematic, complex, unstable relationship between inward character and outward face. On the one hand, faces can be used accurately to read off aspects of character and emotion; on the other, this is not a fixed or determined relationship, so it can be very misleading. If face sutures together aspects of the inner and outer self, the suturing is very variable and uneven, and the facial garment, gauze or gossamer is for ever inverting and exposing different surfaces, real and illusory, in the face of the projections and reflections of viewers. This ambivalence of relationship between face, identity and character is the foundation for the creative and deceptive arts of masking and facial manipulation that both delight and traduce. It also begins to raise the issue of the social life and significance of faces that are not just private property but form a place of negotiation about self,

---

[3]   As I sat at my father's deathbed looking at a face I had known so long and so well, it seemed to metamorphose. As time slowly passed I saw in his face my father, my own face, the face of my grandmother, an elderly Jewish man who I had never seen before (my unknown grandfather?), and an old man – a stranger who I did not recognise at all. It was a very strange experience.

identity, responsibility and belonging. Faces are common and unique, revealing and concealing, skin-deep, yet taken to be profound. There is nothing so private and yet so public as the face, nothing so personal and yet so social. It is within this nexus of paradox that shame and face begin to come together, as we will see in the next chapter.

Chapter 3
Losing Face:
Shame, Defacement and Problems with Face

Love resides in the face – in its beauty, in the music of the voice and the warmth of the eye. Love is proved by the face, and so is unlovability – proved by seeing and hearing, by being seen and heard.

(Wurmser 1995, 93)

I live in the facial expressions of the other, as I feel him living in mine.

(Merleau-Ponty 1964, 146)

Those who remain faceless or whose faces are presented to us as so many symbols of evil, authorise us to become senseless before those lives we have eradicated, and whose grievability is indefinitely postponed. Certain faces must be admitted into public view, must be seen and heard for some keener sense of the value of life, all life, to take hold.

(Butler 2006, xviii)

Mollon (2002, 23) puts it graphically:

Shame involves a hole – a hole where our connections to others should be. In shame we fall out of the dance, the choreography of the human theatre. And at the deepest depths of shame we fall into a limbo where there are no words but only silence. In this no-place there are no eyes to see us, for the others have averted their gaze – no-one wishes to see the dread that has no name.

While Mollon is basically alluding here to psychological shame, the sense of falling into a vortex, into oblivion, out of sight and hearing, and out of positive relationship with others, pervades all kinds of shame, social and individual (Curtis 1999; Pattison 2000).

Having surveyed the nature of face as such in the last two chapters, I want now to explore the relationship between face, shame and loss of face, or what might even be called defacement. 'Loss of face' is a metaphor for losing honour and respect in society, that is, for shamed, defaced or defective identity (Goffman 1968, 2005). It implies diminishment, exclusion, alienation, uncleanness and unwantedness. But it is not an accident that it is thus described; people who have difficulties with face of various kinds, for example facial movement, facial recognition, facial injury or disfigurement, often find themselves shamed and excluded from society, regarded as ugly, and, by implication, evil or ill (Gilman 1988, 1995, 1998, 1999;

Synnott 1989, 1990). If faces are to be saved, if people who have problems with face are to be countenanced, enfaced and redeemed from the shadow of shame, it is, then, important to understand some of the dynamics that pertain to face, identity and the conferment of shame.

In this chapter, I will first briefly discuss the politics of shame and defacement. This makes clear that these matters are not simply of personal, individual significance, though they are certainly that. Thereafter, in the first main section, I will deepen the exploration of the relationship between face, identity and shame by looking at the place that face plays in the formation of individual and social human development.

Facial relations are one of the main ways by which we learn to become persons; they introduce us both to the material and symbolic realities of full social engagement and belonging. Face both enables and symbolises social participation and acceptance. It is also a powerful metaphor for the rejection, alienation and exclusion associated with shame, a very visually mediated and understood condition of selves and groups. But it is more than a metaphor; those who have neurological or other difficulties with real, physical faces also fall into the realm of shame and rejection, suffering an impaired sense of identity and participation. So in the second main part of the chapter, I will look in detail at the situation of those who have various shame-associated 'problems with face', either as perceivers or inhabitants of faces.[1]

The Politics of Shame and Defacement

Shame in the modern Western world is often understood primarily as an inward, individual psychological state. Similarly, defacement, disability and disfigurement can be regarded as essentially personal matters. It is necessary, in the context of this book, to make it clear that there are substantial social and political issues that come to bear on both these phenomena, severally and together. So in this section, I touch briefly on the politics of shame, enfacement and defacement.

In ancient Greek society, shaming stigma was conferred upon criminals by branding them on the face so all could see their new, negative identity (Goffman 1968). In the modern world, defacement, actually rendering people faceless, is one of the ways in which they can be made to seem evil or invisible so that they do not have to be treated as persons. Butler, meditating on the subject of face as the symbol and reality of human frailty, notes how prisoners in Guantanamo Bay were rendered both 'faceless and abject': 'The Department of Defence published pictures of prisoners shackled and kneeling, with hands

---

[1]   Strangely, there is no real word or concept that describes the experience of having a face and relating to it from the inside. Are we owners, inhabitants, users, signallers or something else? Face itself implies the external perspective and view. This lack of vocabulary perhaps denotes a strange ambivalence towards, and possible alienation from, face.

manacled, mouths covered by surgical masks, and eyes blinded by blackened goggles' (Butler 2006, 73). Similar pictures also emerged from the US Army's Abu Ghraib prison in Iraq. By the same token, when the US and its allies want to demonstrate their 'concern' and 'respect' for civilians injured in war, they may select a facially wounded individual victim, maybe a child, for expensive surgical treatment in the West in which a face can be put back together (Ravitz 2012).

The possession, recognition, evaluation and respect of real faces, or neglect thereof, is thus a highly political matter, even if the condition of prisoners in Guantanamo and Abu Ghraib are rather extreme examples of the sorts of issues that I propose to consider in this chapter. More mundane and persistent, but no less politically significant, is the matter of the unjust treatment and unequal chances that may be meted out to people who are regarded as 'ugly' or 'defective' in everyday life. Facially 'attractive' people are likely to get more of what there is to get by way of status, wealth and opportunities in contemporary Western society than those who are deemed unattractive – a case of the 'survival of the prettiest' (Etcoff 1999; Hamermesh 2011).

If there is a politics of recognition of faces, there is also a politics of facial representation. People can be effaced or defaced in representational terms. This occurs by failing to see or represent their faces at all (think of all the dead Afghan civilians whose facial invisibility means that they have not had what Butler calls 'grievable lives'), a strategy of occlusion. It also takes place when people are represented in such a way that they are identified as inhuman or associated with the inhuman (Butler 2006, 142–4). That which might be taken as most human about the person, the face, can come to stand for the absolutely inhuman. Thus Osama bin Laden's face becomes an icon of evil and terror, not the face of a human being. At the other end of the spectrum, the face of the injured girl brought to the West for restorative plastic surgery is then seen as an icon of victimhood and suffering when it appears in media of various kinds.

The tendency to represent the inhuman and non-human characteristics such as fame or fortune with human faces plays upon the connection between identity, character and morals underlying many responses to face. This assumed connection can be deeply misleading and distorting, especially for the poor and underprivileged. But even celebrities can be dehumanised, devoured and distorted by their facial representations, as perhaps was someone like Princess Diana (Kemp 2004, 119). Seeing, understanding and respecting face as both real presence and representation is, then, vital if human life is to be human in the world. Faces can represent the human, the inhuman, or even both simultaneously. And the ways in which they are perceived and represented is a highly political, socially value-laden matter.

I will now go on to explore the ways in which facial relations contribute to individual and social development and relationships, including the generation of shame, before considering the ways in which those who have 'problems with face' can be implicated in shaming relations and issues of spoiled identity so that they lose face.[2]

Face in Individual and Social Development

To have face in society is to belong; to lose face is to be excluded, and often to experience social and psychological shame.[3] Shame reflects relationships and social bonds. It is a powerful indicator of humanity and of personal and social cohesion and belonging (Scheff 1997). It is often imaged in terms of face, gaze, seeing, covering and hiding (Hollander 2003; Pattison 2000, 69–92; Wurmser 1995, 29). This probably reflects the origins of shame in infancy. Here, facial relations play an important part in developing a sense of full, acceptable self and in developing a correlative sense of shame that figures alienation from others and the self.[4]

Emotional communicativeness is central to the formation and sustenance of social relations and personality. Seeing the expressions of others, and being seen by them, provides a road to empathy and understanding, and to predicting their minds and purposes (Cole 1998). This is highly desirable in social animals like humans who need to understand the intentions and mental states of others upon whom they depend for co-operation (Mead 1934; Merleau-Ponty 1964, 1983; Tomasello 2000). Those whose faces register limited or no emotions, for example those who have had strokes, or have Parkinson's disease, can find themselves in considerable social difficulties. They sometimes become non-persons as other people cease to communicate with them.[5] They may also find it difficult to communicate with themselves, insofar as facial expression, and its reflection back from others, seems to be one of the main neural and social feedback mechanisms for discerning internal emotional and mood states (Cole 1998, 114ff.; Cole with

---

[2]   I believe it to be nigh on a human universal that we all have problems with face or with some faces. Who has what problems with whose faces and in what ways changes according to context and perspective.

[3]   I have not defined shame here because I see it as a multi-variant socio-emotional condition. It is enough to understand it here as a negative state of alienation, exclusion and unwantedness that signals a disruption in human relations and community. This can be temporary or permanent. See further Pattison (2000, 2010).

[4]   The nature and causes of shame change and develop considerably over life, time and context; it often becomes a more social than narrowly psychological phenomenon in adult life (Pattison 2000, 131–53).

[5]   A friend of mine who is a prominent academic told me recently that he was no longer able to give lectures as, with the advance of Parkinson's disease, his face no longer moved normally and so people failed to respond to him personally as they had once done. He finds this demoralising and de-personalising.

Spalding 2009).[6] It is upon the face as seat of emotion and the development of personality that I will dwell for a moment as a way of highlighting the importance of the face and vision for making and keeping persons human within social bonds.

Face, Identity and Development

Face and Infant Development

Possibly too much has been made of vision and faciality in infancy. We do not know what babies think at various stages of their development, nor whether psychological theories of development correspond to reality. In this area, there would seem to be plausible stories rather than undisputed facts. However, all I want to do here is create a general picture of the importance of face for being and becoming.

At least some of the salient, largely undisputed, psychological 'facts' about vision and faciality for infants are as follows. First, normally, most infants can see from birth. Opening and shutting their eyes to include or exclude the visual world is one of the few sources of power and control they possess. Babies are 'hard-wired' to be responsive to faces of all kinds, human and animal, from birth (Atkinson 1995; Perrett 2010, chapter 3; Schore 2009; Stern 1985, 1998, 2002; Trevarthen 1995). Within a day, they are able to distinguish their mothers' faces from those of others (Bruce and Young 1998, 250ff.; Perrett 2010, 51). Infants engage in long periods of gaze with their carers, especially during feeding, far longer than would be normal in adult life (Stern 2002). They use their faces and gaze to gain attention from carers by appearing to look interested in, and by responding to, them. Most adults find the gaze of babies an irresistible draw.

Very early on, infants can imitate the expressions of others, and can initiate their own facial expressions; some of these expressions are probably innate, since both blind and sighted babies have them. By six weeks, they can fix eyes and hold the gaze of another; they begin to choose what to look at, and direct their gaze. Over time, babies become more concerned with the eyes of their carers rather than scanning the edges and broader patterns of their faces. Interestingly, within a few months, they are no longer able to recognise the faces of people of other races – vision becomes tribally preoccupied very early on (Hole and Bourne 2010, chapter 5). Very quickly, too, vision and visual clues become important for amplifying or modifying shared emotional experience. Thus, if an infant becomes over-stimulated, it may avert its gaze, while, if a parent averts their gaze, the infant may feel deflated and that it has lost attunement, even experiencing shame (Gerhardt 2004, 49; Schore 2009, 240–47; Stern 2002).

---

[6] For more on emotional expressions as feedback to the self, see, for example, James (1981) and the discussion of the nature and function of emotions in Pattison (2000, 27–38).

The visual experience of face and gaze takes place within the context of a total relationship that also includes smell, touch and hearing. Thus people who are blind from birth can develop perfectly satisfactorily without extensive visual experience (Kleege 1999; Magee and Milligan 1998). Nonetheless, the visual experience of face-to-face relating and engaging in mutual gaze with parents or carers is of enormous importance. Early in life, it is the visual (right) part of the brain that is the main centre for the child's learning about the world, other people and itself. Words and language, associated with the development of the 'verbal self' and the left brain, are only acquired after about a year (Gerhardt 2004, 50ff.).

For infants, visual experience of face and gaze is vital to acquiring information about the world, and also about emotions and the others' intentions and minds. The subtlety of sight and facial gesture is probably an important part of coming to see oneself as having existence in the minds of others and of beginning to internalise social norms (Gerhardt 2004, 33). The child develops a clear sense of who and what they are as they see their behaviour and expressions produce reactions in others (Gerhardt 2004, 41). Visual and facial experience is fundamental in helping the social brain to grow as the sympathetic nervous system is aroused and stimulated by mutual gaze (Schore 2009). Gradually, infants can also begin to process and categorise social experiences and learn how to regulate their own emotions.

Psychoanalytic theories of development that posit the need to be unified with the parent in an attuned gaze to develop a differentiated self are controversial (Stern 1985). However, if psychoanalytic theorising about infant development is treated as loose, plausible myth rather than as scientific fact, it can provide further insightful material about the importance of facial relations of gaze in human development.

Donald Winnicott (1974, 130–38) argues that in the so-called narcissistic period, part of the pre-verbal stage of early development where the infant does not have a clear sense of separate self and identity, it is vital that infants see themselves as acceptable and admired by their carers. The child is mirrored, literally and metaphorically, in the mother's face. Face is, then, the centre for much important emotional communication. To develop a valued sense of self, the baby needs to see itself in its mother's face in order to see itself and its emotions as real and accepted.

When a child sees itself in its mother's face, and engages in mutual, responsive, creative looking, that face is not an inanimate mirror to be looked at, but a place of insight and discovery of meaning, a site of active attunement (Stern 1985). If the relationship works well, the mutual facial gaze of child-mother gives the child to herself and contains her emotions, allowing the infant to begin to explore meanings and feelings. From the infant's point of view, 'what you (mother's facial expression) look like (proto-symbol) is how I (baby) feel (proto-referent)' (Wright 2009, 34).[7]

---

[7]   It is worth noting in this context that the child's image of God is also crucially shaped at this point in development. Rizzuto (1979, 188): 'The mirroring components of the God representation find their first experience in eye contact, early nursing, and maternal

The 'seen' child can see, and so, by implication, begin to value and respect itself and others: 'When I look I am seen, so I exist' (Winnicott 1974, 134). Thus it can take its place socially and emotionally in the human community.

Face is pivotal throughout human growth and development (Wright 1991, 2009). For the infant, it is the visual form of primal blissful experience and comes to represent the mother as a whole (Ayers 2003). As such, it can become the most loved object in the child's world. It is the locus of interface in which infants see themselves through the eyes of the 'other' and it mediates attachment. Because the carer's face is not part of the child, but stands apart from it, it is a means of both separation and connection (Lemma 2010). It may therefore be important in helping infants to have the ability to begin to think symbolically and also to have faith in the tangible and non-real, as the mother's face can be internally represented and carried as a reassurance by the child.

'It begins with a smile', writes Mollon (2001, 9). At the centre of the intimate face-to-face relationship between mother and child is the gleam in the mother's eye or the smile on her face that reflects what she sees, the baby's smiling face in which she delights (Schore 2009, 74). Her smile reflects back the child's aliveness and creates a sense of mutual joy, elation, exuberance and contact-seeking. The mother amplifies the positive affect in the child; they both enjoy mutual pleasure that increases their sense of attachment.

The baby sees in the mother's face attunement and love, so a relationship of mutual reinforcement and affirmation is created: 'Here is a conversation without words, a smiling between faces, at the heart of human development' (Wright 1991, 11). In particular, the 'Duchenne' smile, the smile that lights up the whole face, is the focus of the attentive, responsive, mutual seeing that is essential if humans are fully to develop and to experience joy (Ekman 2004, 205; Hole and Bourne 2010, 65). The face, then, is a 'place of manifestation', that 'suddenly means "I love you" or "I recognise you" or "I'm pleased with you"' (Wright 1991, 107). If this kind of seeing is sustained, over time, the child will internalise a basically positive sense of self as certain views and images of itself are reinforced and shape the brain (Gerhardt 2004; Stern 1985).

---

personal participation in the act of mirroring … When the child is able to connect the word God to his experience he will utilize his experiences of the mirroring phases for this first elaboration. If he has not found himself in the reflection and the object behind the mirror, he will maneuver defensively and fantasize elaborations to compensate by feeling "like God". All these processes are exceedingly complex and encompass multiple experiences and many levels of imaginary bodily sensations and cognitive development. … If the child found in the mirror can pass through it to encounter the mother – at this stage the idealised imago of her – then he can organise his obscure notions of God around it an embroider it with his fantasies.'

The Facial Roots of Shame

In many ways, to be and to become human socially and emotionally is to engage in real, nuanced face-to-face visual relations. However, if the mother cannot let her eye gleam, or 'light up her face' with a smile, then what may be reflected back to the baby is deadness, possibly leading to notions of unacceptability and unresponsiveness, even to primal shame.[8] This unattuned, unempathic, frozen 'Gorgon' face fails to mirror the child so it cannot see and appropriate itself and its emotions in a positive way (Ayers 2003, 78–9). Distance and objectification creep in between carer and child, and internally within the child and his or her own experience. Parents who are depressed, shamed, internally pre-occupied or who do not like and value their children can easily offer this Gorgon face, the 'evil eye' that does not reflect and respond appropriately (Wright 1991, 26). In that context, a small child may feel that they are the cause of this coldness and rejection – they are seen but not valued, loved, accepted. If a child is found acceptable and sees an acceptable image of him or herself in the eye of the other,

> he can relax. But if ... the image formed and reflected is that of a bad child ... there is conflict of being. The child senses that what is wrong is not what the child does but what he is. (Rizzuto 1979, 188)

This sense of being ontologically unacceptable and bad at the core of one's identity lies at the heart of the experience of individual, psychological shame.

Shame and the capacity for shame is a necessary part of being human. Shame marks the boundaries of self with others and the human community. It is important to develop a sense of shame to internalise the norms and expectations of one's own family and group (Scheff 1997; Schore 2009).

The roots of the shame experience are psycho-physiological. If the child receives affirmation of its desires and drives, and an optimum level of reflective response, then it experiences joy and love. If, however, the parental gaze is not attuned or responsive then it can experience abandonment, isolation and pain. Like the feeling of joy, this is hormonally significant:

> disapproving or rejecting looks produce a sudden lurch from sympathetic arousal to parasympathetic arousal, creating the effects we experience in shame – a sudden drop in blood pressure and shallow breathing. (Gerhardt 2004, 49; Schore 2009, 240–47)

Like joy, shame, mediated by disapproving or rejecting looks in response to unwanted behaviour, can be, and normally is, a short-lived experience. However, it requires carers to act if the child is not to be left in a state of powerless despair

---

[8] 'Mother' is used here as it reflects the usage in the literature, but intimate primary carers of either gender or neither are figured by this usage.

and alienation, overwhelmed by an overdose of the inhibiting, anxiety-related hormone, cortisol:

> Shame is an important dimension of socialisation. But what matters equally is recovery from shame. It is important to have a "dose" of cortisol … but an overdose is extremely unhelpful … Just as the child produces cortisol in response to the parent's face, so too does the dispersion of cortisol depend on a changed expression on the parent's face. The young child can't do this for himself, so if the parents don't restore attunement and regulation, he may remain stuck in a state of arousal. (Gerhardt 2004, 49)

Occasional experiences of withdrawal of parental responsive gaze that produce shame are to be expected. These produce a sense of dissonance and disintegration that can usefully bring a child up short and stop undesirable behaviour. However, there is potential here for long-term damage. If the child frequently or continuously fails to capture the approving, attuned facial attention of its carers, for whatever reason, then patterns of self-rejection, disintegration and anxiety may be laid down in its sense of self; chronic shame as a character trait may set in (Pattison 2000, 93–109). Habitually shamed parents may themselves avoid eye contact with others, even their own children. People with mental health problems such as depression tend not to look so often as 'normals' at the faces of others (Argyle and Cook 1976, Hole and Bourne 2010, 194–208). Busy people may not be willing to spend much time in mutual facial gaze with their new children, while some may feel that their children are unattractive or even ugly. All of these phenomena can then contribute to a sense of being unvisible, lack of importance, alienation, unwantedness and self-disgust as children fail to be contained and reflected in a loving gaze (Kilborne 2002). Thus the seeds of lifelong or chronic shame as a dominant attitude to the self and its identity may be sown by poor quality facial contact between parents and children in early infancy.

'Love resides in the face' (Wurmser 1995, 93). However unlovability and sense of shame can also emanate from the same face: 'To be unlovable means not to see a responsive eye and not to hear a responding voice, no matter how much they are sought' (Wurmser 1995, 97). Children can be admired as the apple of their carer's eye, or experience a kind of objectifying dehumanising gaze that violates and damages their sense of self and value (Mollon 1993, 47). If parents continually fail to respond positively to their children, by averting their gaze, or by looking at the child with the 'gape face' of disgust perhaps, then the child may enter into a state of continuous isolation and shame (Kelly 2011, 64; Miller 1997). Untouchability and unvisibility lie at heart of shame, and form proofs of unlovability (Wurmser 1997, 116).

To sum up, visual contact centred round face-to-face contact between carer and child which culminates in responsive mutual shining of faces forms both symbol and experience of being emotionally and physically alive and accepted within the human community. Facial relations enable and stimulate joy and a sense of being loved and positive selfhood. Simultaneously, however, they also allow the possibility of shame and a sense of rejected or unsatisfactory self to emerge.

The narrative I have provided here is somewhat speculative and mythological. However, it has some resonance and veracity in everyday adult experience. If, as an adult, people look at you with disgust, look through you, fail to acknowledge or to recognise your face, or do not notice and respond in kind to the expressions on it, you can feel hurt, unacceptable and shamed. The present acknowledgement of face and identity remains important throughout life, and those whose faces are not recognised and responded to can feel intense shame and rejection. Invisibility and oblivion are seldom comfortable experiences, except, perhaps, for those shamed people who wish to hide from the critical stare of others.

Face and Shame in Adult Life

Shame has some of its main roots in infantile facial experience and it remains facially associated throughout life. The roots of reactive shame in infancy do not necessarily lie in having an ugly, unacceptable or unresponsive face. They can lie in not conforming in some way to some kind of ideal or norm. While this lack might be caused by some kind of direct facial rejection, it is possible, too, that there are other ideals to which children feel that they cannot match up. Nussbaum (2004) argues that an overall basic sense of bodily weakness, lack of control and inadequacy in childhood might produce a fundamental sense of ontological shame in all of us.

Another of source of shame may lie in the infant's embodied sexual organs and desires: 'exposing one's sexual organs, activities, and feelings' is a paradigm of the feeling of shame; in most Western languages, in fact, 'shame is practically synonymous with sexual exposure and with the sexual organs themselves' (Wurmser 1995, 32). This basic sense of shame about sexuality, fundamental as it is to identity and a sense of shame, then gets generalised during the overall socialisation process from the sex organs themselves to the entire body, particularly to the face, where shame is manifested by the dropping of the eyes and head, by blushing and in other ways that indicate that a person is experiencing shame and disconnection. Thus body shame gives way to a broader sense of psychological shame and failure to meet ideals. This is often conceptualised by way of bodily analogies and experiences.

Thus, in adulthood, the face as the most visible and communicative part of the self, in which the identity of the self is taken to reveal itself, easily becomes the locus for the generation and expression of shame. Shame is expressed by way of facial disengagement and looking away. But since face is taken to be the fundamental visible expression of self and identity, it can easily become the site of shame. As we have seen, and will see further below, any kind of abnormality of the face or facial engagement can be taken to indicate that a person is not really a full member of the tribe or of the human race. If satisfactory, 'normal' facial visual experience is disrupted in any way, this can easily evoke shame in both seers and seen.

Lying beneath this kind of disruption and potential alienation are the kinds of assumptions about face and identity that we examined in previous chapters: abnormal = ugly = evil or ill = deviant (Synnott 1989). When seers avert their eyes from the face of another, or fail to find a communicative response, the bond of belonging and potential positive affect is broken and shame is activated. And shame, being a fundamental and early feeling, is very difficult to control or consciously to avert. The irrationality of shame added to the irrationality of assuming that character is reflected in facial features and expressions and that the beautiful and normal is also therefore an expression of personal goodness (so facial deviance equals flawed character) then produces situations in which people can become very depersonalised and alienated indeed. It is the nature of this particular kind of alienation and depersonalisation that will be explored in the next section.

Problems with Face and Shame

Shame is a complex, multifaceted phenomenon. While it may begin with the body and the self, as symbolised in face-to-face relations, it is also social, political and cultural in its causes and effects and it is, of course, implicated in different ways in different lives and contexts (Pattison 2000; Scheff 1997; Velleman 2006). Suffice it to say here that shame is an unpleasant, inhibiting condition that arises in contexts where fundamental relations with self and other go wrong and are placed in jeopardy. The shamed person or group then feels outcast, or in danger of being outcast and unwanted. Shame emerges from a sense of being dirty, rotten, defiled, toxically unwanted (Benthien 2002, 92; Pattison 2000). It is accompanied by fears of rejection, ridicule or abandonment (Benthien 2002, 100). For many, this fear is short-lived, and social acceptance and inclusion are restored. However, for some, shame and the sense of being fundamentally flawed, unwanted and having a 'spoiled identity' become a part of their life; they respond to others and themselves from this basic position (Goffman 1968). This can often be the case for people who have problems with faces, their own or others. Clearly such people have not committed offences against others, and they are not evil. However, they can easily regard themselves as globally bad, seeing themselves through the alienating eyes of rejecting others, or even through their own rejecting inner eyes (Lewis 1971, 40; Lynd 1958, 51ff.; Pattison 2000, 71–8).

Face and facial expression, seeing and being seen, are important metaphors and experiences that bear upon shame and its alleviation. Physically to be seen without disgust and smiled upon in adult life is still to feel included and approved of in an important way that dispels shame and 'gives face'. Here, however, I will not focus on shame generally as it is found in many groups and individuals – I have done this elsewhere (Pattison 2000). I want to draw out some of the ongoing problematic relationships that can exist between those who have problems with face and its implication with shame. This is a close and important, if rather particular, relationship. I will explore its reality through briefly describing a number of case studies from the works of others. Before doing this, however, I need to make a few preliminary remarks.

First and foremost, it is very important not to generalise about the possible involvement of shame in the context of problems with physically dealing with face:

> People vary in their responses to disorders and disfigurements and these responses are not always predictable. Shame and humiliation is not necessarily central or inevitable. Appearance does have an effect in relationships and may be difficult to control – but it is not necessarily shame and humiliation inducing. (Rumsey and Harcourt 2005, 102)[9]

The body, its appearance and functions are an important locus for shame. It is here that both control and the perception of normality and social attractiveness can be lost, threatening social acceptability (Coughlan and Clarke 2002; Ekstromer 2002; Gilbert 2002; Kellett 2002; Velleman 2006). However, shame has many components. They include a social, external evaluative element reflecting social norms, an internal self-evaluative component reflecting how persons feel about themselves, an emotional element, for example of anger or disgust, a behavioural element, for example of gaze avoidance or flight, and a physiological component, for example blushing. These combine differently in different persons and situations to produce very different responses (Gilbert 2002). So, for example, a person who has a high internal sense of value may not be shamed by an external evaluation of their appearance against social norms of beauty. Similarly, in societies where physical facial appearance is not taken to be very important, little kudos may be lost by those who have problems with face. So in reading what follows, it is very important to have a sense of the complexity of face-related shame. It is not an inevitable accompaniment of difficulties related to face.

Secondly, I am, like Cole (1998), and often using his examples directly, using problems with face, pathology if you like, to gain an *entrée* to the whole experience and importance of face. This problem-centred approach is only one way of approaching the topic; it is unhelpful insofar as it pathologises conditions already regarded as problematic by 'normals'. I hope by drawing attention to some of the problems people have with face, and the way these link to shame, I might actually be contributing towards some kind of understanding and shame alleviation. For some people, face – whether their own or that of another – is not a problem, nor are they closely bound up with shame and spoiled identity (Appearance Research

---

[9]   See Appearance Research Collaboration (n.d.) for an empirical study of the very complex social and psychological factors that can affect whether or not visibly disfigured people experience shame and rejection, either internal or external. For many people disfigurement may not be an issue. And it is interesting in patriarchal facist society that the experience of both men and women in this regard is not very different.

Collaboration n.d.). However, I suspect that for many people, at least some of the time, their faces or those of people around them, are a problem to them – consider the face-based shame of many adolescents, for example.

Thirdly, I am highlighting here people and their situations where shame, rejection, alienation and related conditions seem to be prominent. Cole does not name or emphasise the importance of shame in his book and I hope I am picking up on a common and useful association here. However, fourthly and correlatively, it is important to say that it is not necessarily the case that all people who have problems with face are plunged into shame. Shame is a profoundly relational condition, and it is easy to see that where people are not rejected from social and communication networks, shame will not be a persistent part of their experience (Appearance Research Collaboration, n.d.; Gilbert 2002; Rumsey and Harcourt 2005). However, for many people, as I will show, shame and the loss of human acceptance and identity it implies seems to be very important.

Fifthly, shame is not necessarily just associated with facial issues and problems in the lives of many. For some, their problems with face are just an additional shaming factor within, for example, poor, dysfunctional and abusive families that might have made those individuals feel ashamed anyway, for a multitude of other reasons (Fossum and Mason 1986).

This leads to a final important point. While shame is often thought of in visual terms (shamed people often want to hide, turn their eyes away and so on), shame, like love, is mediated through touch, gesture, hearing and even perhaps smell. The rejection of others is not just a visual thing focused only on the face. However, because of the importance and prominence of the face, the visual and facial elements of shame defence and conferral are emphasised here. As we have seen already, physical face and facial reflection have an enormously important part to play in the acceptance and personal and social integration of individuals.

With that, I turn now to my case studies. I will not attempt to describe every possible facially related condition that might have implications for shame, much less provide a guide of how such conditions might be alleviated. All I want to do here is to problematise face and the way in which it can easily become an important locus for shame creation and exacerbation. This is with a view to prompting more creative overall responses to face and its implications.

First, I will consider people whose faces appear often to give problems to others, that is, *inhabitants of face*. Then I will look at some cases of conditions where people have problems with the faces of others, that is, *seers of faces*. Of course, seers and inhabitants are bound up in reciprocal reflective and recursive relations as previously discussed – we see ourselves in the faces of others, or not, as the case may be, and they see theirs in us. Often, people's perception that they have problematic relations with faces is actually the perception of others which comes home to the 'problem holder' through the reaction and reflection of others. So this polarised way of proceeding is just a device; it does not represent a solid line through socio-visual reality.

This, of course, raises an interesting question about 'problems with face'; whose problems are they, anyway? This has important implications for whose attitudes and behaviours need to change to accommodate problems with face. Often shame-related problems with face require a change on the part of normalising society rather than on the part of those deemed to have problems (Betcher 2007). Unfortunately, power dynamics being what they are, it is often those deemed abnormal who have to bear the cost of change – or unwillingness to do so on the part of others. This, of course, multiplies alienation and a sense of inadequacy, failure – shame.

First, then, I will consider inhabitants of face who find themselves living shamed and diminished lives on account of their internalised shame from the gaze of 'normals'. I will look, secondly, at the problems of those who have problems with observing faces and who then may be excluded or treated as less than human because of their perceived deviance from normal behaviour. By the time I have finished giving this very selective account, I hope readers will be able to see how widespread problems with face really are, and how important it is to think about dealing with them differently. They are not the province of a tiny minority of the population, though it may suit the majority population in its alienating complacency to hope that they might be. Face and shame-related problems with face need to be taken more seriously by all of us. But that is the substance of the later parts of this book.

Inhabitants' Problems with Face

Disfigurement
Perhaps the most obvious group of people who suffer the shame and stigma of attributed damaged identity are people who experience facial disfigurement or injury of some kind.[10] It is believed that 'more than a million people in Britain are affected by facial disfigurement each year' (Kemp 2004, 73):

> Perhaps 10% of the population has a scar, blemish or other visible difference that affects their lives. If other appearance-related difficulties such as Parkinson's Disease are included, the proportion of people included could be considered much higher. (Kent and Thompson 2002, 103)[11]

I will discuss two of those people now.

Lucy Grealy was a writer who, from the earliest years of childhood, suffered from a disfiguring cancer of the jaw, Ewing's sarcoma. In her moving book, *Autobiography of a Face*, she recounts the events and attitudes surrounding

---

[10]   Facial disfigurements can be caused by birth defects like cleft palate or birthmarks, by diseases like facial cancers or paralysing conditions and by injuries and accidents.

[11]   People with dementia, acne, Bell's palsy and a number of other common conditions might increase this number considerably (Kellet 2002).

her growing up and the endless attempts made to acquire a beautiful, ideal face that would make her lovable. Although some of her shame is attributable to a generally rather unempathic, poverty-stricken family, her feelings of ugliness and a correlative sense of inevitable unlovability focused on her appearance.

Jeered and stared at by other children and their parents, Grealy grows her hair long to cover her face. Later, during treatment, she can feel more comfortable by wearing a hat to cover her bald head, her scars and her disfigured jaw. Once, she finds freedom in donning a Hallowe'en mask to walk around the streets. But the leitmotif of her early life is constant: 'I *was* my face, I *was* ugliness … ' (Grealy 2003, 7).[12] And for her, ugliness equated generally with being globally unlovable and unwanted – the terrain of shame: 'I thought wanting love was a weakness to be overcome. And besides, I thought to myself, the world of love wanted nothing to do with me' (Grealy 2003, 124).

While not always consciously aware of feeling ashamed, there is a moment where a conscious sense of shame dawns in a very dramatic way:

> One morning I went into the bathroom … I turned on the lights and very carefully, very seriously, assessed my face in the mirror. I was bald … I also knew I had buck teeth, something I was vaguely ashamed of but hadn't given too much thought to until this moment. My teeth were ugly. And, I noticed, they were made worse by the fact that my chin seemed so small … I knew to expect a scar, but how had my face sunk in like that? I didn't understand … More than the ugliness I felt, I was suddenly appalled at the notion that I had been walking around unaware of something that was apparent to everyone else. A profound sense of shame consumed me. (Grealy 2003, 111–12)

Here, the metaphor of losing face, being ashamed, becomes concrete, embodied reality. Grealy's internalised sense of not belonging, not being acceptable, hits her hard and directly. So shamed is she that she believes it is other people's right to make fun of her, employing the 'attack self' mode to avoid hurt and disappointment from others (Nathanson 1992, 303ff.). This involves the shamed person gaining a sense of agency by leading their own abuse:

> I was ugly, so people were going to make fun of me: I thought it was their right to do so simply because I was so *ugly*, so I'd just better get used to it. (Grealy 2003, 145, 194)

Fortunately, she can't quite believe this herself; less fortunately, that means that the words sting. Grealy longs for a beautiful, ideal, lovable face, but in its absence, partly with the help of religion, she aims to climb above her oppressors by seeking

---

12   It is an unfortunate feature of chronic shame that the shamed person not only does not feel that they fail to meet ideals of appearance or behaviour, but they actually embody the antithesis of these ideals (Pattison 2000, 77).

sainthood and forgiving them, again a compensatory response (Grealy 2003, 152). This goes along with a sense of protectively distancing herself from reality, even while being stuck in the terrible sense of self-consciousness as an outsider that is often characteristic of shamed, abused people (Grealy 2003, 167, 178; Pattison 2000).

Years on, and many operations later, Grealy finds the courage to shed her ugly, shamed image, to recognise herself, to find herself lovable and to see herself differently. She can even enjoy looking at herself in a mirror: 'for all those years I'd handed my ugliness over to people and seen only the different ways it was reflected back to me' (Grealey 2003, 222). This does not diminish the sense of anguish and shame suffered over many years described in the book.

Lucy Grealy lived a diminished, less than human life because she internalised a negative image from others. She accepted a role of shame and hiding from humanity because of her disfigured face. Her identity and functioning were substantially impaired because of how she thought she looked to others, and she was not wrong to see the gaze of others as shaming and repulsing. Trapped in the socially engendered facist correlation of facial beauty with lovable, desirable character, Grealy suffered terribly. As did James Partridge, for rather different reasons.

Partridge, founder of the organisation, Changing Faces, which supports people who undergo facial disfigurement, was a young man when his face was severely burned in a road accident. In a self-help book based on his own experience, *Changing Faces: The Challenge of Facial Disfigurement*, Partridge writes, 'The experience of becoming disfigured is total, final and unchangeable – and so is bereavement' (Partridge 1990, 13). For him, acquiring a different kind of face was traumatic and difficult. Disfigured people are in constant danger of being written off (excluded, alienated), and taken at 'face value' so they may be seen as unattractive or a suspicious characters (the correlation between virtue and good looks again).

To avoid this kind of shaming exclusion, people then need to make sure that their real identity is allowed to shine through their new, changed face:

> The process of coming to terms with facial injury or deformity – what I have called "changing faces" is ultimately about showing to the world that your face alone is in no way indicative of your real worth as a human being. (Partridge 1990, 2)

Thus, they must learn to wear 'the mask of disfigurement':

> As a disfigured person, you have to learn to wear the mask of disfigurement like a hospital mask; make sure that your mask does not obscure or dim your real self. If anything, you now have to make your real self that much more conspicuous, just as the nurse who wears a mask will accentuate eye movements and styles of speech. (Partridge 1990, 5)

This metaphor is taken from being looked after by masked health care workers. But it is interesting that Partridge has an idea of essential self that is masked by disfigurement so that an act, or persona-type mask, has to be adopted to be your 'real' self. In a way, Partridge seems both to accept that identity changes, but also to believe that disfigurement should not be allowed to determine a new, shameful or shady identity.

Fighting to be seen beyond the mask of disfigurement is not easy for the disfigured person, invited by Partridge to take control of their situation or to risk demoralisation:

> Every facially disfigured person has to get used to a set of very common reactions in the people they meet: Staring, Curiosity, Anguish, Recoil, Embarrassment and Dread – the SCARED syndrome. (Partridge 1990, 88)

While it is entirely admirable that Partridge affirms the anti-shaming assertion of the person with disfigurement in suggesting that they need to cope with and deal with these sorts of reactions, it seems probable that some people do not so cope. It must be hard not to internalise the invasive, unempathic gaze of others and see oneself as an outsider, someone who is somehow blamed for not being like everyone else amidst narrowly defined ideas of facial normality and acceptability. Partridge, then, actively resists shaming, alienation and exclusion, whether within himself or within society. But the passion with which he argues reveals the enormous potential for shame and alienation that there is here. And once again, it is somehow the job of the 'facially problematic' person to put things right for their own and other people's benefit.

Both Grealy and Partridge, because of facial disfigurements not of their own making, find themselves in danger of being on the edge of society, in the realm of isolation, shame and alienation. It would be easy in these circumstances to internalise a good deal of self-loathing, as Grealy did, and to adopt the perspective of the rejecting surrounding society, in other words, to succumb to shame.

'Empty faced' and 'faceless' people
Some people are not disfigured but they still experience problems with the faces they inhabit and enter the realm of shame and rejection.

An extreme example of this is to be found in people with Moebius syndrome. In this rare condition, people are born with faces that are completely immobile. They therefore present as mask-like and show no emotions, having to turn their whole heads to look in different directions, and being unable to smile (Cole 1998; Cole and Spalding 2009). This makes communication with others limited and impoverished.

One such person, interviewed by Jonathan Cole (1998: 115–30) is James, an Anglican priest. James had a very isolated childhood and youth, keeping himself to himself. He sought to have a valued role in the lives of others by becoming a clergyman, but this formal role with its attendant uniform and ceremonies concealed a sense of worthlessness and depression that eventually led to early retirement. For years, James hated looking at his face in the mirror or having his photograph taken. In later life, however, he has come to value his own feelings and to be interested in his face. It seems, then, that in an attempt to overcome the isolation incurred in Moebius syndrome (nobody named it or discussed it with him till he joined a support group after retirement), James was trying partly to overcome shame-related alienation from himself and others. Whether or not he was conscious of this having to do with his facial expression or lack thereof, it is clear that this considerably hampered his capacity to relate to self and others; in that sense it trapped him in the shadow of shame.

People with Moebius syndrome are rare, but there are many people in the population who have reduced, distorted or no facial expression. They easily then become isolated, unwanted and depersonalised, thus entering the realm of shame-related experience. Cole (1998: 1–12) discusses the case of Mary, an elderly woman who has a stroke so that she cannot speak and her face is frozen. It was noticing how she seemed to fade away as a person that made Cole wonder whether face was not a crucial factor in creating and preserving individual and social identity. There are many thousands of stroke 'victims' who suffer in this way. Add to them people with Bell's palsy, a disease that temporarily or permanently affects facial muscle movement, and those with advanced Parkinson's disease who also lose facial movement, and those with 'problems' with inhabited faces cease to be rare and become quite commonplace. So commonplace, perhaps, that one might begin to think that we need generally to do more to recognise the importance of continuing facial interaction, even if it evokes no noticeable physical response from another. This is vital if people are not to risk being depersonalised, isolated, alienated and effectively shamed as unvisible and worthless.

This tally of people who perhaps need more active facial attention is increased if we include those who are, or rather who are represented as, faceless, so as bearers of an incomplete, impaired or spoiled identity. One increasingly significant group is that of fat or obese people who are sometimes lampooned and stigmatised as 'faceless' or 'headless' 'fatties'. The implicit assumption here is that if facial features are not distinct and 'normal' then somehow the person behind the face is somehow impaired or less than a person, perhaps because they cannot control their weight and conform to the expectations of the world (beauty, virtue and health being linked effortlessly and mindlessly together again). This kind of attitude heaps shame and rejection on people whose weight is deemed abnormal. These are people who may often have very low self-esteem and who can easily feel socially isolated.

Another group that is often represented as not fully enfaced is that of people with Alzheimer's disease or other forms of dementia. These diseases often diminish facial expression and mobility, threatening social relationships. But this is exacerbated by the way in which sufferers are visually represented. Frequently, photographs of Alzheimer's sufferers show them as looking wide-eyed, vacant and disconnected. The semiology seems to be that their faces must be shown as vacant and empty rather than as engaged or happy to represent the fact that 'inside' their faces they have ceased to be quite full persons. Somehow, their personhood has emptied out and so their faces and eyes must look a bit empty, too. This is a very dangerous strategy, because to depersonalise people is to think of them as inferior; once this happens a dynamic of power and shame can be set up that can lead to the ignoring or abuse of such people (Pattison 2000, 171–80; Swinton 2012).

A similar point applies to children with autism and Asperger's syndrome, of whom, once again, there are significant numbers in society. Often, they are represented as solitary individuals and photographed in close-ups of the head and face (Murray 2008, 108). Their faces are often portrayed in such a way as to present them as having a concealed, mysterious character that is isolated and somehow lost to themselves and others. We are invited, so to speak, to peer through their eyes to see some kind of soul, or perhaps autism itself, within:

> Many of the popular concepts of autism that focus on notions of withdrawal and isolation invariably invoke the concept of the "mask" or "curtain" when contemplating the face, an idea that somehow character is concealed. All the usual associations between face and personality are, it is assumed, somehow suspended. (Murray 2008, 113)

Here again, then, the 'normal' community makes judgements about the relationship between face and identity and exercises the power of the shaming, unaccepting stare to fix individuals in the realm of the unwanted other, the shamed, the alienated. The 'politics of the stare' is again a way of creating difference between 'normals' with wanted faces and those whose faces somehow signal an unwanted, spoiled identity (Murray 2008, 107; Razack 1998). This can be positioned in terms of visual rhetoric as wondrous, sentimental, exotic or realistic. But one way or the other, it creates an unequal relationship between starer and stared-at which conspires to the latter's exclusion and lack of recognition of their personhood and belonging. In other words, it incipiently creates the possibility for shame that may be ingested both by autistic people and those who care about them. Goffman (1968) calls this 'courtesy stigma', though, of course, there is actually nothing courteous or respectful about it.

What has been learned about the face, defacement and shame from this brief examination of the problems that inhabiters of face experience? First, and most obviously, there does indeed often seem to be a clear link between problems with face as seen by others and shame. People with the 'wrong' kind of face can often find themselves stigmatised, unwanted, isolated, shamed. This occurs because face and character/identity are linked in the minds of seers, so an impaired or deviant face is taken to imply a damaged or unwanted character or identity. This fatal connection consigns many people to lives of shame and rejection. Not only do they suffer direct rejection from others, but also, as in Lucy Grealy's case, they introject the views of those around them and allow them to shape their sense of self and identity.

It is probably not the case that 'normals' deliberately set out to reject and shame those who have problems with face (which are actually their own problems, not primarily the problems of those who inhabit the 'problematic' faces). Nonetheless, the tyranny of normality in facial perception is mediated through the everyday responses of ordinary people. These responses are not just confined to facial expressions of fear and disgust. However, facial responses, even if temporary, do much to incardinate shame and rejection in those who are seen as deviant or unacceptable against social norms.

We learn who we are to a large extent from the gaze and response of others – if we are ugly, ill or evil in their eyes, it is difficult to retain a separate sense of lovable, desirable self. So we need to re-educate ourselves about the connections between character and face. We then need to orient our gazes accordingly so we don't engender or reinforce shame in individuals who are not responsible for how they look.

Lucy Grealy discovered that animals did not judge her appearance and that there was one person who worked in the hospital under whose gaze she felt soothed – we should perhaps take a lesson from this. The shame lived with by inhabitants of face should perhaps be recognised as the shame of 'normals', not placed on them as individuals.

Beyond this, the most important thing to point up here is that *problems with face are not unusual or insignificant*. There are thousands of people who are made to have problems with the appearance or functioning of their faces from those with acne and birthmarks to those who have had accidents or who have developed chronic conditions like dementia and Parkinson's disease. So understanding and changing attitudes and practices of seeing is not about catering to a tiny minority, but rather part of trying to deal better with a normal part of human experience to enhance mutual personhood and to avoid diminishing, dehumanising, unnecessary and damaging shame.

Let us now, then, turn to those observers who seem to have problems with facial perception and see how shame intersects with their experience.

Observers' Problems with Faces

The relationship between those who have problems in perceiving faces and shame is a bit more indirect and tangential than that between shame and inhabitants of faces that are perceived not to 'work' or to 'fit'. Some of these people may have difficulty in simply seeing faces at all. Others may find it difficult to cope with, recognise or interpret those faces. Yet others seem to fall into a more ambivalent category of people whose vision of faces is disrupted by emotional distress, perhaps even by a kind of shame that makes it impossible to look at the faces of others. I will consider these groups in turn.

For some in this overall group of observers who have problems with others' faces, for example blind people, their problems may be visible to others. However, for others, this may be invisible, for example people with Asperger's syndrome;

they may thus avoid public stigmatisation and be able to 'pass' as 'normals', so perhaps partially avoiding ingesting a sense of shame. However, if their difficulties become apparent they may also find themselves in the realm of isolation, uncommunicativity, unwantedness and unlovability connoted by shame. Anyone who is perceived not to conform to social norms is likely to find life more difficult than the majority, and so to experience an amount of rejection and alienation as a matter of course.

Observers who cannot physically see faces
Perhaps the largest group in this category is that of blind people. Some people may find it difficult that blind people cannot see and respond to them facially, and thus behave towards them in a rejecting and shaming manner. However, so far as I have been able to discover, the lack of ability to see the faces of others is not a major problem for most people who have been blind from birth (Kleege 1999; Magee and Milligan 1998). They devise other ways of knowing, understanding and communicating with those around them, using cues from voice and touch to glean information about others' feelings and moods.

When Jonathan Cole (1998: 13–24) interviewed Peter White and David Blunkett on this subject, he found that both of them agreed there were difficulties in operating in a world where sociality is equated with visible faciality, and where identity is often equated with face. This meant that, for example, they had to think hard about the expressions that they wore on their own faces for the benefit of others, to communicate, and to initiate and control attention. However, both found other ways of representing the individuality of others based on voice. They seem to suggest that while sight of the faces of others would be useful, it is not essential for satisfactory living. Both found living in a sight-oriented world posed problems of normativity and alienation. However, they coped with these, in much the same way as James Partridge perhaps; however, both these people have the high status as broadcaster and politician respectively with which to resist shame and stigmatisation.

Shame of a more particular kind accompanies people who become blind after birth and lose the ability to see faces. Cole (1998, 25–42) interviewed two people who had lost their sight in adulthood, including theologian John Hull. Hull has written extensively about his experience of going blind (Hull 1991, 2000, 2001). One of the most difficult things about it was losing the ability to see human faces, including his own. Losing the image of his own face meant losing his sense of identity, as he thought of the face as being the image of the self (a clear allusion to the identity/face link in popular consciousness). It almost seemed to threaten his sense of being a (powerful) man, as he could no longer see women's faces and bodies. Hull became very depressed and literally hid himself away, feeling that 'if he could not see the faces of others, why should they see his?' (Cole 1998, 30). This very primal response is perhaps based in the 'magic eye' of the baby: if I can see the other, then I am seen and I exist. Correlatively, if I cannot be seen and see others, then I don't exist (Wurmser 1997, 94–7).

This sense of not existing and losing faculties is a profoundly shaming one, not least because it conflicts with the internalised ideal that one may have of oneself – shame can begin in the infant's sense of bodily weakness. It is unsurprising, therefore, that Hull says, 'there's no doubt that the loss of the face is a profound loss. A deeply dehumanising [shaming SP] loss' (Cole 1998, 37). Losing such an important part of oneself, and the ability to see it in others, is shaming and alienating.

Over time, Hull found that he could make more use of voices and other cues to gauge identities, emotions and moods. But this did not entirely make up for the loss of presence signified by the real faces of others: 'Not to be in the presence of the face is a profound loss' (Cole 1998, 41). While there may be a valuable, even priestly, sort of witness in testifying that faces are not absolutely necessary to life, Hull suggests, 'you have to be an extraordinarily faceless person to accept that' (Cole 1998, 41). One senses that the shaming cloud between ideal and reality still haunts Hull's life, or at least did so when he met Cole in the 1990s.

Observers who have difficulties in coping with faces
There are a number of groups of people who seem to have difficulties not with physically seeing faces, but with their nature and identity. Perhaps most numerous amongst them are people diagnosed with autism or with Asperger's syndrome. They are often described as having 'face blindness' or prosopognosia. This means that they have difficulty in recognising emotions and expressions on the faces of others, especially complex or nuanced ones, and so they do not necessarily respond very well to them (Attwood 2006, 128–31; Hole and Bourne 2010, 185–91). Furthermore, they may avoid looking at faces altogether, particularly the eye region of the face, or just look at parts of them.

This is not the place to try to give an account of why autistic people find faces, both their own and those of others, difficult. Explanations range from complex neurological deficits to upbringing and social factors (Frith 2008). Certainly these things seem to combine in the life of Donna Williams, an autistic woman who has written a well-known autobiography (Williams 1999).

Williams was diagnosed as autistic in adulthood, but felt that she had been so all her life. She came from a massively abusive and violent family, so her problems with emotions, faces and shame were almost undoubtedly interwoven. Williams displayed many of the characteristics of shamed people in trying to distance herself from herself and her emotions, avoid others or put on an act to ensure a measure of self- and social-acceptability (Pattison 2000, 110–20).

When he interviewed Williams for his book, Cole (1998, 108) concluded that the reason that autistic people have difficulties with face is because they have difficulties with social interaction. This is then reflected in their response to faces which seem over-complex and engulfing to the fragile self. Faces give out many signals simultaneously; this, too, can be baffling for those who have internal emotional difficulties. Williams, who started off by not being able to look at faces, her own or those of others, and who felt very alienated from her face ('he kissed my face … I wasn't in it at the time' (Williams 1999, 80)), eventually started to have inhabited facial relations with others. However, at the time of Cole's interview, she and her partner still found faces difficult. And if people are not able to respond facially to others, they may shame those others by being unresponsive, but they may also find themselves alienated and shamed by those who cannot understand their apparent inhuman lack of personal warmth and emotion.

Other groups of facial observers who have rare conditions may also find themselves living in conditions of considerable misery and distress which may in themselves be alienating partly because they are simply so distressing. Delusional misidentification syndromes occur when somehow people mistake the facial identity of others in some way and respond affectively in the wrong way to the people involved (Hole and Bourne 2010, 177–82; Ramachandran 1999). They are usually thought to be caused by neuronal disturbance or damage. Oliver Sacks' 'man who mistook his wife for a hat' is one such person who cannot distinguish faces from other objects, so picks up his wife's head instead of his hat (Sacks 1986, 7–21).

Capgras syndrome occurs when people think that the people they are with are somehow imposters impersonating a familiar, known person. Fregoli delusion is the name for the syndrome in which different people are taken to be the same person, but in disguise. Some people come to think that people have changed identity while preserving the same appearance as before – this is called intermetamorphosis. And others experience subjective doubles; they believe that they themselves have a double with the same appearance as themselves, but with different character traits. In all these instances, there seems to be a fault in the link between the facial recognition system and appropriate affectional responses to the face. This can be distressing and alienating for all those involved.

This brings us to the final group of observers who seem to have difficult or different relations with faces.

Observers who experience shame or emotional distress

Hole and Bourne (2010: 209) observe that 'the ability to process facial emotions effectively is associated with the ability to interact with others'. It has been widely observed that those who suffer from emotional and mental health problems focus on faces in different ways from 'normals' or 'typicals' (Argyle and Cook 1976; Hole and Bourne 2010, chapter 8). So, for example, those who suffer from social anxiety take ambiguous emotional expressions to be threatening. People diagnosed with clinical depression seem similarly to have problems in accurately recognising facial emotional expressions, while those diagnosed with schizophrenia have a demonstrably different way of looking at faces, with different scanning patterns that again lead to impairment in processing facial emotion. Meanwhile, there is evidence that abused children may read faces and interpret emotions differently from those who are not abused, being more easily able to recognise different types of anger than other expressions (Pollak et al. 2000).

It could be argued that these different, restricted ways of approaching the face are entirely engendered by some kind of physiological response, but I am not so sure about this. Mental health and other problems occur in a social context and those with them are often stigmatised and shamed. It is a symptom of shame that people drop their eyes and do not look others full in the face. Could it be that one of the reasons that distressed people don't look at the faces and particularly the eyes of others is because they feel ashamed? Perhaps this also accounts for some of the difficulty that some people with Asperger's syndrome have with face; they find it difficult to interact with others having experienced shame, unlovability and unwantedness. This, then, manifests itself in a variety of responses and behaviours that are grounded and symbolised in facial relations with others. This is a highly speculative note on which to end, but there may be some validity in it.

Although shame may not be so directly and obviously implicated in the situation of observers of faces as it is in the case of inhabitants of faces, it is still plausible to argue that shame hovers around the edges, and is sometimes very directly implicated, in the situation of observers. While there is less stigmatisation because of obvious visible facial abnormality, situations of partial communication and alienation arise amongst observers as well as inhabitants of face. This can cause considerable distress, or at least be a symptom of distress for them. Yet again, we have widened the purview of those who have problems with face to include many new groups. Problems with face, and the shame that hangs around them as a penumbra, are really not uncommon.

Conclusion

Face plays a vital part in the development of human beings. As social animals who need to learn what it is to be human and to understand others, physical face is indispensible in helping to shape who and what we are in defining the limits of what is acceptable. We learn love, acceptability and sociality through the faces of others (though as we have seen in the case of blind people, visuality and face are not indispensable in becoming a full person). We also learn about rejection, isolation and shame through the cold or rejecting looks and attitudes of others. Here again, actual face plays an important, if somewhat indeterminate, part. It is for this reason that shame is often imaged in visual terms and the sense of isolation and rejection that people experience in shame is often characterised as losing face. Face remains an important reality and symbol in human development and relations, so where face becomes a problem, there are bound to be communal problems that can result in instances of shame, humiliation, alienation and abjection.

For most sighted people, facially mediated acceptance remains important throughout their lives if they are to function as fully integrated human beings, whether on their own or with others. It is true that your face can be your fortune if it looks like everyone else's and you do not have problems in perceiving or responding to the faces of others. For better, and often for worse, however, the face itself can become a site of shame for those who have problems with faces. Because of the instinctive tribalism and normativity of facial perception, and because of the unfortunate equation of the face with identity and character, those who cannot perceive or present their faces in 'normal' ways are likely to find themselves rejected, isolated and unwanted, to be shamed. Worst of all, they may internalise the rejecting views and attitudes of others and so come to find themselves defective and worthless. Face, such a powerful factor in human formation, thus becomes a factor in destroying and denigrating persons. Shamed people then need to be re-seen in loving and accepting ways if their personhood is to be preserved and enhanced and their social integration is to be assured. They need to be extricated from the 'hole' of oblivion and unvisibility, to see themselves as seen, so that they can see themselves in their own faces and those of others. There are a lot of people who find themselves in this unfortunate position, so this is not special pleading for tiny minority groups. And even if it were, that does not mean that, as a human society, we should not attend more closely to them. Amongst other things we might gain from learning more about ourselves and the social and personal significance we attach to faces and interpersonal relations.

We will come back to more practical responses to the kinds of issue of rejection that I have raised in this chapter later, but I want to conclude this first part of the book by saying something about the notion of 'face behind face' which emerges not only from everyday experience but also from some reflections on contemporary philosophy and theology. This will form a very useful prelude to the second part of the book, where I look critically at the theology of the face of God and the possibility of restoring the face and alleviating the shame of those who have 'problems with faces'.[13]

---

[13]   I should make clear here again that 'problems with faces' and reactions to them are socially defined and maintained, so it is important to emphasise that this is not a matter of requiring shamed people to do the changing, but rather the shamers and the shaming social order. Shame needs to be transferred onto society as a whole, away from individuals who are alienated (Nussbaum 2004). For general consideration of the politics of the conferment of stigma and deviant status onto individuals and groups see Pattison (1997, 83–95; 2000, 131–53).

Chapter 4
Face, Presence and the 'Face behind Face'

In this short transitional chapter, I will begin to explore the transcendence and recursivity of face as a prelude to considering the nature and significance of the face of God. Here we begin to move decisively from the already complex matter of understanding and interpreting human face, perceived and experienced in everyday life, to thinking about its deeper significations and significances, especially as they relate to thinking about and experiencing the face of God.

As we have seen, face is omniprevalent in a world run around the assumption that enfaced recognition and communication is normative. This can have very negative effects for those who are deprived of typical facial contact and expression. So face is very important as an everyday physical reality. But at the same time, it is an enigma. It is openly there on the side of your head for you to feel, and for others to see. But it is so entangled with interpretative and representational issues and deep assumptions about the nature and identity of persons that it almost seems to take leave of physical reality altogether.

Face is person. To ignore or damage the face is to denigrate the person and the people bound up with that person. If the symbol of the human person fully alive is the smiling face, the reality of oppression, denigration and shame can also be enacted and represented facially. In *1984*, a book full of faces, the 'perfecting' torturer, O'Brien, says to the individualist rebel, Winston Smith: 'If you want a picture of the future, imagine a boot stamping on a human face – for ever' (Orwell 1983, 898). This is one of the most chilling sentences in modern English literature.

Superficial and deep, fundamental and ephemeral, stable and always moving, it is very difficult to get a good fix on face. It stands for so much – too much – within and beyond itself. It provides an overwhelming surplus of meanings, many of which are inarticulable. That is unsurprising, because facial knowledge purveyed by visual contact precedes verbal and rational knowledge by some months in the development of human beings.

Like the enigmatic enfaced Sphinx, face withholds the totality of its significances and meanings, allowing them only to emerge obliquely, accessed by fleeting glimpse rather than through the force of systematic gaze. Even the physical entity face can be regarded as elusive and unfinished:

> a face is something that incomplete: a work in progress (that) stands in continuous need of being seen or touched or written upon. And maybe that is a fundamental reason for our fascination with faces: like the personalities they express and the

ideas they communicate, faces need to be used because they are not finished images. (Elkins 1997, 182)

There is, then, a sense in which 'face' is self-transcending, ineffable, even partially or wholly invisible. It is not fully available to the articulate tongue or the observant eye, yet it remains central to the project of being human persons, together and apart. Even blind people seem to find space for the importance of face in understanding existence. After talking to two people blind from birth Cole concludes:

> For them it seemed to represent a preferential part of the body, a site where attention in others was shown. At some level then, the face was buried within us, transcending sight and beyond experience. (Cole 1998, 42)

Face was real and important, but not necessarily visible and accessible.

Lucy Grealy, facially disfigured, talks of an ideal face, perhaps an original face, or a face that is to come – or both – that will make her beautiful and so lovable. This is not so far from St Paul's hope that somehow he will be enfaced and see God's face at some point in the future (1 Cor. 13; Col. 3:3).

A similar kind of concern with the fragmentary and partial nature of faces as they reflect and make present, or make present the absence, of person and identity is recorded in Barthes' *Camera Lucida*, a meditation on photography inspired by his mother's death. After his mother had died, Barthes feels the anguish of not being able 'to recall her features (summon them up as a totality)' (Barthes 2000, 63). He looks through lots of old photographs, trying to find her in the various images in which she appears. Somehow he knows that it is her, he identifies her, but still he cannot find her features, her air, her essential identity and being. So the photographs, like photographs in general, render death and absence rather than presence. Only one photograph, a picture of her in a Winter Garden as a five-year-old child actually reveals 'the truth of the face I had loved' in addition to her identity (Barthes 2000, 67). Wounded by the vivid reality of the truth of his mother in the image, Barthes does not reproduce the photograph in the book, despite the longing he creates for the image in the reader: 'It exists only for me. For you, it would be nothing but an indifferent picture, one of the thousand manifestations of the "ordinary"' (Barthes 2000, 73). Readers are left yearning for the presence of Barthes' mother's face in the Winter Garden, almost able to see it, but left high and dry in the black and white words of text.[1] Face becomes word that evokes but cannot be seen.

---

[1]   Taking the example of Moses, Elkins (1997, 166) similarly notes in relation to the textualisation of lost or absent faces: 'My Moses is in between a person (with a whole catalogue of faces, none of them at all adequate to the task) and an absence (an incomprehensible disfiguration of an unknowable face, hidden in a faceless text). This Moses oscillates between those two poles.'

There are three relevant points to make here. First, any particular image or representation of face or facial expression does not capture the totality of being and personhood in any real way. Indeed, it may bear witness to its fragmentation and to the elusiveness of the real truth and presence of personal being.

Secondly, faces (and the photographs in which they are represented) may frustrate by concealing and making absent the person as much as by making them present – Donna Williams comment when someone kissed her that, 'I was not in my face at the time', is resonant here (Williams 1999, 80). So face and representations of it can seem to be a barrier to personal grasp and presence in relationship, a signifier of absence, as much as they might be an aid to grasping presence.

Finally, here again there is the idea of some kind of face beyond face, identity and presence beyond physiognomy of which physical face is in a sense just a reminder or palimpsest. Which face in which photograph actually represents the real face and person identified in the photograph? And can this face really only be seen by some people, lovers or relatives, for example, who are attached to it, or is it more widely available? Who can see which aspects of whose face, and what do we miss as we look?

All of these witnesses point towards both the importance and transcendence of face, and also to its relative dispensability as a physical organ essential to existence. There seems to be a paradox here that is redolent of some trends in theology with its use of the kataphatic and the apophatic, saying and unsaying, to talk about God (Turner 1995). Before turning to theology proper in the next chapter, it will be useful to attend briefly to this kind of assertion and non-assertion which allows both presence and absence to be important categories in approaching face.

Face as the site of absence and presence is an important notion for exploring not only human faces, but also the face of the divine. I will explore this idea a bit more now, first by considering the significance of the paradox of presence and absence in human faces. I will then consider the notion of 'face behind face'. These themes are related in pointing to the elusiveness and complexity of the meanings and nature of face as both physical entity and signifier of something beyond figuring the ambiguity of presence and relationship. The importance of this is to ensure that, before leaving the realm of common human experience of face to think about God, some of the deeper significances and enigmas attached to face have been recognised. These may then be of assistance when it comes to understanding the significance of the notion of the face of God which will be explored in subsequent chapters of this book.

The Paradox of Presence and Absence in the Human Face

It has frequently been pointed out that, as in the case of Barthes, images of faces, whether in photographs, portraits or other representations, are in many ways intimations of absence (Berger 1972, 8). Indeed, portraits of emperors, gods and other powerful figures were first made to make present that which was either absent or invisible (Belting 1994). People take photographs or commission portraits so that when the subject is not there, either because of death or absence, something of their presence is felt or evoked. This is done in the (at least implicit) knowledge that they will not always be there. So a portrait or photograph can be taken to be an anticipation of death, a *memento mori*, even if a subject physically survives for years beyond their own mimetic image.

An iconic facial image produces 'visible absence' (Belting 2005, 312). Indeed, it may be that which is absent or hidden that draws viewers' attention, as much as its visual availability (Leader 2002, 11–12). There is a power in the emptiness, the void behind the image, that intrigues and attracts (Leader 2002, 68–9). Every representation of a person can be taken as figuring their absence as much, if not more, than their presence. A 'good' portrait or representation makes the person present, providing some kind of life after death, while also clearly figuring their absence and loss, and thus their hiddenness and unavailability: if they were lastingly present and visible in the form depicted (for example when they were young, beautiful, famous), the representation would be unnecessary.

The theme of absence and presence in representations of the face has been taken up by art historians (Freedberg 1989). Icons and other human images, particularly facial portraits of persons, play with the notion of surface and depth to evoke a sense of living presence, hence the enchanting power of such images and their power to appear themselves almost human in their evocation of persons and presence: 'Like a face, an icon is both surface and depth, which combine to create a sense of presence, something that is there yet not fully visible' (Morgan 2012, 89).

The power of facial representations in icons and portraits to evoke living personhood in material media is actually a derivative property of human faces themselves. A face is a 'thick, living surface that begins in the unseen domain of feeling and ends in the visible world of others, limning the threshold of visibility' (Morgan 2012, 92). Physical faces themselves then act like material iconic representations, with the capacity to create a kind of movement between surface and depth that alerts viewers to the reality of personal existence. It is largely because there is a dynamic of surface and depth, presence and absence in actual faces that living personhood is identified as being present. A dead face, a death mask or a doll's face, permanently fixed in expression, all surface with no depth, may not evoke any kind of living presence at all. This underlines the fact that faces necessarily exist in a person-like dynamic of evoking presence and absence. It is the sense of fluctuating, changing presence and absence that makes things appear potentially personal and available for relationship (Pattison 2007b).

The face of another person is as close as we can ever get to their essence, but also the place where we can best experience their absence and the futility of ever trying to get beyond, or beneath their skin. Even when one is involved in an intimate, unitive facial activity like kissing, one is so near and yet so far from the other person. We can never get through someone's face to appropriate their essence. Their elusiveness and absence is as real as their very close presence. Indeed, it is partly elusiveness and absence which establishes what real personhood is, and thus opens up the possibility of person-like relations, either with actual physical faces or their representations, as when people pray to saints using iconic representations to make them real.

This point is well made by psychoanalytic observers of children. Lemma (2010, 39), considering the blissful, unifying, mutually constructive gaze of the mother with the small infant at breast, points out that in this most intimate of relationships,

> the baby cannot grasp the core of the mother – blissful unity of gaze also exposes enigmatic, absent, withholding mother who cannot be seen or apprehended. Appearance conceals absence. *The mother's face is site of presence and absence.*

Thus,

> the present mother always contains the shadow of the absent mother – of the (m)other who is beyond our omnipotent control. At the core of each of us there exists a painful yearning to know the inside of the other who, by virtue of its separateness, can never be fully apprehended and possessed by the self.

Ultimately, there is part of the other that is sealed away and unavailable. To relate to another human being, however intimately, is then also to have to come to terms with the fact that their face represents absence as well as presence. Full human relations, facial and other, have to acknowledge the withheld and elusive nature of the other. Absence, fragmentation and lack of comprehension are necessary aspects of presence and real knowledge of them. The seen face is not only not physically visible to us in all its aspects, all of the time. It also figures a complex dynamic of presence and absence, surface and depth in relationship. Faces evoke what we most want in the way of intimacy and what we may have to accept we can never fully have. They promise and frustrate simultaneously.

This is significant for thinking about human relations with and thinking about God. If God is a living entity capable of real personal relationship, we might reasonably expect to find a mixture of presence and absence, gift and loss in our encounter with the divine. Relating to the divine face is no less complex or ambivalent than personally relating to fellow human beings fully.

'Face beyond Face'

Continuing the theme of surface and depth, presence and absence that evoke personhood brings me to the idea of 'face beyond face'. Elkins (1997, 79) notes that 'a face does not need membranes or living flesh'. Many things can look like, or function as, faces; for example, the simple lines of emoticons, and the geometric patterns on walls.

There is real sense in which face recursively effaces and goes beyond itself. Many people seem to be drawn to some notion of a significant kind of face beyond the immediately visible physical face. Perhaps that is because in Western society we take what is hidden to be more 'true' and real than what is visible (Freedberg 1989, 315). Here I want to explore this kind of thinking by briefly discussing the thought of Emmanuel Levinas, as mediated through some of his contemporary interpreters.

Levinas was a twentieth-century Jewish philosopher, heavily influenced by phenomenology. As a survivor of holocaust Europe, he was very concerned to establish how humans could live respectfully and peacefully together. While not a theologian, his philosophy is partly rooted in Jewish religious thought.

At the centre of Levinas' ethics is the idea of face. Face for Levinas is at one level countenance, the face within perceptual experience. At another level, it lies beyond perceptual experience; indeed, it can be represented not as seen visual object, but as words: 'This attestation of oneself is possible only as a face, that is, as speech' (Levinas 1969, 201). Again, he writes, 'the epiphany of the face is wholly language' (Ford 1999, 37).

Not only is face to be found in language, but it can be represented by another body part. Danchev argues:

> The face may be a face – a human face – but it may also be another part of the body, perhaps even a body part. In *Life and Fate*, as Levinas saw it, the face is the back, or the nape of the neck. "Grossman isn't saying that the nape is the face", he explained in one interview, "but that all the weakness, all the mortality, all the naked and disarmed mortality of the other can be read from it". In his own work Levinas underlined the moral of the story: "The face as the extreme precariousness of the other. Peace as awakeness to the precariousness of the other." (Danchev 2011, 40; Levinas 2006, 201)

For ordinary perceivers of face, this idea of face behind face that then becomes speech or another part of the body seems enigmatic, not to say contradictory. Face does not refer to actual faces, but rather to the essence of subjectivity that lies behind speech and it becomes 'the philosophy of both language and body' that incarnates subjectivity (Sobieszek 1999, 287). It is language, but it transcends language to be inarticulate and inchoate. As such, face can be represented non-facially and non-physically, and it represents the vulnerability and precariousness of existence. It is almost the pre-verbal cry of essential humanity, the humanity that can so easily be shamed, excluded, extinguished:

> The face signifies in the fact of summoning, *of summoning me* – in its nudity or its destitution, in everything that is precarious in questioning, in all the hazards of mortality – to the unresolved alternative between Being and Nothingness, a questioning which, *ipso facto, summons me*. (Hand 1989, 5)

For Levinas, then, the enigmatic and inarticulable symbol of the face represents the demand of the Other and of the Infinite on humans in all their vulnerability. We are addressed by the face of the Other and this precedes ethical language, just as the inarticulate cry of the baby makes a demand on the parent to which they have to respond. It is as if there were an invisible, universal, yet particular, 'archetype' lying within and beyond actual human countenances that inflects and influences them and can, in some ways, become articulate and recognisable as it is responded to. This sounds very like an extreme, apophatic view of the image of God which theologians believe is to be found within human beings. Indeed, Levinas often uses the analogy of God, while disavowing faith. He writes, for example, 'I do not struggle with a faceless god, but I respond to his expression, to his revelation' (Levinas 1969, 197).

Lying behind this kind of thought is the tradition of Moses seeing the face of God in Exodus. In Exodus, neither the face of God nor the face of Moses having seen God are to be represented; their faces are beyond representation (Butler 2006, 160n4). However the encounter with the divine produces words which then create all that can be known of the face of God. God's face is therefore revealed in 'words' or pre-verbal face-like communication that addresses the human race at a fundamental level. The epiphany of God is through language understood as a pre-verbal, multidimensional state of being that represents otherness and infinity. In due course, this finds an ethical articulation concerning respect for the Other through others. God's face therefore remains veiled and known, ultimately concrete, yet also ultimately concealed. This is very orthodox Christian theology, as will be seen later. But what is the significance of Levinas' thought in the present context?

First, Levinas highlights the ambiguity of face. Face is not fixed within physiognomy, nor limited to it. Secondly, he points up the archetypal nature of face and face as the locus of identity and humanity. Thirdly, this humanity figured by face is vulnerable, needy and precarious. Just as physical face can easily be disfigured by a punch or a cut, face as a category figures the precariousness of existence. Face and existence may be uncertain, mortal, weak and therefore prone to shame, denigration and defacement. However, Levinas' concept of face also, fourthly, reminds us of the demand that faces, literal and metaphorical, physiological make ethically upon others (Davies 1993). It is face, not statistics, that requires us to respond to the appeal on behalf of starving children – primordially, ethical and social obligation grows out of facial encounter and recognition. Fifthly, Levinas' ideas of face suggest that there is a kind of face behind face to which we have to respond. This is the demand of Infinity and being, perhaps what Christian theologians would call God. Encountering God in God's words and faces of others made in God's image, showing the face of God so far as we can see it, is the ethical vocation towards which Christians are called, enfacing self and others. Finally, Levinas reminds us that face is a boundary as well as a door. By his insistence on the unbounded, undefined nature of face, Levinas points to the fact that to know or to see a face is not to know the totality of the being that is figured by that face, whether it be human or divine. Face is a barrier to complete knowledge; the fall into words, text or inarticulate sound symbolises the infinite inaccessibility of the other, even as it manifests their presence and availability. So face necessarily frustrates and repels as well as enticing and summoning.

This is the direction which we now need to take as we consider much more carefully what it might be to engage with an enfaced God who enfaces. Many millions of people need to be enfaced or countenanced, to have the shame and stigma removed from their faces, physical and other; to this end they need to see God's face so they can believe that they are seen by God. But what is the face of God, and can it be seen in any sense visually and directly? Or is it, as Levinas seems to suggest, that the face of God is only found in words, which form a kind of veil or indirect trace or reflection of divine presence that can heal rather than destroy?

It is to these kinds of questions that we now turn in our continuing quest to make enfacement for the defaced, effaced and shamed a real possibility. If face figures the fullness of being in all its richness and vulnerability, its sociality and its individuality, as Levinas' thought allusively indicates, then exploring the nature of the face of God becomes a practical and theological imperative for Christians.

Chapter 5

Seeing the Face of God in the Bible

Any religion that does not say that God is hidden is not true …

(Pascal 1995, 74)

Compared to atheistic thoughtlessness, this is the much greater danger for theology and the Christian faith: that God will be talked to death, that he is silenced by the very words that seek to talk about him.

(Jungel 1983, 3)

This book is about saving faces. Thus far I have discussed the nature and significance of human faces which have been both physically and socially lost. In an era of faciality, human faces have in some ways been hidden from conscious, critical attention, and those who have literally and symbolically lost face have been shunned. But it is not just human faces that have been occluded. Within Christianity, the face of God as an important experience and category has also been lost.

In the modern Western world, the idea that God might have a face in any real sense seems bizarre. The idea that God's 'face' might in any way be visible then seems insane! The God of contemporary Christian theology is firmly invisible. The face of God is nothing more than a metaphor or symbol for God's presence – and it may be a very distant, non-distinct presence at that. Robert Orsi (2005, 158) argues that there is nothing students of religion and theology find so disconcerting as experience and presence in believers. And within Western theology in general, and in Protestant theology in particular, there has been an emphasis on the disembodied, rational, cognitive, oral, aural and ethical aspects of divine presence rather on the visual and visible (Pattison 2007). Indeed, it is not going too far to say that many iconoclastic Protestants, following Karl Barth's example, appear to suspect, loathe and denigrate the visual and visible in religion, preferring to emphasise the importance of the Word and divine teaching rather than the seeing of the divine (Ellul 1985).[1] This can lead to a rather thin understanding and experience of divine presence in the world.

---

[1] For theological suspicion and ignoring of the visual, see Pattison (2007b, 84–107). Shantz (2009, 20–66) arraigns contemporary biblical scholarship and theology for its bias against the ecstatic, the embodied, the non-cognitive and the non-linguistic understanding and valuing of religious experience, tracing this bias partly to a desire of some Protestant scholars to distance themselves from the kind of visual and mystical experience associated with Catholicism.

In the so-called Aaronic Blessing, God, instructing Moses on how Aaron should bless the people of Israel, says:

> May Yahweh bless you and keep you.
> May Yahweh let his face shine on you
> and be gracious to you.
> May Yahweh show you his face
> and bring you his peace. (Num. 6:24–6 NJB)

Here God appears to be suggesting that God's shining face, a smiling face, will be available to his people in a direct way.[2] God's face will light up in joy and, in doing so, human faces, too, will light up and smile, so God and humans enjoy mutual blessing. The smiling face of whatever kind has a substantiality that appears tangible and real, even if transient. We can almost reach out to touch this gracious, shining, smiling face through the words of the text.

However, we moderns now read these words in a psychological, metaphorical, disembodied, distanced way. We perhaps hear something like this:

> May you sometimes have a sense that a benevolent invisible being is quite close
> to you;
> May this vague sense of invisible presence feel comforting, so you enjoy some
> inner tranquility.

Shorter and less poetic, this formulation removes any temptation to think that God is anything like us physically. God may identify with God's people, but not to the extent of having a body or a face that really lights up in a smile that humans can tangibly perceive.

Does it matter that God for moderns has become invisible, intangible and faceless? Perhaps this represents considerable progress and advance in truth over apparently more limited, local and 'primitive' anthropomorphic ideas about God?

While this could be the case, I want to suggest that the traditions of seeing God's face in ways other than as psychologising metaphor need to be treated as a much more critical resource and provocation for contemporary theological thinking. To put it starkly, a main tradition of Christian theology has been the hope of seeing God. Jesus promises this to the pure in heart in the Beatitudes (Matt. 5:8), and the vision of God, the *visio dei*, was a central, if now neglected, plank of Christian life and thought; for centuries, the whole aim of Christian life was ultimately to see God's face.

---

[2]   What is the shining face of God but the smiling face of God? 'The face that shines upon you and gives you "the peace of God that passeth all understanding" – surely this soothes and comforts by reaching into that storehouse of early experience deep within the preverbal core of the self where the mother's face "shines" (smiles) upon the baby in her arms and fills its whole perceptual world with light' (Wright 1991, 19).

To be faithful to all aspects of this tradition, I think we need to take ideas and practices associated with seeing the face of God more seriously. The tradition, particularly the biblical tradition, is, at the very least, ambiguous about the material visibility of God's face. The early Rabbis, for example, believed that in principle God could be seen – but the experience would be lethal (Wolfson 1994, 27)! Thus Pascal is only partly right in his assertion that 'any religion that does not say that God is hidden is not true' (Pascal 1995, 74). Much of the orthodox Christian tradition teaches that God is both hidden and visible. And while Jungel (1983, 3) is concerned 'that God will be talked to death, that he is silenced by the very words that seek to talk about him', we should perhaps be equally worried that theological words might help to make God invisible and irrelevant to the real needs of humans inhabiting a visual world. It seems strange that a theological tradition based on revelation, a visual term from the world of appearance and seeing, should be so indifferent to the visibility of God.

But more than that, in the present context where we are considering the place of face, human flourishing and shame in human life, the possibility of being able to find some meaning and value in seeing the face of God may be vital. Let me explain.

Donald Winnicott argues that it is in seeing the face of the other that we believe ourselves to be seen: 'When I look I am seen, so I exist' (Winnicott 1974, 134). In the case of mother and child, the infant and the parent co-construct each other in their mutual gaze. They are real to each other because they see, and so believe themselves to be seen. In other words, they give each other face and countenance; in so doing, they enhance both their mutuality and their individuality. Often, this loving mutuality is encapsulated in smiles. Conversely, when gaze is interrupted, turned away or absent, there is no mutuality and the child may then believe themselves not to exist. They literally lose countenance and become non-persons. This motif of being able to see in order to believe that one is seen, recognised and valued, is carried forward into adult life. If God, then, cannot be seen, it is possible that people will not feel themselves to be seen and so loved by God. This may contribute to a sense of being seen through, non-existent, unwanted or shamed – they may effectively disappear (Ayers 2003; Kilborne 2002). There is, then, a fundamental disconnect between human experience and values, and relationship with God. This seems odd in the context of a God who is regarded as having a deeply intimate, personal relationship with humans.

There is no reason why we should have the God we want, in the shape we want, who meets the needs that we believe we have. But equally, in the light of the tradition of seeing God's face within the Judaeo-Christian tradition, there is a range of important theological and pastoral issues to be critically considered here. There has been a prejudice towards notions of the visibility of God. This has deprived Christians of some important theological and religious resources for understanding humans and the divine.

This suspicion deepens when one encounters judgements from scholars who value the religious experience of ordinary people over the abstract ideas and ideals beloved of many logocentric theologians:

> Religion is the practice of making the invisible visible, of concretising the order of the universe, the nature of human life and its destiny, and the various dimensions and possibilities of human interiority itself ... in order to render them visible and tangible, present to the senses in the circumstances of everyday life. Once made material, the invisible can be negotiated and bargained with, touched and kissed, made to bear human anger and disappointment ... (Orsi 2005, 73–4)

Of course, many logocentrics would condemn both religion, insofar as it is human creation, and, along with that, an emphasis on the visual rather than aural, the Word, perhaps not least because it is associated with popular, experiential, non-cognitive forms of believing (McDannell 1995). But if faithful practice is really to be about full, embodied encounter with the living God, it is doubtful that most people, including apparently iconoclastic Protestants, can really do without some kind of visual, sensual relationship that makes presence real (Harvey 1995, 1999; Morgan 1998, 1999, 2005; Morgan and Promey 2001; Orsi 1985, 1996). Faces are most valued within Orthodox worship where churches are filled with heavenly visages in the form of icons, some of which are kissed. However, even in the most austere Protestant church there are often faces to be found; photos of former ministers, representations of Jesus, sculptures of heroes of the faith (Harvey 1995, 1999).

Characterising presence as a relationship between faces, Orsi (2005, 74) notes:

> The invisible often becomes visible as faces, in heaven (in the face of Blessed Margaret of Castello looking at my uncle Sal) and on earth (in the face of a woman who keeps an images of the Sacred Heart of Jesus in her bedroom dresser and teaches here grandchildren how to pray to this holy figure ...).

However sophisticated, reasonable and logocentric our theology may be, most people need visible mediations and experiences to presence the divine in real and helpful ways. In this belief, I will trace out something of the ambiguous traditions of the visibility of God in the Christian tradition, taking a basically historical approach. Before turning to the Bible and then going on to look at the development of ideas about the *visio dei*, I will say something about the nature of seeing and the cultural construction of sight.

Seeing: It's Not What It Seems

Seeing is not a straightforward, sensory, a-social matter (Elkins 1997; Morgan 2012; Pattison 2007b; Pylyshyn 2003). It is a relational activity, taught and mediated through culture; individual bodies and senses are bound up in an intricate relationship with the social body and it is out of this relationship that the world is experienced sensually: 'To see ... is to see for oneself, but also with others, and thereby to see with the eyes of the social body' (Morgan 2012, 55). Furthermore, visual schemes or 'scopic regimes' are constituted of different ratios of what is seen and unseen (Jay 1988, 4; Morgan 2012, 82; Pattison 2007b, 25–7). Thus people in different places and at different times might be able to see different things; belonging to a community means looking at the world (and not looking at it) in particular ways. This becomes more intelligible if one thinks of everyday experience; an experienced bird watcher or gamekeeper will notice small signs and differences in a swathe of countryside that cannot even be seen by the untrained, unsocialised urban eye.

Social norms and values shape the ways in which embodied humans engage with the visual to create communities of feeling and shared practice that allow people to construct a commonsensical, consensual reality. This is not just a matter of seeing the material world: 'to study seeing is to study embodiment as the mediation of the visible and invisible' (Morgan 2012, xvii). This suggests that the socio-psychological construction of seeing can extend to what moderns might call the spiritual or invisible world of gods and spirits, the world of the sacred. While many Western moderns might, at least publicly, find it bizarre to talk of seeing or touching saints, angels or other figures regarded as invisible and transcendent in our culture, these phenomena have been common in other societies and times and may not be as unusual in our own day as some might like to think (Christian 1999, 2012; Maxwell and Tschudin 1990). Many people, for example, claim to have seen angels (Heathcote-James 2009) and William Dalrymple, travelling near Jerusalem in the later twentieth century, encountered villagers who regularly saw St George (Dalrymple 1998, 343). Morgan (2012, 187) notes that 'apparitions and visions have not diminished, nor has the interest in hearing about them', a view consonant with reports from psychologists I have spoken with. Visibility and invisibility are then cultural, at least as much as natural, events or possibilities (Morgan 2012, 83).

This is an important preliminary point in thinking about the visual world of historic, particularly early, Christianity. One of the most prominent sociological analysts of the Bible, John Pilch (1998, 53), states baldly: 'modern Western science, whether medical or psychological, is so monocultural as to be useless for application to other cultures.' What he is getting at here is that the sense of person, society, culture and so on of sensory engagement and possibility was completely different in what might loosely be called 'biblical times'.[3] In late capitalist

---

[3]   I am acutely conscious that I over-generalise about the Bible, its different cultures, times and books that come from many authors and places. In a work of this kind, however,

modernity, we conceive ourselves to be bounded psychological individuals whose sense of reality is mediated through a highly privileged sense of depth of personal consciousness. Anything that we cannot assimilate to this understanding is seen as eccentric, impossible or non-existent. Thus we understand visions of the heavens or heavenly beings to be symptoms of mental disorder and deviance.

In many other, 'strong group' (Malina 1996) societies, both ancient and modern, selfhood has been much less about total separation and autonomy of the individual, so that some critics have suggested that more corporately bound and collectivist societies consist of 'dividuals' (Malina 1983, 51–70, 1996; Strathern 1988). In these often more pre-modern, pre-industrial societies, not only are persons more porous and overtly dependent on groups and other people, the relationship between the material and non-material realms is different. Hence, in early Hebrew society, the individual was not regarded as having a soul, but rather as being animated, along with the rest of creation, by spirit that indwells the blood. Relations between the material and the immaterial world were closer and less well distinguished. Indeed, the distinction, material/immaterial, which seems absolute and fundamentally unbridgeable in the modern world, could not be thought of or made in the same way. Even desirable goods such as 'honour' seem to have been conceived as material substances that are in limited supply; vision, too, was conceived as a material relationship, more like touching than as a distant scanning; thus the casting of the Evil Eye was not just a figure of speech, or metaphor, but a touching with a malevolent substance (Elliott 1994; Pattison 2007b).

Just as aboriginal peoples are said to have a fundamental relationship of interdependence and belonging with the land in modern Australia or North America, so that people and place cannot be talked of without each other, it seems early Hebrew society did not make the same kind of absolute distinctions between human and non-human aspects of existence that are made in the modern West; they belonged together and were inextricably imbricated, the same kind of seemingly non-dualistic, materialistic thinking applied to understanding the heavenly realms and their relationship with the human world. While the place that the gods inhabited, heaven, could be distinguished from the place where humans dwelt, there was no absolute fixed boundary between heaven and earth. Nor was the heavenly realm invisible or inaccessible in principle to humans: 'The ancient mind drew few boundaries between "imaginary" and "real"' (Flannery-Dailey 2004, 17). Thus visions, apparitions, dreams, heavenly journeys and other apparently strange and bizarre visually-related experiences in which humans encountered the divine quite directly, while exceptional and privileged, were not as unusual or unthinkable as they would be in the modern industrialised world of atomised psychological individuals. Pre-modern people would not see or believe such encounters to be signs of falling out of reality, entering a non-real dimension, or becoming ill. While what might be called Altered States of Consciousness or

---

I do not have space to do justice to the various different kinds and interpretations of biblical experiences and attitudes.

perception were not necessarily common, they were not unusual within the visual or scopic norms of the time (Malina and Pilch 2008; Pilch 1983). In such a world, where human-material-divine-heavenly was not separated as it is in our culture, seeing God is not at all beyond the bounds of reality. It is this kind of mentality that allows for the possibility that the rule of God, preached by Jesus, is not just an ethereal event beyond all human life and experience, but rather a socio-material reality that becomes manifest in the present world.

I suggest that in the thought-experience world of the ancient world, the God of the Bible occupied an analogous position to the present Queen of the United Kingdom. I and many of my fellow subjects have never seen the Queen in person. However, I have every reason to believe that she really exists, that other people, some known to me personally, have seen and met her. In principle, I believe that I, too, could meet her in the flesh. There is no reason why she should want to meet me, and I may never ever encounter her face-to-face. But that does not mean that this is not possible, and no-one, I hope, would think that it was mad or eccentric of me to think that a sensory encounter with her of a very limited kind could occur – at her behest, of course. In the context of the present discussion about the visibility of the face of the divine, this helps make sense of the assertion that people in NT times could have absolutely 'real' experiences of 'other-than-human persons, such as angels, demons, gods, or God' (Pilch 1998, 52).

Perhaps the richness and occasional confusion of this sense of overlapping realms of visible reality is best captured in a passage like Acts 12:1–17. Peter is imprisoned and praying. An angel of the Lord comes and stands in his cell – Peter seems unsurprised. The angel frees him from his chains then leads him out of the prison – Peter is not sure whether this is a vision or not, but again is not unduly perturbed, and confirms that it was not a vision (what was it then, and why was it seemingly less worrying and remarkable than a vision to him?) when he stands freed on the street. He goes to the house of Mary and the maid who answers his knock recognises his voice. But when she goes to tell the other occupants Peter is there, they say, 'It must be his angel' – some sort of person-related doppelganger who looks and sounds like Peter and is embodied enough to knock on doors apparently. Again, they do not seem especially surprised, and only when they go to the door themselves are they amazed to see what appears to be the man himself standing there.

Here, in one short passage, even allowing for the literary and textual nature and purposes of the account, there seem to be intimations of a multidimensional visual world full of beings, not sensorily available to moderns, which is negotiated by the inhabitants of that world with ease and aplomb. This appears to be part of the consensual Christian world shared with the author of Acts. It is a world with very different realms, textures, boundaries and features from the ratio-instrumental technological world which moderns inhabit visually and in every other way.[4]

---

[4]   There is a controversy in studies of texts that purport to deal with visionary phenomena in the Bible and religious studies as to whether these embody actual experiences

Morgan (2012, 69) argues that in any society or culture, by virtue of our cultural participation, we see 'what our participation in the visual field enables us to see. That might be a deity or an angel or a spirit'. Many religions and cultures in the contemporary world, including some kinds of Christianity, prize experiential, including visual, perceptions of the divine (Eck 1998; Pattison 2007b). Western intellectuals may find this difficult, but it is important to respect the different scopic regimes and visual possibilities that have informed the Christian tradition.

Soon, we will start to look more closely at Christian traditions of seeing God in general, and God's face in particular. Before advancing, however, it will be useful briefly to say some things about concepts of visibility, invisibility, hiddenness, concealment, veiling and abandonment which have often been applied to the divine in biblical and subsequent writings.

Various visually-derived terms have been used to characterise God's presence, absence, part-presence and part-absence in the Bible and beyond. If God were visible as other humans can be, we could see God clearly and comprehend the divine (though even here we need to be mindful of the partial, fallible nature of the human sense of sight (Elkins 1997; Pattison 2007b, 25–40; Pylyshyn 2003)). Since the human experience of God, literally and metaphorically, is that God cannot be visibly apprehended at all times, various other visually-related qualities have been ascribed to the divine. God can then be thought of as real, but absolutely and always invisible, hidden from our visual senses – like the far side of the moon. In that case, God may be apprehended indirectly by inference, or perhaps by non-visual perceptions and experiences, for example God's voice may be heard. In a revealed religious tradition, however, God is regarded as literally or metaphorically visible some of the time – perhaps like the transit of Venus across the sun that takes place every century or so. In particular, Christians believe God was made sensorily apprehensible in the man Jesus, the direct manifestation of God on earth. However, there is clearly something beyond the human Jesus in God, aspects of God that are unknown. This, together with experiences of God's presence and absence in the Judaeo-Christian tradition as a whole, has led people to describe God as absent (*absconditus*), or as hidden (concealed or veiled) (Dillenberger 1953). Absence suggests that God, having been visible, has now disappeared so is no longer visible/perceptible. Hiddenness implies that God has been perceptible, and may be present, so potentially apprehensible, at least by some, but is not knowable by

---

or whether they are just literary constructs following certain conventions of presentation. For more on these positions and the variety of visual experiences (apparitions, visions, dreams heavenly journeys, theophanies and so on) see, for example, Collins and Fishbane (1995), Flannery-Dailey (2004), Himmelfarb (1993), Lieb (1991, 1998), Pilch (1998, 2005), Rowland (1982), Wiebe (1997), Zaleski (1987). Lieb (1991) traces the evolution and types of visionary experience and also shows how visionary texts themselves can be direct catalysts to such experience. The Jewish throne mysticism kabbalah tradition also develops the idea that the face of some texts can allow direct access to the divine. See further, for example, Scholem (1991, 1996), Wolfson (1994).

all. Reasons for this sense of hiddenness may include God's partial withdrawal, God's disguising or concealing Godself in whole or in part (perhaps within the flesh of Jesus Christ) to make Godself accessible to humans, to enable them to have independence, to protect them from a lethal or damaging direct encounter, even to protect Godself from pollution, or humanity's inability, unsuitability or unwillingness to perceive God, perhaps because of its sin or unlikeness to God.[5]

Once one gets into the theological understandings of the knowledge of God expressed using these vision-related ideas, the subject becomes complicated and has implications beyond the literal level of physical perception. For example, the ideas of God being visible or invisible can be turned into fairly abstract points about the nature of divine being as both present and absent and so like that of persons – an issue considered in the last chapter. In that context 'eyes' are merely the eyes of faith, not in any way physical sight.

I am aware of the ambivalence of the language and meaning of sight from a modern perspective, but here I merely want to point up and briefly explain some of the main visually-related ideas and concepts that are applied to the experience, presence and absence of God in the Judaeo-Christian tradition. As I have suggested, biblical seeing was undertaken within a different visual organisation and set of scopic regimes from that which is common in modern Western Christianity. It is, therefore, to the Old Testament (OT) that I now turn. We will return to modern ways of seeing and understanding the nature of God's face at a later point.

Seeing the Face of God in the Old Testament

Both Testaments in the Christian Bible are flatly contradictory about whether or not God can be seen, and in that context, about whether God's face can be seen. Reading the Bible through modern Protestant eyes, it is tempting to take the texts that say that God cannot be seen as factual and normative; texts that talk of actually seeing the divine are then treated metaphorically or allusively. Thus all language about seeing God is characterised as mythological talk about the elusive presence of God where paradox can be resolved by simply saying that we are in the world of religious, not referential or concrete, truth. It has taken me many years to recognise that there are, in fact, two basic, and in some ways irreconcilable, viewpoints at work on this subject.

Biblical Hebrew does not have an abstract word for the presence of God – it uses the terms 'face of Yahweh' or 'face of Elohim' to denote a sense of immediate divine proximity. The word used for face, *panim*, is plural; it literally means faces of God (Barker 2011, 72; Terrien 1978, 65).

---

[5]   For more on the perceptibility and hiddenness of the divine, and ways in which the latter has been interpreted as, for example, punishment for sin, see, for example, Balentine (1983), Brueggemann (2009), Bull (1999), Dillenberger (1953), Finney (1994), Koerner (2004, chapter 13), Meyer and Pels (2003).

There are many OT texts where it is made clear that humans cannot see God, particularly God's face, directly and live, for example, Exod. 19:21, 33:20–23; Judg. 6:22, 13:22. But there are other places where people believe that they have encountered God directly and visually. Moses himself talks to Yahweh 'face-to-face, as a man talks to his friend' (Exod. 33:11; Deut. 24:10). He is permitted to see God's buttocks (literally his 'bumps') after requesting to see his face, God placing a hand over him in the cleft of a rock to protect him from direct facial encounter as he passes by (Exod. 33:18–23). A number of the Patriarchs have fairly direct visually-related encounters with God: Abraham encounters Yahweh in the form of three strangers at the oak of Mamre (Gen. 18:1–16), and again when an angel intervenes at the sacrifice of Isaac (Gen. 22:1–19). Jacob in Gen. 28:10–22 experiences an epiphanous visitation with speech in a dream. He later wrestles with Yahweh at the Jabbok ford (Gen. 32:22–32), after which he says he has seen God face-to-face – this moment leads later to Israel being characterised as 'the people that sees God' (Barker 2011, 59). Later on in the OT, prophets like Isaiah have visions of God in the Temple (Isa. 6) and God appears in Ezekiel's vision (Ezek. 1). Many of the Psalms, again relating particularly to the liturgical life of the Temple in Jerusalem, allude to seeing the face of God as the hope of his people (for example, Ps. 27:13; Ps. 42:2).

What can be learned here? First, seeing God, even God's face, is an important aspect of the OT, and of talking about the presence and nature of God. Some of the most important moments and events of the OT involve seeing God directly. However, God is seen only by a tiny number of people, all of whom are men – the women of Israel apparently did not see God.[6] Furthermore, God is not often seen, and not for long when God is visible. And this kind of seeing is not recounted in elaborate or detailed ways – while God appears to have some of the attributes of a super-sized human being, for example buttocks, God is not clearly delineated and defined even by those who see God 'face-to-face' – God remains veiled, concealed, obscure, only partially visible.

Seeing God, then, does not imply having a clear, comprehensive vision of the divine. It indicates a sense of hiddenness, self-concealment, elusiveness and unpredictability that enhances God's power in absence by denoting the awe of his presence. The seeing of God seems to produce a greater sense of mystery than not seeing God; in self-showing, God is revealed to be elusive. Seeing may have been 'thick' and more material than we are accustomed to think, but it was not

---

[6]   Seeing God, whether in the ancient or in the modern world, has political and gendered aspects to it. I am painfully aware that I have not dealt adequately with the gendered seeing of faces, human and divine, or explored the political implications of this in this book. See Jantzen (1995 1999) and Raphael (2003) for excellent introductions to many of the issues that pertain here. Coakley (2002) and Schussler Fiorenza (1983) point up the importance of women having a unique and different experience of seeing Jesus as first witnesses to the resurrection. This is an important, suggestive theological idea which requires far more exploration than I can engage with here.

comprehensive or dominant. Consequently, while seeing God, apprehending the elusive presence of this living, active person-like being who can be both present and absent, is important for the practice and development of Hebrew religion, it is not the sole category for understanding God's nature and relationship to humans. If God's presence is sometimes conceived and apprehended visually, it is also apprehended aurally.

Terrien (1978) argues that presence rather than covenant was the foundational theological idea in Israel's relationship with God, the latter being dependent on the former. While divine presence could be communicated visually through God's *kabhod*, glory, often represented by a cloud, it was also represented aurally by his name, 'I am what I am' or 'I will be what I will be' (Exod. 3:14). Both of these traditions are present in the Exodus account where Moses and others both hear and see the divine. Both name and glory revealed and hid the divine presence; traditions of both continued through Judaism and into Christianity (Terrien 1976, 121).

In Terrien's scheme, the theology of the name and the importance of hearing, words, commandments, equality of access to the divine, morality and obedience were preserved in the Northern stream of tradition in ancient Israel; this is identified with the E textual source in modern scholarship (Terrien 1976, 199). This tradition, which basically opposed images and visual imaging of the divine, substituting the name for the visual form of God, eventually became the dominant way of understanding divine presence. It provided the foundation for the Deuteronomic reforms of the Temple after the return of the exiles. The tradition denied that God could be seen, maintaining the divine could only be heard, in contrast to the tradition that held that Moses and the Israelites could see God (Deut. 4:12; Exod. 24:10). This kind of thinking is very familiar and congenial to Protestant theologians: 'From beginning to end, the Bible deals only with the word' (Ellul 1985, 48).

At the same time, the visual emphasis on seeing God's glory was focused on the Temple in Jerusalem where God was taken to dwell and to be permanently accessible. Here there was a liturgical cult built round the royal family and a priestly caste. People could come to Jerusalem to enjoy face-to-face communion with the divine presence in a richly visual environment. Despite modern assumptions about the perpetual existence of Jewish aniconism and iconophobia, based on elaborations of the command to make no images of the divine, Solomon's Temple was full of visually alluring images and material artefacts used to mediate divinity (Bland 2000). These included an altar, two cherubim, carved figures and decorations (I Kings 6:14–36; Niehr 1997).[7] This then, was a place where people

---

[7]   Despite the forbidding of images of God in the Commandments, it is likely that image-making of God and gods was rife in ancient Israel and found its way also into the Temple. For discussion of the existence of visual artefacts and representations, including representations of the divine (which might have included a throne) see, for example, Assmann and Baumgarten (2001), Edelman (1996), Kuhnel (2001), Kunzl (2001), Mettinger (1995), van der Toorn (1997). Bland (2000) discusses the over-willingness of

might continue to see God's face (Terrien 1976, 141), and also the place where visionary prophets like Isaiah and Ezekiel were formed. While the Deuteronomic heirs of the Northern oral tradition remembered God's name, the priests in the Temple invoked his form and presence (Barker 2004, 38).

What might be called the 'proto-Protestant' anti-visual, logocentric Deuteronomic reformers have decisively shaped the Hebrew Bible. This means that much of the pre-exilic nature of practice and theology is now suppressed and lost; thus it is easy to see the cultic Temple as a place of 'proto-Catholic' materialist, static, 'ethics-lite', routinised, natural religion. In this vein, Terrien (1976, 151) suggests that, while the revelatory hearing of the Name requires active participation of religious adherents in the totality of life, seeing an image or cultic symbol of glory may lull people into passivity and lack of social responsibility.

There is, however, no evidence to suggest that Judaean people attending the Temple to see or to commune with the glory of God were any less ethically or socially committed than their logocentric Northern neighbours. The cult did fall under prophetic moral critique (from prophets whose moral vision and sensibilities were actually nurtured within the Temple), but that does not necessarily mean that its visual emphasis on divine presence was directly to blame. Indeed, a cult focused on the renewal of all creation through seeing divine presence might be deemed to be very ethically relevant, particularly in our own time. It is very important to try not to read Hebrew religion unwittingly through modern Christian theological lenses that conflate visual religion with a supposedly inferior, 'childish', sub-moral form of belief and practice (McDannell 1995).

This brings us, then, to the visual array of the Temple and its practices. It is difficult to know exactly what happened in the Temple, given the Deuteronomists' suppression of the cult and rewriting of traditions to give prominence to hearing, morality and obeying the Law, and their minimisation of the visual aspects of the experience of God (Barker 2004). Methodist biblical scholar, Margaret Barker (2004, 2011), has, however, provided a useful, if somewhat speculative, picture of the pre-exilic Temple, its functions and practices.[8]

Barker argues that the Judaic religion focused around the first Temple was based on the foundation of an eternal covenant that involved the whole of creation that

---

Christian theologians and others to interpret early Judaism through Protestant, iconoclastic spectacles.

[8] Barker seems to infer much of what went on in the First Temple via Christian and other later sources. While her imaginative description seems to make much sense both of the Temple and even more, if accurate, of Christian ideas of the Temple and the Messiah, there is a danger here of circular argument whereby what 'must have been the case before (in the OT)' is inferred from 'what might have been the case (in the NT)'. Whether or not the NT reflects the actual order and practices of Ancient Israel, it is still a valid point to argue that NT Christians created a very substantial Temple-related theology which is of interest in its own terms; Barker has done a valuable job in highlighting the importance of this theological nexus within the NT.

was deemed to have its centre in the Temple at Jerusalem. The cult was focused on renewing the covenant of peace and unifying the creation to its Edenic perfection in which God and humans lived together in harmony; reconciliation to God formed a vertical axis here, while reconciling nature and society formed a horizontal axis. The annual ritual cycle culminated in the Day of Atonement when creation was recreated as the High Priest, dressed in garments representing the earthly creation, entered through the veil into the Holy of Holies, which represented heaven. When the High Priest emerged, reborn, *theosis* occurred. He was seen to be the glory or *kabhod* of the visible Lord God who bore the Lord's name on his forehead. He was an Angel, as were all those who stood and served in the presence of God in the Temple, including priests and prophets like Isaiah and Ezekiel.

The Temple cult was polytheistic and it was adumbrated by visual, material objects. It included: the High God, the Lord, represented perhaps by an empty chariot throne; his son, the divinised High Priest or Angel enthroned on the Day of Atonement; and the Lady, Wisdom, who was a kind of Spirit and Mother, Ashterah, represented by a tree in the Temple. Temple worship involved a rich and complex mixture of sensual experiences, visual, aural, olfactory and other. These were organised around the evocation of presence by a body of priests and singers who summoned God to the Temple and made the divine face (seen in the countenance of the High Priest) shine upon his people for peace and blessing: 'The Psalms show that the shining face of the LORD was central to temple worship, even though we do not know exactly what this meant' (Barker 2011, 55).

Barker does not say much directly about material, multi-sensorial visuality, but the religious experience she describes as 'Temple mysticism' is not the unitive, inward mysticism found in more recent Christianity (McGinn 1991; Turner 1995). Seeing and being with God in the Temple on the Day of Atonement was seemingly a very physical, sensory experience (Barker 2011, 88). In this respect, people really did see God's face, the glory of God in God's Angel. They came to the temple to see the face or presence of God. The scopic or visual regime they inhabited allowed them to have a 'thick', direct and immediate experience of seeing God's glory. And this was not without ethical and human implications. The rebirth of creation, of sight and of the senses, presumably changed people's attitudes to the world and to each other. From a transformation of vision produced by seeing God comes understanding because with vision comes wisdom: 'The mystics saw the world from the holy of holies; they saw it whole and because they looked with new eyes, they saw it differently' (Barker 2011, 40).

This reminds me that Christianity can be regarded, not so much as a set of rules and ethics, but as a way of seeing and looking at God and at the world which produces a different way of acting (Hand 1989; Kirk 1932; Murdoch 1985; Raphael 2002, 101–5). To invert Levinas (1969, 23), it could be argued that optics is an ethics. Sight precedes words in human development and the pre- or non-verbal shapes our fundamental attitudes to people and reality. Similarly, it can be maintained that in religion, beholding precedes acting and witnessing glory precedes complying with law. Iris Murdoch (1985, 31–4) can therefore talk of growing by looking, and by attending to that which is seen. To see differently, then, is to act differently. Personal visual encounter that changes seeing has enormous ethical implications for ways of being and acting which depend on relationships, not on rules. More of this when we return to shame.

In this short, one-sided, account of OT evidence relevant to seeing God and God's face, I have tried to show that while Israelite religious experience may have been dominated by the oral and aural, hearing rather than seeing, thick, sensory visual experience and concepts may be more significant than Western Protestant thinking has generally allowed. God could, in principle, be seen, as well as heard, and there was a significantly visually-oriented cult in the Jerusalem Temple. This cannot be assumed to have represented an inferior or morally bankrupt way of engaging with the real, but elusive, presence of God, despite its eventual decline and the prophetic ethical critique levelled against it. Indeed, much of the prophetic critique from Judaean sources came from those like Isaiah and Ezekiel who were shaped by the visual cult and encounters with the divine within it. Ezekiel, in particular, made huge innovations in understanding that the visible God was not just confined to one particular mountain in Israel, but could be with God's chosen people wherever they went (Joyce 2007). Ezekiel's God was universal, indescribable in many ways, but not invisible.

The visual tradition of the OT points to a God who is visible but not entirely visible. The glory, *kabhod*, of God is to all intents and purposes the face of God, but there is something indistinct and withheld within it as well. God's face can, as it were, be directly seen, but not clearly seen. No clear picture of the divine face emerges from OT texts; it is elusive, in some ways veiled. To see the face of God is to experience God's presence directly, but, as with human faces and persons, there is something beyond what is seen; thus humans cannot comprehend or control the divine. God is both known (revelatus) and unknown (absconditus), indeed, 'He is known as unknown' (Terrien 1976, 119). And this fluctuation between being seen and hidden reflects a sense of presence and absence which came to characterise Hebrew theology (Balentine 1983; Brueggemann 2009a, 91–117; Meyer and Pels 2003).

With this point in mind, it is time to move on to the New Testament (NT) where we will see that some of the traditions of the Temple, God's visible glory and seeing the face of God continue.

Finding the Glory of the Face of God in the Life and Work of Jesus

The tradition of the vagueness yet visibility of the face of God continues into the NT. While no-one has ever seen God (John 1:18), we are faced with the witness of the early followers of Jesus that he is the messiah, the Son of God, the image of the invisible God (Col. 1:15). To see the face of Jesus is, then, to see the face of the divine: 'And the Word become flesh ... we have beheld his glory, glory as of the only Son from the Father' (John 1:14 RSV). The texts of all the gospels are redolent with visually-related language and events – miracles, signs, wonders, angelic visitations, epiphanies such as Jesus' baptism and transfiguration, and resurrection appearances (Terrien 1978). While the synoptic gospels dwell on the fact that Jesus is not seen for what he is, the Messiah, John's gospel, is a profound theological meditation that turns on seeing, blindness, light and dark (Watson 2010). 'For John, "seeing is believing"', and believing is religious sight in the absence of the physical presence of Jesus (Malina and Rohrbaugh 1998, 15; John 20:29).

Amidst all this visually-related text, it comes as something of a shock to realise that Jesus' own human face is completely withheld. While we may almost glimpse his expression as he lifts his face to talk to Zaccheus in his sycamore tree (Luke 19:1–10), or see his anger as he expels the money-lenders from the Temple (Luke 19:45–6), no direct emotional expression or physical characteristic of Jesus' face is conveyed to us. Like the faces of Freud's patients, Jesus' face has been dissolved into non-disclosive text (Elkins 1997, 165). Even as Jesus looks at a young man and 'loves him' (Mark 10:21), or feels 'compassion in his bowels' for a man with skin disease (Mark 1:41), we can only see a blank where Jesus' face might have been.

In this book about lost faces, another human face, then, is lost. A familiar motif is reinforced; while God can be directly seen, somehow he cannot be seen clearly and directly, even in the human face of Jesus. Our vision is partial and occluded:

> The most obvious problem for a theology of the face of Jesus Christ is its apparent vagueness. Nobody can see this face. We do not even have any artistic or photographic evidence of it. So people might imagine any sort of face and project whatever they like on to it. (Ford 1999, 171)

I will deal later with the possible practical and theological significance of the absence of Jesus' face. But here, having dismissed the possibility of discerning the physical face of Jesus, I want to deal with only two aspects of his work and significance that relate to the theme of seeing the face of God and giving face to humans. First, I will explore notions that Jesus was himself thought of by himself and by others as the visible face of God, the *kabhod*, the one who comes to reveal God's face and renew creation as a new Temple. Secondly, I will look at Jesus' work in giving face, raising up a community of the non-shamed and divinely honoured people who could witness to and share in God's glory in the context of a society in which honour was in short supply and shame was easily acquired. Here, as in my coverage of the OT, I proceed by shameless selectivity. Properly understanding the events and significance of the person and life of Jesus is protean, and would involve many other perspectives alongside the ones advanced here.

Jesus the New Temple

The historical Jesus has been characterised as a prophet, a rabbi, a philosopher, a political revolutionary and many other things besides (Bowden 1988;

Pattison 2007a, 229–42; Sanders 1995). What exactly he was, and how he
understood himself, will always be a matter of debate. At least one plausible lens
for understanding Jesus and his work, however, is to see him as the new Temple.
This is consonant with attitudes taken towards Jesus in many NT writings. In the
Epistle to the Hebrews, for example, he is described as High Priest who enters the
sanctuary as well as the sacrificial victim (Heb. 9). Paul's writings, too, are full of
Temple religion references:

> Paul may have baulked at the restriction of access which Temple-based religion
> demanded, but he transferred the sense of special place to a group of people.
> Cultic holiness was now to be found in a group of special people who behaved
> in special ways. (Rowland 2012, 215)

The Johannine writings are also redolent with the theology of the Temple and
of seeing. In the Apocalypse of St. John, for example, the work and role of Jesus is
situated within the context of sacrifice and the renewal of Jerusalem where God's
glory will once again be present as God is enthroned. Like the High Priest in the
Temple, Christians in Revelation have the name of God written on their foreheads,
and they see God face-to-face:

> And I did not see a temple in [the new Jerusalem] for the Lord God Almighty
> and the lamb are its temple. And the city has no need of the sun or the moon to
> illuminate it, because the glory of God will light it, and its light is the lamb. …
> And the throne of God and the lamb will be in her, and his slaves will offer
> worship to him, and they will see his face and his name will be on their foreheads.
> And there will be no night and they will have no need of the light of a lamp and
> the light of the sun, because the Lord God will shine upon them, and they will
> reign for ever. (Rev. 21:22–3, 22.4–5. My translation.)

Unfortunately, not much is known directly from contemporaneous accounts
about the theory, theology and practice of the Temple in Jerusalem in its first and
second forms. So much of what it might have been and meant has to be inferred
from Christian and post-Christian sources. Thus there is a real danger of eisegesis
from the more recent past to the ancient past, which is then used as an explanatory
lens for understanding the former.

However, if we take the work of Barker and others to be a reasonably responsible
and plausible reconstruction of the Temple (and even if we do not, there can be no
doubt of the use of Temple-related concepts in understandings of Jesus in the NT),
then many of the attributes, roles, actions and titles of Jesus seem to be consonant
with his seeing himself as an embodiment of what went on therein. Sacrifice,
atonement, the invocation of direct divine presence, the incarnation of God in
the form of his Son as the human image of God, resurrection and the renewal of
creation, the bridging of the gap between heaven and earth, *theosis* (when the High
Priest becomes God's Angel), the presence of angels, the importance of the Mother

of God and the identification of the High Priest as Son of God, were all part of the life of the Temple; they find resonances in understandings of Jesus' life and work (Barker 2004, 11). Indeed it can be argued that early Christians' understanding of Jesus' life and work was expressed in terms of Temple theology, so that they conceived themselves as parts of the Temple, angels on earth, holy ones who have seen and reflect the glory of God (2 Cor. 3:18), sons of God like the Temple priests, 'sons of light' (1 Thess. 5:5). In this context, Jesus saw himself as a High Priest, sharing the glory of God like a priest in the Temple (John 17:5; Barker 2011, 11). Having had an experience of being exalted to the throne of heaven at his baptismal anointing, Jesus knew that he was the Lord because he had been with the living creatures and the angels served him (Mark 1:13; Barker 2011, 104,108).

Barker is not alone in seeing Jesus in terms of the Temple. Perrin (2010) also believes that this thinking goes back to Jesus himself. For Perrin, Jesus was an apocalyptic teacher who came to see himself both as the new Temple and the high priest in the new Temple, effectively the presence of God on earth. Jesus, like John the Baptist and members of the Qumran community, was part of a reforming movement that believed the Temple in Jerusalem to be corrupt because of the injustice and sins of the priestly caste which ran it. The Temple, the place where God's footstool or throne on earth was placed, could not discharge its function as a place of worship where God's presence could be realised and experienced because it was polluted. Jesus then saw himself and his followers as the place where the eschatological Temple was coming into being in the Kingdom of God, the place where God would be present and could be encountered and worshipped.

This purified, holy space, built without walls, was a place where the poor were accepted and justice reigned – this was the *sine qua non* for being able to participate in the Temple and for its realisation. Heaven and earthly rule were integrally connected, as were forces of good and evil, angels and demons. So wherever there was injustice and corruption, for example by the priests in the second Temple, then the demonic was involved. Jesus purifies it and his followers with his practices of casting out demons and his ethic of standing with, and seeking justice for, the poor. The healings he performs, and the meals he provides for his followers, are not primarily acts of charity or ethical concern as such. They are part of a whole socio-political project enacted in prophetic symbols to actualise the new Temple, which is coincident with the land, the place where God should reign (Sanders 1995, 253). Thus Jesus was inaugurating and realising a new Temple community that would replace the old, and restore both vertical (religious) and horizontal (political) relations that would allow God properly to be worshipped again. Thus the cleansing of the Temple was not just a single casual act, but rather the culmination of Jesus' ministry of creating a new Temple, a new order in which 'he will feast with his disciples, there will be a new or improved Temple, and he will be "King"' (Sanders 1995, 264). It was part of a systematic and necessary programme of purification and rededication that would allow Israel once again to see God. And the new Israel starts to see God in Jesus, his Son, acting on earth and inaugurating the Kingdom.

Jesus was probably executed for his anti-Temple activities (Sanders 1995, 265). In his lifetime he created a new, purified Temple, the reign or Kingdom of God. This was manifest in a body of people who experienced the vanquishing of demons, participation in messianic feasts and the presence of the glory of God in Jesus' own face as Son of God. It was not a non-material, ethereal or 'spiritual' matter. The Kingdom/Temple, cleansed so God could reign and be seen within it, was a tangible group of people who could be seen and who engaged in real activities. The Kingdom existed on earth, not just in heaven, even if its final realisation was not possible during Jesus' own earthly lifetime.

I now want to say a bit more about a relevant part of Jesus' ministry which is the redistribution of honour and shame, the giving and taking of face. This can be seen as part of the tangible work of creating a new heaven on earth.

Jesus and the Saving of Face

In modern Western society, shame and the loss of face implied by it are regarded basically as emotional, psychological and individual states (Pattison 2000). While the basic sense of worthlessness and dishonour that modern shamed persons feel has some continuity with shame in the ancient world, the shame in ancient societies, as in many 'strong group' societies today, was essentially much more social and substantial (Jewett 2010; Malina 1983) . It is important to make this distinction before launching into a discussion of Jesus' work of reconfiguring shame.

According to scholars who approach the NT sociologically, peasant societies, such as Palestine was around the time of Jesus, were characterised by the following features (deSilva 1999, 2010; Elliott 1992, 1995; Malina 1983, 2010; Moxnes 1988; Pilch 1998; Watson 2010).[9] First, in a group-oriented society where members were governed by the opinions of others so that value came from outwith the individual, honour and shame were fundamental dynamics for making and keeping social order. The informal but all-powerful communal 'court of reputation' was the place where people were rewarded with honour or punished with shame for conforming or failing to conform to the norms and expectations of their group (DeSilva 1999, 4–7). Shame and honour affected all parts of life. Honour was regarded as a kind of limited substance like gold; if someone gained it, this was to the loss and shame of the person from whom it had been taken – thus social relations were essentially conflictual in nature:

> Persons achieve honour not only by acts of bravery and beneficence, but also by successfully challenging others and calling their honour into question. Ignoring this challenge and failing to publicly defend one's honour and reputation results in shame. (Elliott 1995, 168)

---

[9]   For a critique of the sociological approach to the NT and the dangers of applying concepts of shame and generic 'mediterranean peasant society' models to early Christianity see Sawicki (2000, 61–80).

To be engaged in the competition for honour and successful exhibition of oneself to significant others, you needed to be recognised as a member of the relevant group, often a kin group. Strangers and slaves were essentially non-persons, shamed and non-existent to start with (Glancy 2006). In addition, honour could only be gained and embodied by men, while women folk in their groups were a liability insofar as they embodied the risk of shame – they could lose the honour gained by men.

It is in the context of this society, structured round a hierarchy of visible, tangible shame and loss of face – in which men exhibited themselves to be viewed to advantage and thus gain what the Romans called 'glory' – that Jesus' ministry occurs (Jewett 2007, 50). It might be thought that Jesus would himself have nothing to do with shame and would want to abolish it. A modernist understanding of healing might presuppose that it is possible to have a society in which shame can be eliminated. But this would have been unthinkable to Jesus and his followers. Shame and belonging were inseparable in any group. Jesus is the founder of a new group, not based on kinship but on discipleship (Mark 3:31–5). To cohere and have identity, this group must devise its own standards of approval, inclusion, exclusion, shame and honour (Malina 1996). In this context, Jesus challenges the distribution of shame and honour (Watson 2010).

Jesus was criticised for eating and consorting with tax-gatherers, Samaritans, gentiles, women and many other types of shame-hidden non-persons from outside the bounds of honourable social groups. Much of his ministry was spent living and working with those who were without honour. His teaching that the first would be last, and the last first, inverted the general view of how honour might be distributed (Mark 9:35). In this redistributive quest, however, Jesus did not opt out of shame. To form a community with a distinctive identity of its own in such a society, shame was needed to mark the boundaries and reinforce the norms of the new community. Shame was also redistributed to other groups whose values contrasted with those of the Jesus group. In his teaching and works, therefore, there is a good deal of shame meted out to non-insiders of the Jesus group. Scribes and Pharisees, for example, are publicly accused of not knowing, not understanding, not being able properly to interpret the scriptures – thus they lose honour and face before Jesus and in front of the crowds (deSilva 1999; Watson 2010).

In some of the miracle and healing stories it is possible to see some shamed persons gaining honour, being able literally and metaphorically to hold their faces up to the world, while others who see themselves through the eyes of others as unpolluted and respected lose this. In Luke 13:10–16, for example, a crippled woman with a spirit of infirmity comes to Jesus in the synagogue on the Sabbath. She is unable to stand upright. Thus she presumably could not look into the faces of those around her. Jesus heals her so she can stand straight and, by implication, see people face-to-face. The bystanders, however, think this is a shameful act as it pollutes the Sabbath. Jesus then refutes their objections by a piece of masterly scriptural rhetoric and 'all his adversaries were put to shame'. Presumably, they are then in a position of not being able to look into the faces of others. Like many of

Jesus' other healings, this one can be seen at least as much as an enacted prophetic sign that makes clear that 'the Kingdom of God has drawn near', as an act of healing compassion (Mark 1:15, Luke 4:16–21).

Jesus rejects and redefines the shame-honour system that prevails in contemporary society. He reverses the flow of shame onto the visibly socially respected, unpolluted and honourable and redirects it in favour of the poor, humble, abused, alienated and despised who are the members of his new Kingdom or Temple, the in-group that he inaugurates (Watson 2010). He also teaches that in the Kingdom of God there is no place for the kind of shameful, community-corroding envy that fuels the quest for worldly hierarchical honour. In parables like that of the labourers in the vineyard (Matt. 20:1–16), the envy of the Evil Eye is condemned. The parable, directed as shaming rebuke against Jesus' critics, shows that God is generous towards the undeserving and that within God's rule or Kingdom, unlike in earthly shame-honour societies where goods are strictly limited, 'one person's gain does not entail another's loss' (Elliott 1992, 61). The Kingdom community is thereby warned against destructive competition for favour and status and encouraged into loyalty, commitment, 'trust in God's unlimited care, and solidarity with the poor and "undeserving"' (Elliott 1992, 62).

Jesus, whose face might be seen to embody the glory of God, looks on people in his community in a new way. Their status, together with the meaning of glory is transformed into something different in light of the rechannelling and reconceptualising of shame. The poor are exalted and the mighty are cast down from their seats (Luke 1:46–55) – the shadows of shame, though present, are cast in a different direction; there is the possibility of something totally different in a community of justice whose identity is shaped by the presence of the actual reign and presence of God. The faces of those who have dwelt literally and metaphorically in the non-being of shame are illuminated and shine in response to the love of God, while those who fail to recognise God's glory are cast out of the Kingdom and shamed themselves (Luke 9:26). To reiterate, this is not just a spiritual or metaphorical experience, it is the inbreaking of new ways of seeing and sensing in a material world in which God justly reigns in a purified Temple of worshippers who accept his patronage and grace. Seeing Jesus meant to see God's face and glory; in seeing God's face, the world and the community were transformed.

A Speculative Theory of Face Saved to Glory

Trying to stay near to the close connections between seeing face physically and its metaphorical implications of inclusion and exclusion in a world where social relations were thought of in non-dualistic, substantial terms, I have suggested that Jesus believed himself to be the Son of God and the manifestation of God's glory within a movement that sought to purify or destroy the old Temple to allow God's shining face to once again be present, accessible and visible to God's people. In this context, Jesus creates a new community of justice. It is bounded by re-directed and redefined shame conventions, in which the poor, alienated and dishonoured, including slaves, children, women and gentiles, who enjoy God's glory in the face of Jesus, see God, others and themselves in new inclusive ways that are not based on blood kinship. At the same time, those who enjoy honour and respect in the public square and in their own kin groups are blinded, and so excluded. In this community of redefined honour and shame, healing miracles, epiphanies and other signs confirm that God's reign has begun. Jesus' brothers and sisters share his privileged access to God, seeing the Father's heavenly face (Matt. 18:10). This participation in the Kingdom and in seeing God is also enacted in the messianic feasts that Jesus hosts, fulfilling the prophecies of Isaiah, a former Temple official. Jesus, then, appears to be the High Priest who has entered within the veil of the Temple and made accessible and visible the glory of God, the face of God, to God's people.

This theory perhaps gains further force by reflection on the rending of the Temple veil which occurs at the moment of Jesus' death on the cross in all the synoptic gospels (Mark 15:38–9; Matt. 27: 51; Luke 23:45). The veil, with its embroidered guardian cherubim, representing the angels guarding the way back to Eden, was there to divide off heaven from earth, to protect the holy from the less holy. Its rending would, then, seem to be a theophanic event, a clear indication that the gospel writers thought that visible access to God had been obtained by Jesus. Heaven, hidden within the veil, had been opened to earth, Eden was restored, and God was now present and visible to those who were part of the new Temple. The righteous could now enjoy the eschatological blessing of sharing fellowship with God, for the first time since humankind was expelled from Eden. Interestingly, in Matthew's account, gentiles like the centurion are included in this new vision of God, and Jesus is named by him as Son of God (Gurtner 2007). The death of Jesus thus provided 'unprecedented accessibility (both physical and visual) to God' (Gurtner 2007, 191).

Linking this directly to Isaiah, one oracle reads:

On this mountain, for all peoples,
Yahweh Sabaoth is preparing
a banquet of rich food,
a banquet of fine wines,
of succulent food, of well-strained wines.
On this mountain, he has destroyed
the veil which used to veil all peoples,
the pall enveloping all nations;
he has destroyed death for ever.
Lord Yahweh has wiped away the tears from every cheek;
He has taken his people's shame away everywhere on earth,
for Yahweh has spoken. (Isa 25.6–8 NJB)

It seems plausible to suggest that in the life and death of Jesus, this prophecy was thought to have been fulfilled.[10] God's people saw God; the veil that separated them from God was removed, a feast was prepared, shame was dissipated and fellowship and presence was enjoyed by the dwellers in the new Temple, now found to be people of all races and conditions, including slaves, sinners and women. At the centre of all of this was material vision of God mediated through the actual vision of the face of Jesus and the enfacement of members of his movement. This was not thin, metaphorical seeing, but a community of mutual facial seeing and enfacement between people and God. And somehow, indeterminate though this relationship was, and difficult to recapture in its detail now, this mutual physical enfacement, based on real seeing and mutual shining of faces, was integral to allowing a new community to come into being that shattered traditional social taboos and boundaries guarded by shame. This enabled the poor and humble to find their place in a Kingdom of God that was materially coming into being. Thus, it can be suggested that mutual seeing and countenancing were integrally linked to the re-construing and redirecting of shame.

Without the vision of the glory of God in the face of Jesus, shame and loss of face would have been the order of the day. With this transforming vision in a community of new sight and presence, sorrow, sighing, shame and loss of face fled away before the glory of God's face in Jesus. Terrien (1978, 288) writes, 'Response to presence in the awareness of love is the foundation of ethics'. To paraphrase, loving joyous response to the present God whose face is seen in that of Jesus and the community of the new Temple is the beginning of a new humanity invigorated by other-respecting love and service that can give face and respect to itself and to others who have been made invisible within the miasma of shame. Like any ancient community, strong boundaries between insiders and outsiders indicated by shame are to be expected (cf. Segal 1990, 166; Watson 2010). However, shame and lack of honoured place is now cast over those who cannot, or will not, recognise the face of God in Jesus' brothers and sisters. The community of the vision of God is now constituted on the basis of new relationships that are transformative in terms of personal and communal attitudes and behaviours. Seeing was behaving as well as believing.

This kind of scenario sets the scene for the contribution of Paul to ideas of seeing the face of God and its relationship with shame and honour. Before moving on to that, however, I need to acknowledge a number of things.

First, my account here has been quite speculative, I hope helpfully so. Secondly, in some ways, it removes the kind of seeing and enfacing that moderns might find congenial a long way away in terms of experience – it is difficult to imagine belonging to a religious group in which God's face is directly visually present and available. Thirdly, however, linking seeing the face of God to shame redistribution and enfacement provides a useful challenge to our thin, abstract non-physical ways of thinking about divine-human relations.

---

[10]   I owe this text and putative connection to Robert Jewett.

Theological exploration within the Christian tradition should raise questions about taken-for-granted contemporary assumptions; indeed, that is part of the joy of inheriting a pluriform, puzzling tradition. In this vein, perhaps we should change our ways of seeing rather than rejecting the insights of the kind of approach to the tradition of seeing God in the Bible which highlights the importance of enfacement as a remedy for shame, alienation and loss of face. We can, then, use aspects of the Bible to help 'redescribe reality' (Brueggemann 2009a; Swinton 2012, chapter 1). The materiality of seeing and including/excluding is something that might usefully find a place in thinking about God today. Jesus' contemporaries inhabited a spiritual-material world that was full of thicker, more substantial relationships than we can mostly imagine in the urban West. We cannot import a total alien worldview from ancient Mediterranean culture uncritically *in toto*. However, there is something to be said for valuing the connections between physical seeing, the distribution of shame and social enfacement, and we might have things to learn here.

Finally, I am struck by the real sense here that God and humans have a partnership, a mutual if unequal relationship that requires both to do something if God's face is not to be lost and human faces are not to be consigned to exclusion and shame. There is, perhaps, an important theologico-moral implication here that can be taken further later on in this book.

Paul, Shame, Face and Glory

Because Roman society was fundamentally oriented around shame and honour, it is not surprising that these are prominent themes throughout the NT. 1 Peter, for example, is preoccupied with them and they creep into other writings as well (deSilva 1999, 2010; Elliott 1995). But the most prominent exponent of its significance in the NT is St Paul.

Paul is just as complex and controversial figure as Jesus. Every generation of scholars finds a 'new' Paul who might be composed of different elements in different degrees of, for example, Pharisee, tortured guilty soul, mystic, charismatic, rhetorician, systematic theologian, apostle, prophet, shaman (Ashton 2000; Malina and Neyrev 1996; Mitchell 2010; Sanders 1991; Segal 1990; Shantz 2009). Paul's writings are similarly interpreted through all manner of lenses. Ashton (2000) aptly characterises him as 'Paul the enigma'. Here again, then, I must be extremely selective and one-sided. In this section, I will consider the possibility that Paul in some way sees the face of God. Furthermore, this is integrally, if obscurely, linked with his ideas about shame, honour and the reality of living the life of the *agape* love, in the community of the risen Jesus. Once again, I will be guided by some recent social-scientific approaches to Paul.

One trend in recent Pauline scholarship has been to thicken portraits of him to make him less like a rationalist proto-systematic theologian, primarily cognitive in his concerns, and more of an embodied religious experiencer (Ashton 2000; Segal 1990; Shantz 2009). In this context, Paul can be seen as an ecstatic, a charismatic, a person who had direct religious visions of God, perhaps in altered states of consciousness; and these should not be regarded as non-material, inward psychological experiences (Malina and Pilch 2008; Pilch 1983).

It seems likely that Paul and other early Christians were 'physical mystics', people who had an all-encompassing relationship with Christ like marriage (1 Cor. 6:13–20), so that 'mind, heart, spirit and other "spiritual dimension" of the human psyche are completely integrated with physical, sexual dimensions' (Jewett 2007, 434–5). Believers then shared a direct vision of the face of God in Christ through charismatic experience within the community of the faithful (Jewett 2007, 406). Quite apart from the apparitions that are reported around Paul's conversion in Acts 9:1–9, Paul states that the resurrected Christ appeared to him directly (1 Cor. 15:8), and elsewhere he seems to talk of himself as being caught up into the third heaven (significantly, perhaps, he could not distinguish this as a bodily or non-bodily experience) (2 Cor. 12:1–10).

Particularly in 2 Cor. 3–4, a passage situated in an epistle that deals centrally with honour, shame and boasting, Paul suggests that he has seen 'the glory of Christ, who is the likeness of God' (2 Cor. 4:4 NJB). The glory of God seen in the face of Christ is God's *kabhod*, God's face: 'Christ represented for Paul the visibility of God' (Young and Ford 1987, 234n25). And since Paul had seen Christ directly, he had seen the face of God:

> Paul believes that the Glory of God is something that one actually sees … He himself had visions confirming the identification of Christ with the Glory of God. This illumination gives him sure knowledge of the "Glory of God in the face of Christ" (2 Cor. 4:6). The centre of Paul's gospel is the identification of Christ as the Glory of God. (Segal 1990, 156)

It is not clear whether Paul thought all Christians could share this vision (though it is probably the case that he thought that through the gift of the Spirit, they were all bearers of the image of Christ (2 Cor. 1:22, 5:5; deSilva 1999, 125)). This might be part of his rhetorical strategy in the Corinthian correspondence. Here, he is trying to argue for his own authority and importance as himself the living visual and biographical re-embodiment of the living Christ. People who see Paul's face see the face of Christ in that of his envoy, Paul (Mitchell 2010, 7, 11). Those who fail to acknowledge this, and the authority that flows from it, should then themselves feel ashamed.

It may be that Paul thought of the full vision of God as being in some ways eschatologically deferred, veiled and indistinct, as in a mirror (1 Cor. 13). He introduces both the veil and the mirror into Christian theology – these are both devices which both focus attention, yet block it, allow a partial glimpse, yet deny access to the whole (Mitchell 2010, 62). Paul can thus be seen as the inaugurator in Corinthians of 'the hermeneutics of clarity *and* obscurity, because this was true of himself'. He invents what Mitchell calls 'the veil scale' whereby there is a 'tension between the hidden and the revealed, between clarity and obscurity – clear eye and obscure object, occluded eye and clear object' (Mitchell 2010, 58–9; 1 Cor. 13:12, 15:9). Nonetheless the glory, the face of God in Christ, shines now in his people whose unveiled faces along with Paul's are then changed 'from one degree of glory to another' (2 Cor. 3:18 RSV).

Paul's motives in 2 Cor. may be largely to establish his own authority, deriving from his own personal embodiment of the face of Christ, and to reverse the shame that has been directed at him because of his poor appearance and presentation in the flesh (2 Cor. 10:10) – he might have had a sight defect and so been accused of having the Evil Eye (Elliott 1992; Malina and Neyrey 1996, 207–11). He wants to argue that his critics should be ashamed for not recognising Christ's face in him, using his considerable rhetorical skills to rebut them and assert his own power to open and shut the scriptures as an apostle (Mitchell 2010, 26). This brings us to the matter of shame and honour that goes along with the world of 'boasting' that Paul deals with at length in the Corinthian correspondence and elsewhere.

As we have noted a number of times, shame and honour were key axes of the ancient Mediterranean social order. In Roman civic life in particular, there was a 'pyramid of honour' surmounted by the Emperor (Jewett 2007, p. 46). This led to the pursuit of public display, and the competition to gain honour and glory was a major feature of life (Jewett 1999, 8; 2007, 50). Women, slaves, strangers and barbarians could not take part in the competition for honour – they had no public face to gain or lose. However, these groups were quite well represented in Christian congregations like those in Rome, included amongst the faithful (Jewett 2007, 65; Watson 2010, 142).

It is in this context that Paul reverses the contemporary ideology and practice of honour and shame. Rather than being concerned with sin and forgiveness, scholars like Robert Jewett (1999, 6) suggest that Paul's basic message is about receiving honour from God in the form of grace. Grace, then, is the overcoming of dishonourable status, not the forgiveness of individual sins. Rather than coming from external human sources, from social systems and from power games that distort relationships, honour or grace, now comes from God. 'This undercuts the superiority claims of every system of gaining honour through performance or inherited status' (Jewett 1999, 10).

In the divine economy, 'all fall short of the glory of God' which was intended for Adam and Eve in Eden, but this original honour and glory is restored, not by achievement, but by God's grace and gift (Rom. 3:23). This then changes the position of all those who belong to the community of Christ. The shamed are raised to a new status. They share this equally with their brothers and sisters, following a saviour who died a shameful death on the cross that now reinterpreted as noble. To share the burdens of the shamed and suffering then becomes a new form of honourable behaviour (Jewett 1999, 15). The *agape* love is shared, and respect and care for others who are not members of one's original class or kin group becomes possible (Malina 1996). A new understanding of the glory that belongs to God and to God's new community comes into being so that face and place are bestowed on slaves, women and the other despised people who are excluded from the gaze of the ruling-class men who run the public world. The glory of God is now reflected in the faces of those who belong to the church, whatever their external status, background and position, without distinction.

Paul saw the face of God in Christ and believes that he represents this to fellow believers who can also see this glory in some way. In the social context of the time, this would be a physical seeing, not an intellectual, mystical or psychologically understood event. Paul also spent much of this time addressing honour and shame in his work, reversing the hierarchy of dishonour and oblivion that confined many to the position of being non-persons in Roman society. Is there a connection between these two features of Pauline writing and experience?

It is difficult to create a clear and direct connection between the seeing of God and the redirection of shame. However, it is worth noting some possible connective possibilities. First, the community and the values that it enables seems to have some continuity with Jesus' new Temple community where people see God and act differently towards others, reordering their social relations and obligations. Secondly, in 2 Cor. Paul himself seems to suggest that seeing the vision of God in the face of Christ is a main reason for reordering hierarchies of honour, shame and boasting. Thirdly, it could be argued that by becoming acceptable to God, being pure and holy in God's sight, by God's grace, direct access to the presence of God is implied. To be honoured and recognised by God, to share the life of Eden as God did with Adam, is to be in God's presence; that means to see, and be seen by, God in an immediate way. Those who are like God, who share the Spirit, can see God (Matt. 5.8). Fourthly, Paul characterises the Corinthians as a Temple: 'Do you not know that you are God's temple and that God's Spirit dwells in you?' (1 Cor. 3:16 RSV). A Temple is clearly a place where God is expected to be present and to be seen directly. Fifthly, Paul (1 Cor. 11:23–34) dwells on eucharistic practice and exhorts his Corinthian readers to discern the body of Christ, that is to recognise and see the presence of the others who share the image and identity of Christ, before helping themselves. This would seem to be an instruction to see and recognise the face of Christ in the charismatically inspired corporate body. This is an inclusive, respectful, shame-reducing strategy that honours and cleanses both people and place, thus allowing God's face to shine and to find a place there, too.

To conclude, here is a very speculative and over-generalised picture. Christians in the first century came from all manner of backgrounds, many without social honour. If they were slaves, they were unable to control access to and the boundaries of their own bodies. They would have lived without rights and been subjected to actively shaming practices every day, including routine anal rape and vaginal sex (Glancy 2006, 50–57; Jewett 2007, 180–81). These dishonoured and excluded folk became members of a new Temple, a place where the Spirit dwelled in their corporate midst. Socially resited by the grace of God, they found themselves in a community where they could give and receive respect in the *agape* love. And in this community, if they discerned aright, when they met to celebrate the messianic feast, like Paul, they could see the face of Christ, the *kabhod* shining in their midst and lighting up the faces of those around them, fellow-bearers of the image of God. This seeing and experiencing made their citizenship of the Kingdom of God a reality. In seeing and being seen, they were transformed, living and behaving differently. The *agape* love, modelled by the shamed saviour in his life and death, became a possible enacted, material response for people who now found themselves in a moral community where shame was incurred in failing to recognise God's grace and to share the burdens of other seers of the divine face. This was to have a real experience of the glory of God, which would be finally realised when God's reign became fully present on earth and the whole creation would once more be God's Temple. The earliest Christian community was then, perhaps, a group of people who saw and were seen by God with transforming implications for their relationships.

Conclusion

In this chapter, my main aim has been to suggest a number of things about sight and seeing in the biblical tradition, understood in a rather broad and unnuanced way.

First, seeing and being seen by the face of God in a variety of ways and contexts was likely to have been an important and continuing aspect of religious experience. It has been somewhat downplayed and ignored, perhaps sometimes even actively repressed, both by Deuteronomic reformers and by contemporary biblical scholars.

This seeing was not understood or experienced in the same ways as we would understand it (cognitively, psychologically, metaphorically) because it was made available in a different social context. It was probably a thicker, more material and physical kind of seeing that involved various means such as visions, dreams, liturgy and heavenly journeys.

It seems impossible to determine the exact types and nature of visual experience of the divine face that people had in biblical times. This is partly because we cannot see past and through the literary texts that record that experience. It is also because people who saw God's face were theologically reticent and inarticulate about what they saw. This is analogous to the difficulty that any human might find in trying to articulate exactly what they see in the faces of other human beings; faces and seeing are not words and hearing, so it is difficult to represent the former adequately in the latter.

Seeing the face of God revealed a God who can be both present and absent and whose presence is somewhat indeterminate. To see God's face is not, then, to comprehend that face, but rather to realise that it figures a presence beyond comprehension. The living face of God, like the face of a human, points to depths that are not available for inspection. The language of veiling, mirroring, concealment and so on points to a kind of person-like relating that is based on seeing and not seeing as equally important. So there is something withheld within and beyond the visible face of God. God's face is seen in reality, but not in a detailed, over-determined way.

The sort of seeing we have considered took place in the context of communities of sight was ethically and socially significant and transformative – issues of justice, purity and sight were not separable. To see differently was, and is, to act differently.

It is not possible to say just how seeing and including/excluding in community were related in exact terms. However, to be included in the people that see God was to have different boundaries for shame, pollution and exclusion from members of other communities. Those who could not see God in the same way were excluded, shamed, as the gospels make clear. In that sense, the later term 'orthodoxy', right giving of glory in worship, right seeing of God's glory, was appropriately seen as a social and ethical marker.

It was the pure in heart, those who were in the new Temple, those from whose faces divine light was reflected so God was visible to them, like with like, who saw God. They began to make real the reign of God with its social and ethical consequences. In the Kingdom, to be finally realised by God's action in the future, the alienated, dishonoured, shamed and unwanted were included in a new vision of heaven and earth. Here, values were transformed, even reversed, and they could see God's face reflected in human faces all around them. The veil between heaven and earth had been torn apart and the face-to-face messianic feast had begun. When God finally appeared, his purified adoptive children, sharing the essence of likeness and light that allows recognition and affinity, would then be able to 'see him as he is' (1 John 3:2).

Nothing I have said here is intended to denigrate the place of words and hearing in the Judaeo-Christian biblical tradition. Encounter with the presence of God was a multi-sensate experience, involving whole persons with all their senses, including the oral/aural. However, in light of the logocentric bias to the aural in much Christian theology, I have sought to bring a thicker notion of the importance of sight and seeing the face of God into consideration as an important aspect of religious, cultural and ethical experience in the biblical tradition. If God's face in the Bible is regarded as visible but obscure, that is theologically accurate. But not being able to see or describe God's face in detail is a very different matter from denying that it can ever have been seen or from holding that the visible face of God had no real importance in biblical Christianity.

As we will see in the next chapter, finding the image of God and seeing God's face remains an important theme in early Christian theology as the radical inversion of norms and values inaugurated in Jesus' new community continues to ramify and develop.

Chapter 6

Seeking the Face of God in Post-biblical Christian Life and Theology

By focussing on the face we feed our love and take delight in it.

(Scruton 2012, 144)

Where there is love, there is seeing.

(Richard of St Victor, quoted in Wilken 2003, 184)

Christians in biblical times expected the consummation of the vision of God's face on earth when the Kingdom of God materially and finally came: 'we know that when (God) finally appears we shall be like him, for we shall see him as he is' (1 John 3:2 RSV). This expectation of a direct, physical, this-worldly encounter with God changed as time elapsed. Christian hopes became focused on life and experience with God beyond the present world. Although the aim of seeing God face-to-face as the culmination of the Christian life remained paramount, understandings of what it meant to see God's face changed. On the one hand, the eschatological vision of God gradually transmuted into a more mystical, contemplative matter (Lossky 1983). On the other, finding the face of God, whether in other people or in visual representations such as icons in the present world, retained enormous significance. In neither case, however, was embodied sight discarded.

In this chapter, I will very briefly and selectively trace some relevant themes in seeing face, human and divine, from the first to the thirteenth centuries. I cannot provide a comprehensive account of seeing the face of God. I simply aim to establish the possible importance of this theme as a corrective to its being so ignored in recent theology. This exploration is undertaken to discern whether there are insights, concepts, practices and ideas that might usefully problematise or inspire contemporary Christian attitudes to faces, divine and human.

First, then, I explore the nature of early Christian attitudes to seeing the divine in general terms. Thereafter, I consider the significance of Jesus' gaining a representational face. I go on to look at the idea of the *imago dei* and the way in which this contributed to enhanced respect for humans. Finally, the theological vision of God, developed over the first millennium and culminating in the thought of Thomas Aquinas, is outlined and discussed.

Seeing the Face of God in Early Christianity

Christians in the Roman Empire lived in the context of a world where deities were ubiquitous, normally visible, and sensually perceptible in everyday public life through their images, the scent of sacrifices and incense burnt to them and other devotional practices (Harvey 2006).[1] Moderns have tended to screen out the fully embodied sensual engagement that worshippers had with their patron deities. In this general context, early Christians continued to have a complex, important relationship with seeing the face of God. From within Christianity itself, the incarnation of God in Christ, God being found in and sanctifying matter, provided a profound impetus for taking the body and all things material and sensual seriously. In a tradition shaped by the treatment of believers' bodies, including suffering and martyrdom, there was every reason to value embodied experience (Pagels 1982; Perkins 1995; Walker Bynum 1995). Following the example of Stephen, whose face looked at his trial in the Temple like that of an angel (that is, a Temple servant who reflects the shining face of God at the very place where heaven and earth intersect, Jerusalem), and who saw the glory of God and Jesus in heaven while being stoned to death, martyrdom offered the possibility of seeing and reflecting the divine vision (Acts 6:15, 7:55–7; Malina and Pilch 2008, 224–5). And as martyrs saw into heaven in their earthly lives, their earthly relics were also places where the radiance of God's glory could be glimpsed, as body and person remained integrally linked (Belting 1994, chapter 3)

To touch on the theme of shame and alienation for a moment, it is arguable that the pre-Constantinian martyrdoms can be seen as public displays of shame that shame the shamers and affirm the values of the Christian community (deSilva 1999). These allowed the martyrs to transcend their shamefulness so they and their co-religionists could see God and strengthen their own identity. This kind of self-humbling in a shame-honour society allows 'in exchange for the sacrifice of face a joyous opening of the subject within grace'; it redefines what honour might be (Burrus 2008, 8). Arguably, the idea and importance of bodily resurrection into glory was generated to overcome 'the dishonour of being treated as a common criminal after death', so this fundamental doctrinal theme has its origins in facing down shame (Walker Bynum 1995, 48). Many of the martyrs were women. One of them, Perpetua, is recorded just before her death as 'beating back the gaze of the crowd with the power of her eyes' (Perkins 1995, 112). This looking back with confidence at the dishonouring crowd is sign and symbol of the redefinition of shame in the Christian community. It embodies a new way of seeing that allows a different way of responding in the world over against other communities that would seek to shame Christians.

---

[1]   To have a completely invisible God was highly unusual in the ancient world, and it must have been difficult to maintain the sense of that god's presence without visual or sensual engagement. It is not clear why the Hebrew tradition forbade images of God, when most surrounding religions would expect their presence (Barasch 1995, 18).

In this context, seeing was not a distant, disengaged, disembodied beholding. The 'eye of faith' was materially involved and informed – spiritual knowledge began with 'things that can be seen with the eyes and touched with the hands' (Wilken 2003, 240). While Christians could not reach God through the use of their senses, God could come through the senses to impart knowledge of Godself so that the whole body and person were transfigured (Harvey 2006). Through the realm of the seen, it was possible to come to see the God who could not be seen. Matter was filled with divine grace and power.

If the face of God is found displayed in the icon of Christ's face, then the scriptures act as an icon for Christ, 'the face of God for now', as Augustine characterised them (Wilken 2003, chapter 3). But it was not just in beholding Christ in scriptures that visual encounter with the divine was pursued. God could also be discerned throughout the material order, in liturgical action, water, oil, bread, wine, milk, honey, salt, the bones of the saints and in places touched by Jesus in his earthly life. In a process of relational seeing and being seen, believers were transformed into the one sought and seen. Sharing in light, they could be seen and enlightened as they cultivated likeness to, and fellowship with, God by growing in love and faith (Wilken 2003, 21).

All of this depended on some basic, common philosophico-cultural assumptions about seeing and light. First, people become like what they see and desire, or love – formation takes place by attraction (Miles 1985, 127; Wilken 2003, 21). Secondly, only like can recognise and commune with like – light can therefore only commune with light (Harrison 2010, 33). Thirdly, impressions, images and visual representations continue to have a real and continuous relationship with their originals, as wax continues to bear the imprint of the seal (Barasch 1995, 42). Thus the original can be discerned and related to through the copy or impression in a kind of great chain of being (Wilken 2003, 254). Fourthly, the way to the transcendent God who is light occurs through and by means of the body and its senses, particularly the sense of vision: 'early Christian thinkers favoured the metaphor of seeing, not hearing'; they divinised the eye as the highest of the senses, essential for gaining knowledge of God (Frank 2000a, 113ff.; Wilken 2003, 20). Indeed, hearing may have been distrusted as inaccurate and misleading in the journey and quest to see God (Frank 2000a, 114ff.). Following Aristotle, seeing was haptic, conceived in terms of touch; as images were stamped on the retina, sight was a kind of touching in which the seer and the object were interpenetrated (Frank 2000a, 131; Miles 1985, 45; Pattison 2007b, 41–60).

Early Christianity was 'an affair of things'; bread, wine, water, relics and other material objects were the means for sensual education and transformation towards the full vision of God:

> When the faithful look at the relics, it is as though with the eyes, the mouth, the
> ears, indeed all the senses they embrace the living body itself still blooming with
> life. (Wilken 2003, 238, 261)

Thus Gregory of Nyssa (335–c.395 CE) believed that looking at a martyr's remains was seeing the saint face-to-face; a glimpse of the face of God could be found reflected there. At around this time, people also visited holy places that bore traces of what Gregory described as 'the footprints of life [i.e. Christ] itself', hoping to stir their inner eye (Wilken 2003, 250). Seeing the faces, and even the beards, of monks and other ascetics could also be revelatory (Frank 2000a). These successors to the martyrs, who rejected the way of the city to clarify their own vision of God, revealed the glorified body of the resurrection and reflected the glory of God like Moses' face. By a kind of holy physiognomy, the eye of faith could read the face of the ascetic and see through and beyond it, to gaze at the holy person of God (Frank 2000a, chapter 5; 2000b). Holy faces were windows of the soul, and ultimately to God.

Having established the overall constructive, engaged sense of sight understood in material, multi-sensorial terms as an important undergirding way of apprehending the face of God in a creation redeemed in the human Jesus, I now want to say a bit more specifically about the development of relationships with the face of Christ, about the growth of visually related ideas about the *imago dei*, the image of God in humans, and then about the growth of the contemplative tradition which developed ideas about the *visio dei*.

Jesus Finds a Face

There is no portrait or physical record of Jesus' face or body in the NT. Similarly, there were no images of Jesus in early Christianity until the second century. Sometimes, this has been attributed to an inherent puritanical aniconism. This may have been operant in relation to images of God, held to be invisible not only by Christians but by many philosophical sophisticates in ancient society, so that to visually represent God would seem embarrassingly naïve. But in relation to images of Christ, it seems more likely that there was a lack of space, money and skill to create public images, as well, perhaps, as a lack of clarity about distinctive Christian identity. Once this identity was clear and opportunity presented itself, Christians wanted to make their religion public and visible (Finney 1994). For Roman religions, 'nothing is more important to gods than image. If a god's image should fail, how long could he survive?' (Mathews 1999, 11). In the competitive polytheistic marketplace they found themselves in, Christians, like others, made images of their saviour.

It was, however, only around the fourth century that images of Jesus began to proliferate in wall paintings, mosaics and other media in churches. Before this time, most images were of symbols or narratives, for example healing miracles. Now, however, dogma-driven portrait images of Christ became more normative. In apses and on walls, direct images of Christ's body and face were now depicted (Jensen 2000). His eyes could search out the eyes of believers so that face-to-face encounters might take place (Jensen 2000, 26; Mathews 1999, 96).

Representations of Jesus were surprisingly pluriform and polymorphous, drawing mainly on depictions of non-Christian gods like Apollo and Dionysus (Mathews 1999, 193). Jesus could be young, old, masculine (indicating victory), feminine (indicating nurture), bearded (like Zeus), clean shaven, short-haired, long-haired, a god, an emperor, a philosopher, a magician, a bishop (Mathews 1999). Jesus, then, seems something of a chameleon with no fixed appearance. Much depended on who was depicting or looking at him; maybe through this pluriform representation Christians worked out some of their theological problems in trying to establish who and what Christ was in terms of being both God and human, just as contemporary Christians portray Jesus differently, for example as black or a woman, to try and understand him today (Jensen 2000, 131; Mathews 1999, 141).

To fall under the gaze of Jesus depicted on an apse or wall was to fall under the gaze, presence and power of the person of Jesus who looked at you. Image and original were connected, so gods were treated as inhabiting their images. Christ's face and image made present his archetype and accepted its honours (Jensen 2000, 67; Mathews 1999, 190).

The instability and changeableness of the physical depiction of Jesus might have been expected to be a problem for theologians. But it was recognised that this had to do with imagination and the perspective of different viewers. While Jesus the man must have had a single visual appearance, salvation did not depend upon visual verisimilitude or likeness as it was the invisible divine image in Jesus that accomplished reconciliation with God. Augustine concluded that it was,

> ... not the image which the mind forms for itself and would perhaps be far different from what it actually was that leads to salvation, but what we think of the man according to his kind. For an idea has been impressed upon human nature as if it were a law, according to which, when we see any such thing, we at once recognise it as a man or as the form of a man. (Augustine 2002, 11)

With some variations, the facial image of Christ stabilised and became standardised into the image we recognise today, bearded and long-haired (Morgan 2012, 55–67; Pelikan 1997). Eventually, it came to be thought that there were acheiropoetic images which had been created, not by human hands or imagination, but by the image of Jesus' own face before his crucifixion. These were pieces of cloth like the Mandylion and the Veil of Veronica, which were held to provide an accurate, direct representation of Jesus' visage (Belting 1994, chapter 4; Jensen 2005, 134–7; Kemp 2011, 13–43; MacGregor 2000, 85–115). This image, and copies and derivatives of it, became widespread in both Eastern and Western Christianity; indeed, it forms the basis of the face of Christ that is best known today:

> ... by the end of the fifteenth century there was an agreed likeness of Christ; "everyone" throughout Europe "knew" what he looked like. For one thing, he

wore a beard. His appearance varied, but only as the appearance of someone we know varies in photographs. (MacGregor 2000, 93)

If the image of Jesus' face was in due course to spread across the Christian world, in the first millennium it was most important in Eastern Christianity where the icon became central. While relics and the Eucharist formed the main way of presencing God in the West and seeing God's heavenly glory, a limited range of significant images known as icons was important in the East. Much of the thinking about relics as a means of glimpsing and making present the divine was then applied to icons, including images of the face of Christ (Belting 1994, 59).

Icons were probably first produced in the fifth century. While the full theological understanding and justification for them only evolved at the time of the so-called iconoclastic controversy, in which opponents of icons thought them to be idols, there can be little doubt that from the earliest times they were thought to make God present and to connect believers to the reality of heaven on earth (Besancon 2000, 109–46). If Jesus was a real man, it was legitimate to make images of him as a reflection of the incarnation. By an implicit belief in the idea that image and archetype were linked and shared properties (often verified and authenticated by the fact that images could actively perform miracles), it was thought that icons could transform person and reality (Barasch 1995, 185–253; John of Damascus 1980; MacGregor 2000, 86; Ouspensky 1992). Belting (1994, 209) summarises the importance of the image of Jesus thus:

> The desire to see the face of God was inherent in human nature and included the expectation of a personal encounter with the "Other". Christianity offered the hope for a preliminary vision of God, for eternal life was understood as a permanent vision of God. In the "genuine image," the earthly features of Jesus, which could be seen by human eyes, merged with the divine features of God – visible reality with an invisible mystery … The very act of viewing in its turn implied the desire of viewers to resemble the One whom they had in view. The image and its beholder … related to each other like archetype and copy, like Creator and creature. The material image, as a mediator, thus became the tool for a contemplation of the lost beauty of humankind.

Defenders of icons and images of Christ against the charge of idolatry always made it clear that it was the archetype and original who was being worshipped and honoured through the image (Barasch 1995). However, it is likely that then, as more recently, people often effectively blurred image and archetype, visible and invisible, in a face-to-face relationship of mutual seeing (Belting 1994, 213; Freedberg 1989). Encounters with icons became living re-enactments with life and presence that aroused people's feelings and imprinted themselves on the heart (Belting 1994, 261–3). One can only feel sympathy with the human impulse that drove a fourth-century woman to ask for a portrait of Christ so she could embrace more fully the core of her new religion, Christianity, or with the sixth-century woman who asked of Jesus, 'How can I worship him if he is not visible, if I do not know him?' (Belting 1994, 144). Seeing the image of the face of Jesus became, and remains, an important way of seeing God and growing in love of the divine (Morgan 1998, 2005, 2012). This was not just an imaginative, spiritual or aesthetic matter, but a thick, sensory engagement.

The *imago dei* and Respect for Persons

If one thrust of early Christian life was towards seeing the face of the human Jesus in images and icons so that earthly life could be transformed towards the vision and love of God, an important theological dynamic was the development of ideas about the image and likeness of God in living humans. Perhaps this can be seen as another aspect of the outworking of the Christian inversion of values and of the rechannelling of shame and honour.

One of the most radical outworkings of incarnation, witnessing to and seeing God becoming human, seems to have been the development of the idea that all humans – slaves, lepers, women, poor people, beggars – are created in the divine image (Harrison 2010; Young 2011). They are also restored by the Christ, the model of what full likeness to the divine might be, and the visible image of the invisible God (Col. 1:15).

The image of God might be thought of as the basic divinely bestowed potential with which each person is born. It can be understood as a kind of stamp on the person, like the image stamped on a coin by a die. But it is can also be conceived in more naturalistic, relational and dynamic terms; it represents continuing and continuous contact with God who thus renews God's image within humans all the time (Harrison 2010). The indelible and inalienable image of God is often thought as existing within individuals, but it can also be thought of as something that is shared between humans. Thus Gregory of Nyssa argues that the image of God as an archetype is shared within the whole of humankind; it is not just a property of individual persons (Schaff and Wallace 2007, 406). God's image is also to be found in nature (Harrison 2010, 5).

Humans with the potential of the divine image have the freedom to become more or less like God, to develop and move into greater likeness to the divine (Harrison 2010, 7). In its most extreme form, growing into the likeness of God can be expressed as *theosis*, fully participating in God and seeing God face-to-face. At the very least, the reality of divine being connected to each and every person and all creation implies a model of respect for the royal dignity of all persons and of the material world (Harrison 2010). It is in this light, perhaps, that this saying of the second-century apologist and theologian, Irenaeus, should be read: 'The glory of God is a human being fully alive and the life of a human being is the vision of God' (Harrison 2010, 50). The aim of life is to become godlike and so to come to see God – and also to allow God to be seen through the human, as happened in Christ. This requires growing into God's likeness, for only like can see like.

Brueggemann (2009b, 59) notes that 'the notion of humanity in "the image of God" plays no primary role in Old Testament articulations of humanity'. So while it is in Gen. 1:26 that the doctrine of image and likeness is first articulated, it is only after the end of the NT era that this transforming idea for human destiny and dignity is properly developed. It is not necessary to outline the evolution and variants of this doctrine here, though the revolutionary importance of idea of finding God in humans and then finding his face through human development cannot be underestimated.

Briefly, then, it is maintained that people, men and women, are made in the image of God. Like all aspects of creation, they share in God's image which is diffused. This basic foundation cannot be shaken or taken away, for people are in constant contact with the creator renewing the divine image in them. However, people have the potential to become more like God in beauty, truth and love, and so to draw nearer to God. This is growing into the likeness of God; it is brought about by God and humans working together to allow humans to see and reflect God's light and glory. In their natural state, humans are like mirrors covered in dust, or iron covered in rust (Gregory of Nyssa 1954, 143–53). In Christ, however, the model for being both image and likeness has been revealed, and Christ, like an artist, can clean the image so it reflects the glory of God, as his own being does. Christ, 'like a good painter paints in those who believe in Him and constantly behold Him a portrait of the heavenly man, in His own image, by the power of the Holy Spirit, out of the very substance of his ineffable light', as the desert ascetic Macarius put it in the fourth century (Lossky 1983, 115). Athanasius makes a similar point:

> A portrait once effaced must be restored from the original. Thus the Son of the Father came to seek, save, and regenerate … For, as when the likeness painted on a panel has been effaced by stains from without, he whose likeness it is must needs come … to enable the portrait to be renewed on the same wood. (Athanasius 2011, 36–7)

By working using physical and spiritual senses to create pure and virtuous living, for example by prayer, people can move through the visible world to see God in the invisible world. And when God becomes visible, then the image of God in others will also become apparent.

This is not just a matter of life beyond this world, or something that is confined to individuals. Once again it has implications for the present material world and the embodied persons in community who, all together, according to Gregory of Nyssa, represent the image of God (Harrison 2010, 173; Schaff and Wallace 2007, 406). 'The human likeness to God is participation in God's life and immortality; it is abundant new life here and now and eternal life in the age to come' (Harrison 2010, 194).

Seeing, or aspiring to see, God aright is a radical catalyst for changing views of the self and the world. Shame and dishonour are subordinated to finding an inclusive view of humanity. This has enormous potential for creating witness to God's glory and for motivating the quest to find God in self, others and in the whole material creation. While the consummation of the journey to see God may lie beyond the material world, the quest for this vision starts firmly in the sensual, embodied world and with the example of the human Jesus. The divine face and working towards seeing it thus becomes an important driver for moral revisioning and resituating oneself in the world. Seeing is believing, is changing and being transformed, along with the whole creation. There is no room here, then, for 'worm theology' that denigrates the human race and the material world – God does not discard people (Harrison 2010). Indeed, God creates them and draws them to Godself to share the divine glory. Thus we should reverence others as present embodiments of the image of God.

I now move on to further consider the theological tradition of seeing God. While the *visio dei* may go beyond the body and senses in some ways, prizing some aspects of the *imago dei* over others, the way to the vision of God cannot entirely leave the body and senses behind. It is the incarnate Christ who has ascended to heaven and continues to reveal the glory of God, not a disembodied spirit. The vision of God's face includes resurrected human bodies, not just souls, spirits or mind.

The Theological Vision of God

The vision of God, of God's face and glory, was the aim and end of Christian life for over a millennium. With the decline of a real hope of eschatological completion in the present world, and beginning in the second century under the influence of Platonism, theologians began to try to understand what it might be to see or attain the vision of the face of God beyond the present material world (Lossky 1983). This development is sometimes seen as the beginning of mysticism, even unitive mysticism. However, modern critics warn against seeing the early Fathers as mystics at all (McGinn 1991). Mysticism is a nineteenth-century invention; there is no agreed understanding of what it is. Furthermore, there was no particular experience which thinkers like Augustine were trying to theorise or cultivate. Rather, they were theologians working dialectically in language shaped by neo-Platonic concepts. Insofar as they used the language of senses, hierarchy and inwardness, they were working with a set of common metaphors, not cultivating particular esoteric or ecstatic experiences (Turner 1995). The language referring to interiority was thus about epistemological inference (how and in what ways is it possible to know and talk about God who is beyond experience and understanding?) not psychological introspection (how can I unite myself with God?) (Turner 1995, 88). These early theologians, then, were not esoterics, but rather normal practitioners of Christian life and work, shaped by routine worship and prayer, not by rapture. They were engaged in the quotidian, but demanding, work of loving God and neighbour as a means of coming ultimately to the vision of the face of God as the end of the Christian journey.

Thus Louth (1989) argues that, far from producing treatises on mystical theology, the fifth-century theologian Pseudo-Dionysius was writing theological commentaries on actual liturgy, itself an opportunity for corporate theophany in which participants are drawn into God's light and possibility as God processes towards humans (Pseudo-Dionysius 1987). The ascent described is not that of the mystic's solitary inward ascent to God, but rather that of the bishop to the altar in worship. In this context, mystic union and deification does not mean having privileged, extraordinary personal experience, but rather 'letting God's love be the principle of one's life' (Louth 1989, 103). This then allows worshippers to manifest God's love in the world.

Saying this perhaps makes these non-experientialist thinkers then sound like proto-systematic theologians, interested primarily in the intellect and the invisible. This is misleading.

First, they valued the material world and saw it as a 'book' in which God's presence could be read and interpreted in both physical and spiritual senses (Harrison 1998). The material and immaterial, visible and invisible, human and non-human were all interconnected and valuable in God's sight. For Pseudo-Dionysius, for example,

> The world is a theophany, and manifestation of God ... The world is God's glory made manifest: it exists to display his glory and draw everything into contemplation of his beauty. ... God is immediately present to his whole creation as creator; created reality is not ... an obstacle to his glory. (Louth 1989, 85)

So these early theologians were not as dualistic or spiritualising as they might at first seem.

Secondly, while they did not believe that God was to be comprehended and limited as an object in the sensual, material world, early theologians did not exclude the importance of the bodily senses in perceiving the divine. While not thinking of God as a physical object who could be comprehended corporeally, they did maintain that the senses were the beginning of trying to obtain knowledge of God. The corporeal senses, however, had to be transformed into parallel spiritual senses that ultimately apprehended God in God's non-corporeality, that is intellectually (Coakley 2002; Gavrilyuk and Coakley 2012; Rahner 1979, 81–103).

In this context, Augustine provides a good case study of thinking about the vision of God. He wrote a great deal of influential material about this; it became the normative understanding of how God was seen in medieval theology (McGinn 2005). Here I follow Miles' (1983) authoritative account.

Augustine thinks it is possible for the faithful to have three kinds of vision in this life: corporeal vision, veiled inner vision related to internal images and comprehending vision in which the mind directly grasps the truth of God (McGinn 2005). God can grant any of these types of seeing, but they are fleeting and partial. They cannot be complete or permanent now, except for exceptional individuals like Moses and Paul. For Augustine, physical sight is the best analogy and metaphor for understanding the vision of God:

> The visual ray of the physical eye which unites the soul to the objects of its habitual attention provided Augustine with a powerful description of the vision of God, a coordination of physics and metaphysics which grounded his "vision" of the process and goal of human life. (Miles 1983, 142)

Physical sight was understood to be an act of extramission by a ray from the eye (Pattison 2007b, 42–5). This was initiated by the perceiver, and the visual ray then touched the seen, visual object, uniting sender and object; thus, what is seen actually impresses itself on the mind of the sender. The seer is thus defined and shaped by the objects of its attention and affections. With the eye, one actively reaches out to, and is also drawn by, the object.

While God is light and draws the inner eye to Godself, it requires will and energy in terms of the metaphorical 'inner eye' of the mind or soul to see the deity. There must be faith that there is something to see. Then, it is necessary to engage in exercise and training, cleansing and strengthening. Cleansing requires the recollection of oneself from the variety of images that occupy and structure the soul, so that one becomes focused and continent. It is then necessary to cultivate longing which functions as the visual ray of the mind's eye that is able to touch God. The cultivation of the soul's longing is the concentration of love. Where this occurs, humans can attain a glimpse of God as love. No visual image of this is left on the soul, but in the life to come believers will be able to gaze endlessly on God.

Like many other early Christian thinkers, Augustine emphasises that God can be further seen in present earthly life by loving one's neighbour. In loving, one shares in God's love and life by being like him. So here again, the end of the quest for the invisible is to see God and Christ in the faces of real people around one. The full recognition and enjoyment of God, and the enjoyment and recognition of other people made in the divine image, are integrally linked.

Augustine thought that physical vision itself had a spiritual aspect to it that was powered by God. There was continuity between physical and spiritual vision (Miles 1983, 141). Physical sight could be used to see beauty and other humans and through the visible world to the invisible God. He acknowledges, with some difficulty and puzzlement, that while God is not to be apprehended in God's essence through physical sight, God can be seen bodily if God so wishes; this is what happened with select biblical figures (Augustine 2003).

While God is love, basically invisible, and only fully available to spiritual sight, Augustine doggedly sticks to Christian orthodoxy, believing that humans will be united with their glorified bodies in the resurrection (Augustine 1982, 230). And if there are bodies in the resurrection, 'there will certainly be something that bodily eyes can see' (Augustine 2003, 349). The eye of the body and eye of the mind will both be present in the resurrection; there may well be some kind of physical sight of the immaterial. Augustine admits that he is confused and uncertain about exactly what the nature of seeing will be. He suggests that the saints will have spiritual eyes with their new spiritual bodies whereby 'we shall discern, by means of our bodies, the incorporeal God directing the whole universe'. Alternatively,

> … perhaps God will be known to us and visible to us in the sense that he will be spiritually perceived by each one of us in each one of us, perceived in one another, perceived by each in himself; he will be seen in the new heaven and the new earth, in the whole creation as it then will be; he will be seen in every body by means of bodies, wherever the eyes of the spiritual body are directed with their penetrating gaze. (Augustine 1972, 1087)

Augustine is clearly working at the edge of knowledge and speculation here, but he is determined to insist that there is some kind of body in the resurrection. This body, albeit different from present bodies and eyes, has a place in the beatific vision which is the end of Christian life. Perhaps this body will see God directly. Maybe, however, God will be found by looking at the bodies around us and in ourselves, in other humans and in beings who are, in some ways, the image and vision of God. Either way, it is not clear; Augustine admits that he finds Scripture of limited value in understanding how things will be when bodies and spirits are reunited in the resurrection and the blessed see God face-to-face.

Augustinian thinking about some kind of bodily seeing of the face of God continued to be normative till the thirteenth century (McGinn 2005). During the first Christian millennium, there were differences of opinion as to whether God could be seen in God's essence through knowledge, the view largely adopted by Western and Latin theologians, or whether God could only be encountered in God's revealed energies or powers, so that God's face and essence could never be directly or finally known (Lossky 1983, 131). The latter tradition is mostly associated with Eastern Greek theologians like Gregory of Nyssa and Pseudo-Dionysius (Gregory of Nyssa 1978; Lossky 1983, 88, 122–30; Pseudo-Dionysius 1987). God's essence and image could never be finally grasped; it was God's back, seen in darkness, rather than God's face, that could be known. Thus, 'to follow God wherever he might lead is to behold God' (Gregory of Nyssa 1978, 119; Young 2007, 18). To see God would be to circumscribe and contain him. Thus, there is a perpetual, unfinished dynamic journey of discipleship and desire towards God as Christians are gradually transformed into God's likeness.

Both Eastern and Western theologians would basically have agreed on the importance of this journey of discipleship. They would also have shared other commonalities of approach. These would have included:

- the basic need for cultivating love of God and neighbour in this world as a way of moving towards seeing God by becoming like him;
- the primacy of God graciously wishing to make Godself known;

- the unfinished and partial nature of seeing God in the present world;
- the possibility of deepening love and sight of God hereafter;
- the continuing existence of some kind of transfigured physical human existence in seeing God, even if God is not to be seen through the bodily eye.

At the apex of the Western tradition of the *visio dei*, St Thomas Aquinas (1225–74 CE) argues that no-one can see God fully in this life because humans are stuck in the corporeal realm; they cannot grasp God because God is not confined within the realm of the senses. Beyond death, however, in heaven, 'a place and not simply a spiritual state', bodies, as well as souls, will participate in life with God in a glorified, but personally identifiable and dimensional form (Wawrykow 2005, 45–6). Here, 'the blessed see the essence of God' by means of the intellect, not the continuing body; some will see it more perfectly than others (Pegis 1997, 82, 95). Having been illuminated by grace, by the light of God's glory, the intellect acquires a kind of deiformity in which the divine essence is united to it; the image and likeness of God are completed in the human (Pegis 1997, 100, 105). Thus humans can move from sensual knowledge to the vision of the essence of God, but only by the action and will of God beyond death. Furthermore, the beatific vision that fills the soul or intellect will overflow 'from the soul in its enjoyment in contemplation, to the body' (Wawrykow 2005, 45). However, even in seeing the divine essence, a created intellect 'does not see in it all that God does or can do' (Pegis 1997, 103). At the point of ultimate beatification, the face of God, like a human face, is not wholly self revealing. There is a sense in which, as with the Eastern tradition, God cannot ever be completely or finally known.

Lossky perhaps unifies both Western and Eastern perspectives:

> To see God face to face is to know Him as He knows us, just as two friends know each other reciprocally. Such a knowledge-vision, presupposing reciprocity, excludes all idea of finality in the face to face vision of God. (Lossky 1983, 31)

And it should not be forgotten that before life in heaven, both Western and Eastern traditions bear witness to the possibility of seeing God in the world through various means and, significantly, in other embodied humans. Commenting on Albert the Great in his interpretation of Pseudo-Dionysius, Tugwell (1988, 93) writes, 'If Dionysius and Albert are right, we are bumping into God the whole time'.

What Can Be Learned Theologically about Seeing the Face of God from Christianity in the First Millennium?

It is not to be expected that looking at early Christian thought and practice will produce a ready-made, easily applicable theology of seeing faces, human or divine. Christian ancestors were not apparently directly very interested in physical human faces (though there was some interest in the faces of Jesus and the saints), nor do they have detailed knowledge of the face of God. We do not know much about how they looked at themselves or others physically, or about what their conventions of gaze were. The culture and context of this thought is different from our own; it was not constructed to address our concerns. In fact, one of the real advantages of looking back in time at the Christian tradition is to expose the pluriformity and apparent irrelevance. It is at least as problematic as it is helpful. Thus, it is usefully provocative in helping to disrupt assumptions and suggest questions in contemporary discussions.

So what might be learned from this excursus into early Christian ideas and practices? First, the idea of seeing the face of God, the *visio dei*, formulated in the NT and perhaps drawing on OT traditions of seeing God in the Temple and in Jesus, continued, and was developed, over the first millennium. The beatific vision, promised to the pure in heart as the end of Christian life, was important throughout this period, but the consummation of the vision was transferred from the present world into a future world beyond death. Seeing itself, however, was more valued as a sense than hearing, so it was not theologically downgraded, as it was after the Reformation.

Secondly, ideas and theories about seeing God remained closely related to the body and the senses. The journey to the vision of God began in the sensual world; it was understood through language about the senses that was substantial and materialistic. The senses and the body, while they might not be able to reach the ultimate vision of God's essence in knowledge and love, were not to be discarded or left behind at any point; redemption was both physical and spiritual. Senses were transformed rather than discarded, and new 'spiritual senses', different ways of perceiving, were developed (Coakley 2002; Rahner 1978).

Thirdly, the journey of discipleship and love that eventually led to the vision of God did not mean ignoring the present world. God could be seen in and through the present material world, as well as in visions, theophanies and so on, so its significance was transvalued. Material objects such as images and icons could be a link between heaven (understood as a place, not just a spiritual state) and earth. People were linked to God in a fundamental way by being made in the image of God. If they responded to God's love shown in Christ, they could then be enlightened to the state of being able to see the light of God. In doing this, a main part of their training was to love others, to see the image of God in those around them – this contributed to a revaluing of the human as made in God's image and to the redemption of alienation.

Because sight, both physical and spiritual, was important, in due course it became important to give Jesus a face. However, it is interesting that his face was not standardised for a long time – there were many images of Christ. As images became icons, they, too, became an important bridge between heaven and earth and part of training in seeing the divine and transforming the vision of the world.

All of this took place in a corporate, non-mystic context in which bodies were to be redeemed as much as souls. Ultimately, the meaning of the quest to see God's face, to be transformed into God's likeness and share divine light, is possible but enigmatic. At the end of the journey, God's essence is perceptible but unfathomable, like relations with humans. What it means cannot be spelt out. As in the Bible, the nature and meaning of the final vision of God's face is withheld. God remains veiled and elusive within the eye of faith that firmly hopes, but does not yet fully see. In the meanwhile, however, the bodies, faces and souls of humans and of the creation provide many opportunities for 'bumping into God' directly or indirectly.

In many ways, then, the search for the ultimate beatitude of the *visio dei* is an outworking of I John 4:12: 'No one has ever seen God; if we love each other, God dwells in us and his love is completed in us' (my translation). There is much, then, to be found in the shining and despoiled faces of the human community that will eventually lead directly to the discovery of the image and essence of the divine vision as humans grow into God's likeness in love, repainted in the image of, and with the grace of, Christ, the image of the invisible God. In that sense, perhaps humans, like the desert saints, can become icons of the invisible God.

What then can be taken from this brief, partial glance into a thousand years of theological development? In the first place, we cannot derive a theology of physical human face directly from this material. However, it might prompt us to think that seeing has been and perhaps should be more important in Christian understandings of the world.

Seeing God is not just a disembodied, otherworldly matter, though it is indirect and imperfect in the present world. It also involves seeing the image of God in others as love is practised and Christians grow into the likeness of God. If God's presence is made available through the world and through people, then perhaps there is a need to take the physical reality and presence of others generally more seriously.

In this context, it might be important to revalue the human face as itself a kind of icon of the living God. It, too, has qualities of presence and absence, knowing and unknowing that are also found to be true of God. If God has a face, even if it is not easily visible, then it might be inferred that all enfaced beings are in principle important, particularly those who embody the image of God. Furthermore, it may be that we cannot, and will not, understand the face of God unless we also take the faces of other humans with absolute seriousness.

In terms of ideas for constructing theologies of face, it is fascinating that the image of Jesus was so polymorphic as people made their own images of him in response to their own beliefs and perspectives. It may be that this is an idea which can be worked with creatively today. It is intriguing and suggestive that it was thought that different people would see even the essence of God differently and God would appear differently to people according to their needs and abilities. This suggests a good deal of possibility and flexibility in thinking about the nature of divine and human faces.

My main aim in the last two chapters has been to highlight the importance of faces and embodied seeing within the Christian tradition in an attempt to counterbalance an excessive emphasis on the word and hearing. If God is made totally invisible and cannot be seen, this may contribute to a devaluation of sight and faces in the contemporary world. I have sought to question whether the early Christian tradition will support this, and suggested that in some ways it does not. At least some kinds of Christianity support the view that embodied seeing is central, both in heaven and on earth. In the next chapter, I will go on to discuss briefly the disappearance of God into complete invisibility before looking at some contemporary theological resources and approaches for funding a theological imaginary for responding to, and thus saving, faces, human and divine.

Chapter 7
Modern Theological Resources for the Saving of Face

God is wholly other to the world and yet God's face "peers out from the windows, peeks through the lattice work". That face contains within it all the faces of humanity and each of them contains the face of God.

(Raphael 2003, 8)

Having surveyed some biblical and historical aspects of the traditions of the *visio dei*, the present chapter brings the theological story up to date so we can begin to develop a creative practical theological response to the saving of faces, human and divine. I will devote most of this chapter to looking at some modern theological understandings of the face of God and of human faces as a preliminary to creating practical theological horizons for different ways of seeing and responding to faces. Before that, however, I will give a brief account of the decline of the importance of the notion of the vision of God as a doctrine, and of the increasingly non-material notions of divinity and human encounter with the divine; these led to the present situation in which God is held to be entirely invisible.

It is my hunch that the increasing invisibility and immateriality of God has undergirded the development of Western spiritualising capitalist materialism, whereby we see through the material world, including the physical world of humanity. It may also have colluded with a downgrading of theological attention to human faces and bodies (Pattison 2007b, 159–66). This trend has only recently begun to be reversed with an increasing emphasis, initiated largely by feminist, womanist and liberationist theologians, on embodiment and valuing the material world (Betcher 2007; Jantzen 1984, 1999; McFague 1987, 1993, 1997; Morris 2008).

Losing the Visible Face of God

The theology of seeing the face of God, the beatific vision, which was the end of Christian discipleship and living, seems to have reached almost its most complete formulation by the thirteenth century. As we have seen, the fullest and final vision of God's face, the direct encounter with divine essence, was not by this point really a sensual, this-worldly possibility, though some kind of bodily involvement was not ruled out.

Vision – physical, spiritual and metaphorical – continued to be an important part of trying to engage in theology and discipleship beyond the thirteenth century

(Denery 2005; Hahn 2000; Hamburger 1998, 2002; Jantzen 1995; McGinn 2005). But while early medieval vision experience was experienced momentarily by an individual in community, late medieval experience was more systematically shaped by physical and metaphysical ideas; it was more the product of the solitary contemplation (Hahn 2000). Increasing use was made of images and of imaginative visionary techniques (Hamburger 2002, chapter 8). The details and disputes as to what was practised, and why, need not detain us here. Suffice it to note that,

> Visions and visualisations, both here and in the *visio beatifica* to come, were never simple, uncontroversial, and generally agreed-upon aspects of Christian belief and practice. (McGinn 2005, 245)

This was true at the time of the Reformation. Then iconoclasts destroyed and defaced images to witness to the invisible God whose face was to be seen in humans and in the book of creation, while other reformers like Luther found a place for devotional images (Koerner 2004; Wandel 1994). However, Calvin, Luther and others would all have agreed with the Fathers in thinking that the main place in which the image of God was to be discerned was particularly in humans:

> For the Puritans ... the whole of life, in its patterns and structures took on the character of an icon of God's presence. And in the midst of this theatre of God's glory, it is the individual person as the special image of God that stands out as the dramatic focus in the narrative of salvation. (Dyrness 2004, 238)

Thinking about the vision of God's face and God's glory has not, it seems to me, fundamentally advanced beyond this. And although it might seem to suggest that the world of the seen, including the experience of those human faces that reflect the glory of God, should be taken very seriously, theological engagement with the face of God and the significance of human faces has not progressed far. Words, including theological words, have conspired to maintain the invisibility of both human and divine faces , despite facial relations being of great everyday significance within the Christian community. Serious thinking about the *visio dei* as such seems largely to have disappeared except as some kind of pious metaphor, or obscure, apparently peripheral, point of doctrine which relates to a world beyond this one. Why, then, has the *visio dei* been downgraded within Christian theology and practice? Why have we effectively lost sight of the face of God?

Why Has God's Face Been Lost?

The entire Judaeo-Christian theological tradition bears witness to the, at least partial, invisibility and obscurity of God. God cannot be apprehended visually and directly in God's essence. Nonetheless, much of the tradition we have examined suggests an immediacy of presence and experience of the divine which was understood as seeing God. Some of it suggests that this is a thick, physically related experience rather than being characterised by intra-psychic events and imagination. So what has happened since the times of St Thomas Aquinas to have made seeing the face of God a matter of such minor concern for Christian believers, and especially theologians?

This is not the place to write a history of the changing form of theism in the West over the last millennium, but a few pointers can be offered.

Buckley (1987) ponders why the idea of an active, present God became implausible after the Enlightenment, while atheism quickly became thinkable and relatively non-controversial. The roots of this change lay in the adoption of abstract philosophical ideas and reason for establishing theology, from Aquinas onwards. Theologians defending Christianity bracketed out the lived experience of the religious community, the personal, the experiential and the importance of Jesus, to create a philosophically acceptable God. But this God was then abstract and non-personal, without real presence in the natural, material world. The irrationality and the intrinsic religious reasoning that accompanies thick, revealed religion was eliminated. Impersonal nature understood by reason was substituted for the God disclosed in Jesus Christ and then found to be a poor basis for belief in a personal God. This way of looking at theology did not conflict with the world of science, because religion had imported the latter's ideas and conventions of reasoning. However, theology then had nothing really to contribute to understanding the nature of reality. God was objectified philosophically, then found not to be either knowable or interesting. Figured as invisible, God was easily considered to be non-existent, not a part of the common material world of science and experience. The latter thereby attained a kind of autonomy, free of religious control.

At the same time, personal religion and religious experience in ordinary life were downgraded as far as theology was concerned. God and theology became matters of the mind, not of the heart and the body. There started to be a separate invisible realm of the supernatural or mystic in which religious experience occurred. This could be dismissed as esoteric or paranormal, outwith the shared common world:

> With "nature" now deemed single, homogeneous and self-contained, we labelled "supernatural" that other world inhabited … by demons, angels and suchlike extraterrestials – and by God. (Lash 1996, 168, 171)

Around the end of the sixteenth century, especially in Protestant countries, the quest for experience of God took an individualist, inward, personal turn. The outward, physical world was subordinated to an inward, contemplative journey:

> The inner space of medieval Catholicism was physical, it was a space people could share. The inner space of Puritanism was the space of the most radical individualism and was impalpable. The Puritan eye could only see within itself. (Sennett 1992, 45)

In many ways, Protestant culture, building on a previous Catholic philosophical abandonment of the material, experiential realm of inhabited, revealed religion, led to the neglect of the outer, sensual, communally shared world. In this context, eyesight became feeling-toned insight into the self (Miles 1985, 3). Symbolic of this, in many Western churches, people still shut their eyes to commune with God through their minds and selves, rather than looking around at the faces of others who bear God's image.

At the end of the sixteenth century the senses had also been divorced from the Augustinian worldview that allowed a unity between symbolic, spiritual and material worlds. The arts and sciences were divorced from the medieval symbolic order of word and light:

> The Augustinian tradition – as a unified symbolic horizon of word and light, verbal and visual, hearing and seeing, ears and eyes, words and things – lost its grip on the western imagination. Eyes and ears defined independent fields of discourse, knowledge, and power divorced from their sacred convergence and interpenetration in any symbolic synaesthesia. (Chidester 1992, 132)

Simultaneously, there grew to be a suspicion of the capacity of humans to understand or be active in finding the face or image of God. Divine and human natures were now understood to be very different, and to lack many points of similarity or identification. Gone was the lifelong pilgrimage to realise and discover the *imago dei* undertaken by humans with discipline and divine grace. The Reformation, in particular, emphasised human frailty, passivity and incapacity faced with the huge gulf between divine goodness and human lostness which has continued to this day (Robinson 2011). In this context, only the radical action of God could enable humans to encounter the divine; there was no longer any pilgrimage way upon which Christians could gradually progress towards God.

As heaven and earth, humans and God, decisively separated out from each other, the human face ceased to be regarded as a window of the soul, a lens or book that could be read to help access and understand the divine in the human and natural world. The turn to mechanical thinking and philosophy closed the book of nature as a way of finding God while the material and theological realms became autonomous and disconnected.

In this context, the human face became no more than an interesting site for speculative parlour games or a means of seeking an appropriate sexual partner. The discipline of physiognomy, regarded as a religious discipline in medieval times, changed from being an adjunct to spiritual discernment to becoming a more or less trivial parlour game. This movement can be characterised as a change 'from praying to playing' or 'regeneration to recreation' (Porter 2005, 220, 244). For better and perhaps for worse, no longer was physical appearance taken as a sure guide to the qualities and spirit of a person within. Eventually, for many, morality and carnality were completely separated: 'Dislocating spiritual identity from appearances, Protestantism enables a subject's nature to be constructed in opposition to his carnal nature' (Baker 2010, 52).[1]

The upshot of these, and other trends, including widespread secularisation, is that God's face has been almost completely lost to sight and to reason. The abstract God of contemporary academic Western theology cannot and never will be seen. Indeed, perhaps no-one would less like to have an experience or sense of the visible God than most contemporary academic theologians. For us, experience and presence are problematic as they disrupt our cognitive captivity of a thin, uninteresting God who is kept apart from the material world (Orsi 2005).

This, however, is not the case with many ordinary Christians, including the supposedly cerebrally confined rationalistic Protestants, who continue to have rich visually related experiences of God and beings like angels, with images beautiful and ugly, in visions, apparitions and in the faces of those around them (Christian 1992, 1999, 2012; Harvey 1995, 1999; Heathcote-James 2009; Morgan 1998, 2005, 2012; Orsi 1985, 1996, 2005; Wiebe 1997; Zaleski 1987). Significant visual experiences of, and with, the transcendent remain important and impervious to theological and philosophical abstracting minimalism. But they are not well supported from within the formal academic, word-focused theological tradition. Seeing and taking faces, human and divine, seriously is not theologically supported either.

If God's face is invisible, and so irrelevant, we may be inclined to believe human faces are also relatively insignificant. If this is so, then it is time to write God's face back into theology, partly so the faces of our fellow human beings can also be seen more adequately. In the remainder of this chapter, therefore, I consider some recent theological work that may help in a recovery of face. I will then move on to suggest some theological motifs and prompts emerging from the whole discussion about face that may help in constructing a provisional practical theological approach to faces, human and divine.

---

[1]   The de-sacralising of the face did not take place in one singular moment and a variety of attitudes persisted across time. It is misleading to think that any one practice of seeing or thinking prevails without challenge or diversity in any society (Otter 2008). Notions of the sacrality and theologically revelatory nature of face survived into the eighteenth and nineteenth centuries in places. Blake and Lavater, for example, were exponents of a version of 'sacred physiognomy', and Duchenne also saw the face as an entrée to understanding the divine. It is likely that in any culture there will be many different perspectives on this that co-exist alongside one another. Modern ideas about the face revealing the spirit or mystery of the person can in this sense be seen as transmutations of the idea that the outer reveals something profound about the inner. See further, for example, Duchenne de Boulogne (1990), Hartley (2001), Lavater (1978), Porter (2005), Pearl (2010).

Recent Theological Approaches to Face

The visual dimension of existence, including the vision of God and seeing the faces of people, has been generally been occluded and neglected in Western theologies. Now, with turns towards the body and the senses, this *aporia* is beginning to be addressed. The recent works that I have been able to find on this subject are small in number, but high in interest and quality. I will consider them now.

David Ford's profound theological meditation, *Self and Salvation* is 'an invitation to see the face of Jesus Christ with the eyes of the heart' (Ford 1999, 267). In this context, face is taken as a main symbol for the self. Modern philosophers and theologians, as well as with biblical and other sources, are engaged to create a theology of 'facing'. This is understood as a symbol of salvation, addressing problems of identity, crisis and transformation amidst the polyphony and cacophony of contemporary life. The community in which Jesus' face is realised and turned towards all people is a community of salvation. Here, worshipping selves live before the face of Christ in 'an economy of superabundance' and manifest health, hospitality and worship (Ford 1999, 9).

'We live before the faces of others', as well as before the face of God (Ford 1999, 17). Faces are a crucial interface between inner and outer worlds where vital communication occurs. However, Ford quickly moves from the concrete physical particularities of human faces to begin to discuss facing in transforming 'communities of the face':

> Christianity is characterised by the simplicity and complexity of facing: being faced by God, embodied in the face of Christ; turning to face Jesus Christ in faith; being members of a community of the face; seeing the face of God reflected in creation and especially in each human face, with all the faces in our heart related to the presence of the face of Christ; having an ethic of gentleness towards each face ... and having a vision of transformation before the face of Christ "from glory to glory". (Ford 1999, 24–5)

Ford explores what it would mean to be a hospitable, non-idolatrous, worshipping self so that one becomes a witness to the glory of God in the face of Christ. It is Christ who reconfigures the worshipper to become part of an inclusive community of mutual and joyful ethical responsibility characterised by love and abundance. This worshipping community is comprised of singing selves. Facing God and Christ, they give face to all in non-coercive speech and action and respectful communication. Selves are embodied, particularly in Eucharistic participation. Here, people enjoy blessing in facing each other and Christ in the community of the baptised; they experience the glorious face of Christ: 'The eucharist is an apprenticeship in being blessed and blessing before the face of Jesus Christ through whom the face of God in the Aaronic blessing is recognised' (Ford 1999, 215).

Christ's face is thought of in terms of immense glory and historical reliability. The 'abundant particularity' of the face of Christ is to be found in face-to-face relations with others (Ford 1999, 176). It is not possible to say much about the glorious and historical face of Jesus. While there is complete continuity in it, there is a disturbance of recognisability in the transformation of the resurrection, as the gospel accounts make clear, so it is intrinsically vague: 'We do not have the detail of a physical face but we are allowed to imagine well enough what it was like to be before this face' (Ford 1999, 181). There is continuity between physical historical face and risen face, but we cannot say much more than this. The important thing is the facing that goes on between God and man. Jesus' face is not dominating or coercive (Ford 1999, 184ff.).

Significantly, the dead face of the crucified Christ has been neglected as a focus for doctrines of atonement. Ford goes on to explore what this face might mean for the doctrines of sin and salvation, representing as it does the hiddenness of God's own face. It should act as a touchstone for love and power (Ford 1999, 205). It represents an absence that then requires human responsibility; it puts an end to sacrifice and idolatry:

> To worship in faith before this face is above all to be faced by him. Whatever refers us to this face – whether the faces of fellow human beings, or the imagination aroused by scripture and worship, or works of art, or joyful responsibility, or "the face of the earth" – is seen with an iconic, not an idolatrous gaze: it leads us to "see" Jesus Christ only to find ourselves "more radically looked at", loved, delighted in and accountable. And even "seeing" this face in faith is to find it a self-effacing face, referring us to the face of the Father and to the faces of fellow human beings … (Ford 1999, 214)

To concretise this kind of thinking, Ford looks at the 'polyphonic' lives of two saints who faced God: St Therese of the Child Jesus and of the Holy Face and Dietrich Bonhoeffer. Bonhoeffer famously wrote of living before the face of God and of Christ. He found the great joy of being face-to-face in community in his devotion to the freedom and responsibility of living in a world in which God is hidden, Luther's *deus absconditus*. Bonhoeffer believed that God's hiddenness in the face of the crucified Christ creates a space for human activity and response and so it enables, as well as requiring, human responsibility.

Ford's book ends with a meditation on feasting, the opportunity for humans and God to face each other in joy. The only persons who are excluded from the Christian eucharistic joy are those who themselves cannot accept and imitate God's generosity, the envious and non-communally minded presumably (Elliott 1992).

Self and Salvation is a rich, complex text, combining erudition, scholarship, imagination, devotion and poetry. Its non-linear way of tackling the theme of face and facing is apposite. There are many important and suggestive ideas in the book which can frame a rich theology of facing. These range through the importance of the worshipping community, the public and communal nature of facing, the inclusion of all, the transformation of persons, the significance of seeing God and Christ and the ethical and social implications of being bound up in this facing in a world where God is present in absence. I will return to some of Ford's creative thinking when I try later to do some constructive practical theological thinking myself later on.

However, the book does have some limitations from my present perspective. First and foremost, it is frustrating that Ford moves so quickly to consider the abstracted symbols of face and facing rather than spending more time exploring the experience and reality of face and enfacement, thus missing some of the richness and complexity of his topic (Hull 2000). He says very little about the concrete reality of the kind of face that is seen in the street every day. Like many theologians, he may have been caught in words and the Protestant emphasis on meaning amplified by some anxiety about the possibility of faces themselves becoming idolatrous and attracting 'the wrong kind of fixations' (Ford 1999, 23).

For Ford, and for me, salvation and facing are bound together – to find face is to be saved. But in his case, presencing or facing God directly, which is the meaning of salvation, seems to be almost entirely indirect and metaphorical – God cannot be directly or materially apprehended in this life, so the material reality of faces and facing drops away. Ford then appears to be primarily interested in trying to educate the eyes of believers' hearts, not their physical senses and responses. Ford shows little interest in sociological and anthropological approaches to the Bible. These might have brought to the fore the importance of the community and the relation of face to shame and honour. Inclusion and exclusion are important themes in Ford's thinking; the eucharistic community and the positive view of hospitality he commends implies a high commitment to shame inversion. However, the concrete means as to how this might be brought about are left obscure.[2]

Ford provides positive and attractive general theological horizons for valuing face and facing and, implicitly, for giving countenance to people. However, his vision is somewhat idealised, abstract and a bit too non-specific and disembodied to touch everyday reality. It is none the worse for that; no author can deal with all aspects of a subject. However, it will be important to move from general ideas about facing and finding face to more specific approaches to actual physical and other faces in the everyday world. This will help to concretise more specifically how this kind of thinking can really help ordinary face-seers in this era of faciality. Persons are more than faces; in that Ford is correct. But the specific faces of persons, human and divine, need careful consideration if they are to attract the respect and honour flowing from the face of God in Christ. Physical face, I would suggest, deserves to be treated as more than symbol or cipher.

Roger Scruton is a theologically-minded philosopher rather than a theologian. In *The Face of God* (2012), he tries to redeem the abstract, transcendent face of God that means nothing so that it becomes a discernible presence in the world. Like

---

[2]   Ford does deal with shame elsewhere in his work. See Hardy and Ford (1984) and commentary in Pattison (2000, 195–6).

some Catholic critics, he believes that God's face, which he understands as God's presence, has disappeared because people are looking in the wrong way, and also in the wrong direction (Buckley 1987; Lash 1996; Moser 2008). They make the mistake of thinking to find it in the thin world of metaphysical philosophy: 'The God of the philosophers disappeared behind the world, because he was described in the third person, and not addressed in the second' (Scruton 2012, 45).

God's presence, like the human conscious self, is not to be found as an object in the world of nature understood by scientific enquiry in terms of cause and effect. It is realised by participating in the believing communion of human beings. Here Godself is revealed in complex personal dialogue and in face-to-face encounters:

> The communion is the real presence of God among us, and it is from such acts of participation that we come to see who God is and how he relates to us. It is through the communion that we come face to face with God. (Scruton 2012, 20)

Scruton goes on to argue for the importance of the face as the place where conscious persons are known and interact in the world of actions, intentions and responsibilities. Adopting a very traditional, basically pre-modern view of the relationship between inner and outer aspects of the person (Porter 2005), he claims:

> The science of the human being ... does not acknowledge the thing that makes faces so important for us – namely, that they are the outward form and image of the soul, the lamp lit in our world by the subject behind. It is through understanding the face that we begin to see how it is that subjects make themselves known in the world of objects. (Scruton 2012, 72)

The face is a kind of 'balcony of the soul' from which a light shines through that is not of this world (Scruton 2012, 78). I take it that implicitly it is something of the divine in the human that is alluded to here, though this is not clear. The physical face, then, is a vehicle for subjectivity to shine into the world of objects 'as though lit from behind', revealing self-conscious and interpersonal states of mind with, and to, others (Scruton 2012, 81). The face is both vehicle and symbol of non-objectified human subjectivity that is like divine non-objectified subjectivity. It should therefore not be treated as an object.

Objectification occurs, for example, when faces are commodified in celebrity and consumer culture. Here, faces cease to be a relation between subjects and are converted into relationships between objects so that 'the light that is not of this world' is extinguished:

> Through the face the subject appears in our world, and it appears there haloed by prohibitions. It is untouchable, inviolable, consecrated. It is not to be treated as an object, or to be thrown into the great computer and calculated away. (Scruton 2012, 49, 109–10)

Scruton agrees with Levinas that faces and the subjectivity they represent form the foundation for ethics; they are the locus of the search for righteousness, responsibility, trust, guilt and so on (Scruton 2012, 74). When faces are commodified and detached from subjectivity, shame and alienation set in:

> ... when people become objects for each other, love withers and dies. The result of this defacing of the erotic is not hatred, but an ever-expanding heartlessness. (Scruton 2012, 113)

If humans are temples, sacred spaces for God to dwell in, this kind of defacement and desecration of the subjective pollutes the sacred, so God cannot dwell there. Sacredness should protect from this kind of denigration, whether it concerns the faces of persons, or the face of the world:

> Persons can be harmed in ways that are not adequately summarised in the idea of a violation of rights. They can be polluted, desecrated, defiled – and in many cases this disaster takes bodily form. (Scruton 2012, 158)

The real presence and face of God, God as subject, or 'I AM', is to be found in the worshipping community. This group prepares for the experience of God and has revelation granted to it in response. Here God is present in the relational subjectivity that characterises human relationships, presenting a vision of sacrificial love exemplified in the human face of Christ, the real presence of a human subject. At the eucharist, then, there are moments of both communion and gift. These constitute non-objectified presence; they renew the world and its inhabitants as subjects to be revered, not objects to be used. Adopting a subjective view of God and others thus preserves truth, goodness and beauty within the perimeter of sanctity.

There are a number of important positive points to note about Scruton's analysis. He gives priority to face both as physical entity and as symbol. This is linked to important ethical issues of respect and shame. Face-to-face relations, properly construed and intersubjective, create sanctity in a world in which people easily fall into alienation and commodification; Scruton has some very useful phenomenological observations to offer here.

Scruton also finds a way of writing the face of God back into the world as an important category that underwrites subjective relations. Indeed, God cannot be found outwith a community that is prepared to seek relationship with God because God is not an object. This is a very important theological move, sometimes made particularly by Catholics (Moser 2008). It has the possible downside that God then becomes in some sense experientially captured within a particular community, only finding significance in the wider world through that community. However, this also highlights the importance of the believing eucharistic community as the place where God's presence and glory can be seen and encountered in different kinds of subjective engagement. Not for Scruton the 'bleak theology of Karl

Barth' where 'there is nothing to be known of God except that he is unknowable, concealed behind every image, every story, every idea even, which purports to reveal him' (Scruton 2012, 143). In the community of faith, the face of God can be seen and known, particularly in sacramental activity, though Scruton does not really dwell on the nature and features of God's face beyond considering the moral features and face of Christ that inspire sacrifice and love.

Scruton's 'take home' message is a practical and important one: enface the people and places around you with subjective significance and respect and then you will avoid desecrating and defacing the world, creating shame and alienation as modern consumerist and ratio-instrumental practices do. The face of God, then, here again acts as a catalyst to respectful living and acting in the world.

Some of the most illuminating, challenging approaches to thinking about the face of God and what it means for the recovery of the sight of human faces theologically have been inspired by those interested in the Jewish concept of *Shekinah*. *Shekinah* denotes 'the personification and hypostasis of God's "indwelling" or "presence" in the world' (Scholem 1991, 141). This presence may be hidden or visible, but it denotes God Godself, insofar as God may be present in a specific place or event. It may be denoted by a supernatural radiance or light, and can be equated with *kabhod*, God's glory. Its roots lie in the pillar of cloud in Exodus (Exod. 33:9, 11) that denoted God's presence, but also it relates to the theology and experience of the Temple where God's glory was seen. Significantly, this hypostatisation of God's essence was something that accompanied Israel, the people who see God, even when they were exiled. It therefore shared Israel's joys, sufferings, persecutions and hopes. In medieval kabbalistic theology, *Shekinah* increasingly acquired feminine qualities and was seen as almost separate from God so that she/it faces God as well as facing humans as the creative power of God in the world (Scholem 1991, 1996, 111–16).

Two modern theologians, one Christian and one Jewish, have developed the significance of *Shekinah* for seeing the faces of God and humans in the world, Moltmann and Raphael. I will deal with each of them in turn here.

Jürgen Moltmann is one of the few post-Reformation male Protestant theologians to affirm that embodied humanity has a place in collaborating with God actively in partnership to bring about the reality of redemption on earth (Robinson 2011). His collection of essays, *Sun of Righteousness, Arise!*, explores many of the themes that I have raised in this book. Against the 'gnostic Christianity of our own time', Moltmann emphasises the embodied and immanent significance of theological ideas, calling for a new spirituality of the senses, the body and the sensory world that is attentive to bodily life and witnesses to the present redemption of the body as well as the soul (Moltmann 2010, 181, 65). Taking up the theme of *Shekinah* as developed in kabbalistic theology, Moltmann argues that this makes God self-differentiate and give Godself into Israel's fate and condition. God is thus placed in a position of dependence upon humans, for it is they alone who can sanctify God's name and redeem God from alienation (Moltmann 2010, 107–8).

It is in this light that the incarnation of Jesus should be interpreted; the indwelling, self-surrendering God or *Shekinah* is seen in Jesus, and the movement from and towards God is made manifest as participation in human life and suffering. Against the Jewish *Shekinah* tradition, however, Jesus dies and rises again, rather than suffering with Israel and leading them home. Furthermore, Jesus' self-sacrifice is seen as being for the sake of the world, not just for Israel. This opens the way for a wider Christian love in the power of the Spirit in which 'there comes into being the reciprocal *Shekinah* of God in human beings and of human beings in God' that brings present concrete hope, healing and liberation for life to human kind in all its dimensions (Moltmann 2010, 115).

Going on to meditate on the significance of seeing God, Moltmann starts with human facial experience in rather general terms. He then distinguishes *Shekinah* as God's face in descent into creation from God's glory, and differentiates this from God's exalted face that cannot be beheld in this life without lethal consequences. The *Shekinah* of descent is a friendly face on the same level as human faces. This was the face that God showed to God's friends like Moses and Jacob in the OT; it is available in the contemporary material world as God's living and transforming presence. This presence is physical, involving all the senses. It is communal not individualistic, and it is fragmentary and partial, a foreshadowing of the vision of the full glory of God, when deified humans and God will know each other fully in a joyful, mutual and reciprocal way as friends in community and likeness. There will not be union with God, but mutual knowing as humans have the full enjoyment of God.

In the meanwhile, the Holy Spirit brings the future into present and moves people into the orbit of the shining face of God:

> To see and know God face to face is not simultaneous now, but will be a simultaneous seeing and knowing then. Now it is just that God knows us from his side; then it will be a mutual knowing. It is not enough to recognize that "the light of God's countenance" rests upon us in blessing. That light is also meant to reflect the glory of God which will shine on our "unveiled faces" (2 Cor. 3:18) ... [H]ere Paul is evidently insisting on complete reciprocity, as the phrase "face to face" seems to suggest. Why? Because it is one in the same light in which God sees human beings and human beings see God. (Moltmann 2010, 183)

God and world become fully mutually indwelling or present to each other, 'then the perfect perichoresis of God and world comes into being as the environment in which God and human beings look upon each other face-to-face' (Moltmann 2010, 186).

In the context of the present work, Moltmann's sense that the seeing of God's face is in some way physical, this-worldly, communal, multi-sensorial, figured and experienced in this world now, not just beyond it, in the future, is valuable. The idea of deification as the thing that makes it possible for humans to see God, and the idea that presence is real and mutual, so that God and humans dance together to reflect and enjoy, perhaps even helping to create, each other's image, also seems very significant. But at the same time, this thinking seems loose and non-referential. It is not clear what the concrete outworking of discerning the *Shekinah* amongst us now really is in terms of seeing and relating to others, and to God. The future vision figured in the present quickly becomes a deferred vision, even a denied one, because it is not apparent what it means on earth.

Moltmann himself sometimes slips into using the language of contemplation rather than physical encounter. Although he wants to talk concretely about bodies, faces and material realities, his consideration of sight and seeing face-to-face as a human experience seem disappointingly non-specific. There are no mechanisms or clues as to how seeing of God and other humans in community might be better enabled or recognised in advance of the eschatological completion of mutual recognition. If one were harsh, one might say that it is not clear that his approach is much more than a set of readily available commonplace truths, for example, about the importance of faces in human encounters, that then have an idealising, sensualising theological gloss placed on them. Moltmann is usefully influenced by *Shekinah* theology and the importance of mutuality and recognition in friendship between humans and God. Unfortunately, he does not pin down his vision and what it means firmly enough. He does not want it to be a disembodied, heavenly abstraction, but neither does he not really make it a realisable bodily and earthly possibility.

For real depth of encounter with the idea and importance of *Shekinah*, particularly as it relates to real faces and earthly possibilities, one has to turn to the stunning work of Jewish thealogian, Melissa Raphael in *The Female Face of God in Auschwitz*. By contrast with many of the other works mentioned here, Raphael (2003) takes a phenomenological, experiential approach to creating a constructive and imaginative theology of human and divine face and face-to-face relations. To do this, she correlates the concrete experiences of women in Auschwitz, cleaning and preserving each other's faces, with the theological motif of *Shekinah*.

Shekinah understood through the kabbalistic tradition represents a basically female divine immanence in creation and with God's chosen people, Israel, the people who see God, wherever they may be. The people of Israel can only be fit for, and see the face of God, if the image of God is pure in them and in their faces. To be clean and pure is to be visible to God and so not to be forgotten by God. Because God has placed *Shekinah*, his image and face in Israel, if God's people are defiled, then God's image cannot be seen – the people cannot see God. But equally, God cannot see Godself reflected in Israel. Israel must see God if God is to see Israel.[3] If this does not happen, God is alienated and exiled from Godself. Both God and God's people then need to be healed and purified so that they can

---

[3] This perception is remarkably similar to the psychoanalytic perception of the child's 'magic eye' whereby to be seen, it is necessary to see the seer in some kind of mutual gaze. See Winnicott (1974), Wurmser (1995, 94–7).

see each other again. This is work that has to be done by both God and Israel. God is at risk and cannot be healed if God's people are not also healed.

Raphael places alongside this the facial experiences of Jewish women in Auschwitz. Although she does not use the word shame much, if at all, in her book, she clearly describes a process of pollution, desecration, erasure and defilement of women's faces and bodies where faces, whether in photographs or real life were destroyed, mutilated, covered with faeces and dirt and disparaged. Amidst this, women cared for and enfaced each other by small acts of washing and care using dirty cloths, spittle and other means. These real acts of compassionate care for the faces of others were analogous to lighting the Sabbath candle at home to invite the mother-face of God, the *Shekinah* into the home (Raphael 2003, 61).

In a context in which God's face could not be seen because of the impurity and defilement of Israel in the concentration camps, a glimpse, a spark of *Shekinah* could then be seen. God's face could be seen in the faces of humanity which contains the face of God:

> When a woman in Auschwitz saw the face of the other and went out to meet her she can also be said to have gone out to meet God. Auschwitz was a mirror onto the suffering face of God; God was seen and authoritative in the face of the suffering other. (Raphael 2003, 105)

Patriarchal models and theologies of God failed in the face of perverse patriarchal power at Auschwitz. Rejecting the tradition of God's presence as absence, *deus absconditus* (particularly valued in Christian Lutheran theology and often characterised, as we noted with Bonhoeffer, as God opening up a space for masculine development and responsibility), Raphael asserts that God as *Shekinah* was never absent in Auschwitz. Like the moon in daylight, God could not be seen, but remained present:

> Presence, a keeping watch, is a function of love. A present God paces back and forth, circling the object of her concern; an absent God seems to have walked away. (Raphael 2003, 47)

God's face could not be seen, being obscured, disguised and made imperceptible by the impurity and defilement of the situation. However, God was not either hidden or absent:

> In Auschwitz, to have seen only God's back was no longer to witness a God whose power and glory is too mighty to behold, it was to see a God whose humiliation and sorrow was such that he could not face us; could not bear the sight of us. (Raphael 2003, 50)

Where acts of relational cleansing and care took place in the context of excremental assault, God's face was recognised in the faces of Jewish women.

God became immanent and redemption could be experienced, for relational care 'is the sign and medium of God's care within the world':

> The transcendent God is immanent in the aperture made between the one seeing and opening to the other. That is the redemptive moment. (Raphael 2003, 41, 42)

Far from God being unrepresentable, 'God's face is visible and his love figurable as it passes across the face of the Just Man or … Just Woman' (Raphael 2003, 57). Thus Auschwitz 'could yet be a mirror of God's looking and seeing face', and profanation could be overcome at the interface between faces (Raphael 2003, 81). God is then 'the face between faces' whose glory is reflected back into the world by the redemptive work of women (Raphael 2003, 88). Amidst the mass erasure of faces, it was possible for people to make real, restore and heal the face of God, thus redeeming it and making the face of God visible to God once more.

Raphael's is a rich, suggestive text; here I simply want to note a few, particularly relevant points that may prompt further reflection later. Raphael takes human faces and real experiences of care seriously. The practical and theological significance of what seeing the faces of God and humans really means in concrete, physical terms is elucidated. The face of God becomes not pious vague hope, a doctrinal optional extra, but a vital accompaniment for life and survival. Her thoughts about healing, restoration and theology are rooted in a real praxis of care in the context of the shame and defilement.

A very particularly Jewish emphasis in Raphael's thought is the idea of mutual partnership between God and God's people. In much formal Christian theology, while humans have a part to play in seeing and reflecting God's glory in the world, God in Godself is not affected by human suffering. Thus humanity can only be the beneficiary of God's grace, it has no role in restoring or making God's face to shine and be visible (Robinson 2011). The theology of *Shekinah* makes partnership and mutuality between God and humanity more central in the process of saving face. If humanity's face is besmirched and defiled, so it does not shine, then God's face cannot shine either – humans and God find face together.

Arguably, Christianity can also lay claim to a similar notion of shared face. However, in practice, the face of Christ is seen to be more important than any human face. Christian theologies, as we have seen, then tend to focus around God's mysterious absence in the dead face of Christ, seen as a challenge for humans to take responsibility for the world. The radical mutual presence of the face of God and cleansed human faces in Auschwitz challenges vague, non-specific Christian claims that somehow God's glory will shine through human faces to some kind of eschatological completion. Raphael's theology roots the mutual seeing of divine and human faces within the context of a challenging world in which faces are lost and defiled. If humans and God need each other to find their faces, then the quest for lost faces becomes a lot more urgent and also much more practical.

Turning specifically now to practical theological perspectives on face, the nearest thing that I have found to a practical theological approach to face is Shults' and Sandage's *The Faces of Forgiveness* (2003). The authors, a psychologist and a theologian, conduct an inter-textual dialogue between a 'hermeneutics of face', by which they mean real, physical faces, and a theory of forgiveness as dynamic relationality. They aim to get beyond forensic and economic understandings typical in some theories of redemption to provide an account of facially related forgiveness as transformative reality.

For Shults and Standage (2003, 17),

> The human face is an embodied symbolic mediator of intersubjective communication that shapes the relational episodes that we call forgiveness and unforgiveness.

If forgiveness is intersubjective and relational, face is the important locus, symbol and metaphor of where it occurs. Indeed, face can actually mediate the process of forgiveness, whether it be intra-psychic or interpersonal. It is here that 'facial hermeneutics', 'the ability to read or interpret the faces of others' become important (Shults and Sandage 2003, 44). The face of recognition signifies forgiveness when offences have occurred. Thus face is saved.

Unfortunately, recognition is hindered by sources of systematic alienation or shame production by means such as totalisation, scapegoating, exclusion/ assimilation, self-objectification and denigration and narcissistic wounding (Shults and Sandage 2003, 71 ff.). These systemic and interpersonal dynamics that impede the acceptance of forgiveness need to be overcome by creating a sense of common humanity with empathy and humility. This allows people to experience a forgiving and accepting facial presence, the 'smile on a beloved face', as Simone Weil characterised God's love (Shults and Sandage 2003, 90).

The book explores biblical material on the face of God, but emphasises the notion of God's face as being a loving, saving presence. It is 'a faithful and loving face that will never go away' that meets a fundamental human desire (Shults and Sandage 2003, 106). It cannot be escaped or manipulated; it reveals and conceals God simultaneously. In this context, the face of Jesus, enigmatic though it is, allows people to see the glory of God which is also reflected in the face of the Holy Spirit, all three persons of the Trinity being faces of God. All of these faces mediate grace and peace.

Salvation and forgiveness are understood as union with Christ and the Spirit. This occurs through life in community created around the dynamic Trinitarian relations in the Godhead. Forgiveness is not, then, a substantial, forensic or legal matter, but an intersubjective, relational thing, a way of being in proper dynamic relationship, as the persons of the Trinity are. People are incorporated as sharers in the divine. So forgiveness is rooted in divine grace and made real in *koinonia* (fellowship) that reflects the Trinitarian God and intensifies personal being. It is a sharing in the fellowship of divine glory as people are gradually transformed into the image of Christ: 'The divine glory is the shared relational being of the triune

God, not an attribute of the heaviest single person in the universe' (Shults and Sandage 2003, 168, 209, 212).

Transformation of individuals within fellowship, mediated through the faces of those in the community, allows guilt and shame to be dealt with relationally. Being forgiven is like seeing the smiling face of a child restored in relationship (Shults and Sandage 2003, 254). The eucharist and worshipping life of the church community are taken to be exemplary and paradigmatic here.

Shults and Standage provide a theologically sophisticated model of the relational Trinity rooted in biblical insights and Christian orthodoxy. This relational life is opened up to include humans who share in the glory of God that abolishes shame. This model is dynamic, social, communal and helpful in providing a basis for dealing practically with shame and guilt, especially since it clearly implies that the shame-reducing effect of the face or presence of God are mediated in lived communal life.

Less positively, however, Shults and Sandage are inclined to seeing God's face rather metaphorically and theoretically. Furthermore, I am not sure that forgiveness is the most appropriate organising category to use for the importance of dealing with shame, as it is more guilt/offence rather than shame/person-oriented (Pattison 2000, chapter 8). Perhaps acceptance and reconciliation would have been more apposite categories to use to include both offence and alienation. However, it can clearly be seen, once again, that the face or presence of God, mediated through real faces and communal experience is integrally linked with the overcoming of shame and alienation. Shults and Sandage are right to take seriously the relational image of God, the relational nature of glory, and to apply these categories to human predicaments and communities.

Conclusion

What are the overall themes and resources provided by the theological sources considered here, and what are the weaknesses and areas that need possible development?

There are some clear areas of consensus. The vision and face of God is an important category. However, mostly, it is not clear what this vision/face is like. This may be due to an appropriate theological humility that preserves the ultimate unknowability of God, God's hidden essence. Equally, it may represent intellectual and cultural reservations about thinking hard about what the face and vision of God might be. This tends to result in the vision of God being deferred in any very substantive form to another place and another time in the eschatological completion of creation, something that is hoped for, but not really sensually grasped in the present.

Having acknowledged the ungraspability of the face and presence of God, all these writers agree that it is important for human beings in the present age. If God cannot ultimately be grasped, God can be sensed, and has a transforming real effect on embodied sensual people now.

In the community of belief, God's face and vision can be seen proximately and presently. The affirmation that the main place in which we glimpse the vision of the face of God is here and amidst fellow human beings is enormously important. However, it is often difficult to see exactly what this means. Christian theologians emphasise the life of people in the community of believers. They particularly point to the eucharist as a place where God and those who reflect God's face and image can encounter each other and gradually be changed into God's likeness. However, what this means in practice is mostly not adumbrated, other than in terms of general hopefulness.

All the Christian theologians considered emphasise that the seeing of God has communal, physical and sensual aspects, so the vision of God affects the real material world. However, they are mostly not specific about what this really means either. While some theologians talk specifically about aspects of human physical faces and their meanings, they do not mostly go into the significance of this theologically or practically. They mostly remain at the level of general attitudes and, as with the face of God, use face as a metaphor to talk about presence, and attitudes to it. So real, physical human faces remain in some ways as hazy and obscure as the divine face, but not because they are unavailable for inspection, as the divine face might be held to be.

All the writers considered, even if they do not give much direct attention to it, imply that seeing the face of God and the reflection of God's face in others has important implications for respecting and honouring others. The face and presence of God eliminates pollution and shame; it opens up a world of acceptance and belonging in which people can see God and each other properly and respectfully. This is an interesting continuity with the biblical witnesses discussed earlier.

That all of the theologians we have considered here should lay emphasis on the ethical difference and responsibility that seems to correlate with seeing or trying to see the face of God in humans is perhaps unsurprising; they have all been directly influenced by Levinas' philosophy of face as the source of ethics and relationship. But it is noteworthy that the revaluation of the world and people, enfacing both, seems intrinsically linked to seeing the face of God.

And it is perhaps not coincidental in that context that nearly all these thinkers then favour notions of relationality and possibly even some kind of mutuality and partnership (at least amongst humans) in realising the vision of God. Raphael's Jewish theology is the only one that goes so far as to make the vision of God dependent on human as much as divine activity, so that God cannot be healed and restored to vision of Godself without human engagement. However, all the others seem also to be pushed in the direction of some kind of dynamic relationship of mutual reflection and change that engages humans and the divine together. In joyous, personal face-to-face relationships, all the faces involved shine and smile.

Perhaps there is a sense in which that is true for divine-human relations, too. It certainly seems to be an impetus within thinking about seeing the divine face.

So to the limits and weaknesses of present thinking about the face of God. First, there is not much of it; what there is seems somewhat sketchy and rhetorical. It mostly seems to be based more on hope than on the experience of seeing and doing things differently. The vision of God, then, seems rather far off, and in some ways uninspiring compared to other themes that might be explored in theology, for example the nature of the Trinity, the implications of resurrection. While divine presence is certainly an important theme, it is assumed, not fleshed out, despite the incarnational thinking and other doctrines that might point to this being a central theme of Christian theology. The face of God remains hazy, lost amidst words about it, basically deferred till the *eschaton*.

Similarly, the real, specific faces of humans do not seem to appear much in these theological accounts. Faces are mostly turned into symbols, generalities and texts, losing their specificity and visibility. As with the divine face, they are mostly regarded as symbols or surrogates for some general sense of presence or for ideas about persons and face.

Allied to this, there is then a lack of specificity about behaviour and practice. How does one recognise, honour or enhance the vision of the divine face in everyday practice and face-to-face relationships? While Raphael, and Shults and Sandage, give concrete examples of how physical faces can be cared for and mediate theological realities like the presence of God and forgiveness, even they do not really suggest extensive concrete ways of evaluating and changing actual behaviour. They thus contribute to the general sense that paying attention to actual faces is a 'good thing', but not really to changing facially based practices.

In this context, it is perhaps worth highlighting that shame, a visual and facially related emotion, is not dealt with in any depth. It is assumed that the vision of God, either direct or indirect, abolishes shame and produces joyous inclusion. While this is a positive thought, shame is a complex phenomenon used by all human groups to police their communities and values (Pattison 2000). Ford mentions that those who are not generous like God will exclude themselves from God's feast to live in the realm of shame – this is an acute and very relevant observation, but this kind of awareness of limits and exclusion highlights the fact that there are serious issues here that need more attention.

This brings me to my final point. Seeing the face of God, whether directly or indirectly through the faces of humans made in God's image, should surely imply a change in the praxis of seeing. Coakley (2002, 130–52) suggests that redemption/salvation, like resurrection, should have a physical effect on human bodies and senses. To see the risen Christ is to have one's senses transformed. Those who share in the resurrection of Christ should see, and so treat, others differently as they are transformed physically and spiritually into the likeness of God. It is not enough to think and believe cognitively differently; our ways of seeing and acting on an everyday basis need to be transformed so that lost human faces are saved and God's face, too, becomes more visible. It is this practice of seeing in such a way as to recognise and respect faces, human and divine, that I want to explore further at the conclusion of this book. The next chapter, however, is devoted to creating some theological horizons for developing a positive, critical and practical theology for seeing faces.

Chapter 8
Shining Up the Face of God: Practical Theological Horizons for Enfacement

Anoint and cheer our soiled face
with the abundance of thy grace.

(Veni, creator Spiritus)

We are united with God in matter, in our flesh and his flesh.

(McCabe 2010, v)

I want, now, to take some suggestive images and ideas emerging from the broad historical tradition of seeing the face of God to develop some practical theological horizons. These might form a basis for taking faces, human and divine, more seriously, so that lost faces can more easily be found, recognised and restored. In doing this, I adopt an imaginative approach. I do not intend to provide a consistent, coherent theology for seeing faces. Rather, I intend to play with some themes and ideas that may be evocative and illuminative, opening up possibilities for saving the faces of humans and of God. So I will be using theological language and concepts unsystematically, loosely and as an inspiration or provocation to seeing faces differently. At best, what I hope to do is to create a few theological 'handholds' that might help to get a better grip on engaging with faces in practice.

I do not defend any single orthodoxy or ontology here. My thoughts will be informed by the ideas and insights that have struck me as insightful and valuable in considering the previous theological material, including material from the Jewish tradition. Similarly, I do not try to prioritise any particular aspect of doctrine as more important than others. The only theological norm adopted is that the aim of the Christian life, and of Christian theology, is to prepare people to see and recognise the face of God, however understood. Beyond that, I will simply draw on ideas and motifs, even repressed and minority ideas and motifs, that might prompt a fuller appreciation of saving faces in the contemporary world. This loose, multi-perspectival approach is, I hope, consonant with the mercurial, multifaceted nature of faces themselves.

By constructing a loose, but interlinked, 'web' of ideas and concepts, my intention is to fund a critical 'theological imaginary' that might inspire and support further practical and theoretical exploration (Brueggemann 1993; Taylor 2004). I aim to create horizons – horizons being things that do not necessarily touch, and which are situated in different directions – for practical theology, rather than creating a unitary, normative practical theology that can then be rolled out and applied. Having created this practical theological imaginary, I will then go on to look at practices of seeing faces in the next chapter of the book.

Seeing Differently

Perhaps the most challenging aspect of the theological traditions we have been examining has been the material and physical nature of seeing the divine. While in the modern Western world we can cope with the idea of some kind of metaphorical idea of seeing as denoting the presence of God, at least the early parts of the Christian tradition appear to insist on some kind of real physical seeing of God as God comes to reign on earth. As I noted *in situ*, seeing is a culturally inflected and enabled capacity; in different cultures and contexts, different kinds of things can be seen, and in different ways. Thus in some cultures people see what many Westerners would regard as invisible beings like angels, demons or saints.

While writing this book, I have been asking professional academic theological colleagues, why can't we see God? Most of them, understandably, look at me with mild surprise and then mumble something about God being invisible, not an object in the world and so on, and then change the subject. One of them, an Eastern Orthodox theologian, bucked the trend, saying that we probably could see God but do not do so because we are not looking![1] This seems to resonate with Tugwell's comment on Albert the Great and Pseudo-Dionysius: 'If Dionysius and Albert are right, we are bumping into God the whole time' (Tugwell 1988, 93).

If seeing is culturally influenced, so that the ways that we see are in some ways arbitrary, and if put alongside this is the idea that perhaps God can be seen with the physical eye, even if Westerners do not see God, what emerges is a challenge for us to think more broadly and creatively about practices of seeing (Morgan 2012). Generally, Western intellectuals live in a world of thin, objectivist Cartesian seeing in which intellect is separated off from the sensual world (Chidester 1992, 131–5; Jay 1988; Pattison 2007b, 31–7).[2] We also tend to privilege the word and concept over vision and experience (Orsi 2005). This is not something that can be changed by fiat of the will. We inhabit the scopic regime that we have inherited; the habits of a lifetime or of a culture cannot be changed overnight. However, the tradition of

---

[1]   The theologian concerned was Andrew Louth. He went on to point out to me that in the Eastern tradition for at least the first millennium visions of God were regarded as essential by some for appointment to ecclesiastical office and for valid celebration of the liturgy (Louth 1989, 99–100).

[2]   For an interesting account of how vision can be socially inflected and changed so that it is possible even for Western rational academics to see supernatural or transcendent beings, see Haberman (1994). Haberman, a cultural anthropologist, has an unexpected, unwilled vision while taking part in a pilgrimage in India, which he then has to make sense of. See also Orsi (1985, 1996, 2005). For thick seeing in religion, see Morgan (2005), Nightingale (2005), Pattison (2007b).

a thicker, more sensual kind of theological seeing, not solely based on inward or mystical ideas of vision, might usefully question assumptions about seeing God's face in the human world. If our senses can be educated and changed, along with our hearts and minds, then there is perhaps the prospect for a richer seeing of God and humans. At the very least, this possibility should not be arbitrarily dismissed, particularly if the reign of God is conceived to be partly a material reality in this world, not just an aspect of the world to come.[3]

The tradition then challenges our present assumptions and practices relating to seeing God and might be taken to suggest broader, more material approaches that are also creative and imaginative. These are figured in the work and thought of Nicholas of Cusa and William Blake.

Nicholas of Cusa and Creative Sight

Nicholas of Cusa, a fifteenth-century theologian, did not believe that God was in any simple sense visible to the human eye. However, he had a sophisticated theology of God's engagement with the world. Taking the words, '*theos*', God, and '*theoria*', sight, to be integrally related, he thought that it was God's sight and seeing that brought into being, and sustained, all created things: 'You … are my God who sees everything, and your seeing is your working. And thus you work all things' (Nicholas of Cusa 1997, 242). God's sight was creative and sustaining of the whole created order; through that order God could be indirectly discerned.

This kind of thinking might then be a spur to contemporary Western Christians to take seeing the material creation and all the creatures within it more seriously. We are seen by God, which is what allows us to become and to be; by the same token, we can see God in God's creation. This would seem to add force to the idea that we might 'bump into God all the time'.

If we want to see the faces of God and of humans better, then we need to think more creatively about seeing. The Christian tradition will not easily allow all seeing to be just a metaphor for thought and presence. Part of undertaking this thinking, which might be specifically addressed by theologians concerned with words and understandings about God, might be to enrich and reconnect the language and metaphors of the senses and physical world to embodied, everyday experience.

---

[3]   I am very conscious that I have not discussed the relationship between inner and outer images of God thus far. I do not intend to do so here, but it is important to recognise that there is an integral link between the images that people have of God in their hearts and minds and what might be seen of God in the external perceptual world. Images can flick across media and through societies and persons in conscious and unconscious ways, and the face of God is no exception to this. And it is inner images and impressions that can then enable the recognition of external images (Pattison 2007b). See further Auge (1999), Belting (2005), Gruzinski (2001), Koerner (2004), Pattison (2007b, 74–5), Rizzuto (1979), Schaap-Jonker (2008).

Augustine, and others before and after him, used the language of the senses beautifully and almost synaesthetically, to describe and give substance to invisible, spiritual things:

> You called and cried out loud and shattered my deafness. You were radiant and resplendent, you put flight to my blindness. You were fragrant, and I drew in my breath and now pant after you. I tasted you, and I feel but hunger and thirst for you. You touched me, and I am set on fire to attain the peace which is yours. (Augustine 1991, 201; Chidester 1992)

In the modern age, physical and inner sight have become completely separate. God is mainly to be found within the self and in the realm of the invisible. Perhaps, then, the time has come to reverse the Platonically inspired spiritualisation of the senses and of God better to understand and relate to the physical, material world and divine presence within it.

New theological metaphors and language are needed that help us recognise the physical presence of God so the world can be appreciated God's visible body, not just as a passing epiphenomenon (Jantzen 1984). If Origen produced a theological language of spiritual senses, we need a language of sensual spirituality that will help us to see the face of God and others better and to restore something of the concrete reality of God's visible presence in the world (Coakley 2002; Gavrilyuk and Coakley 2012; Jantzen 1984; McFague 1993; Rahner 1979, 81–103). This reversal will demand much poetic imagination so that bodies and faces are revalued as something more than pale shadows and unsatisfactory imitations of the invisible God (Alves 1986; McFague 1993). Cusa was able to create a thick language and concept of the vision of God as a seeing that brings the world into being and sustaining it. We need similarly to find thicker and richer languages to enable the seeing of a God who 'bumps into us in everyday life', to find words that redress the dominance of the aural and invisible.

William Blake and the Value of Faces

A perhaps rather unlikely exemplary seer, and one who serves as a benchmark for the distance that needs to be travelled in the development of thick seeing of faces here, is the poet and artist William Blake (1757–1827). Blake is often regarded as otherworldly, eccentric, even mad. He owes this reputation partly to the fact that he saw visions constantly throughout his life. When he was four, 'God put his head to the window and set the child screaming', and he was beaten for telling his mother that he had seen the prophet Ezekiel under a tree in the fields (Bentley 2001, 19). While Blake's visionary experiences are often linked to imagination, it needs to be remembered that Blake was an acute observer of human life and of human faces. He was a devotee of Lavater's work and illustrated an edition of his book on physiognomy, as well as taking great care to depict faces, even of visionary beings, very carefully (Bentley 2001, 118, 368–88).

For Blake, the divine and human realms were not separated as they are in consensual modern consciousness; human faces were one means of reading divinity on earth (Porter 2005, 279, 288–9). Blake,

> challenges the way in which we divide human and divine, body and soul, the sacred and the secular into mutually exclusive opposites, rather than allowing "contraries" to exist alongside each other in creative tension. (Rowland 2011, 233)

Blake regarded all humans as being partakers of the divine nature. Like him, all could see the world and other people with the transfiguring eye of God. Therefore all people were potentially prophets and seers who could enjoy *theosis* in relationship with other people and with God (Rowland 2011, 172).

Blake was also sharply critical of institutional religion and all political structures which constrain the indwelling divine potential of all humans. Through inspiration, imagination, art and experience, this potential could be realised on earth, not just in heaven: 'if the doors of perception were cleansed every thing would appear to man as it is: infinite' (Rowland 2011, 86).

Blake thus has a high doctrine of material reality and human physiognomy and potential transfigured by imagination and vision. It is something of this kind of specific, yet creative, imaginative vision that fights human oppression and shame that is needed to transvalue human faces and help us to take them, together with the divine face, seriously. It is a measure of how far we have to go that Blake's approach may seem fanciful, far-fetched and unrealistic. We need his closeness of attention to the material order along with his width of human vision to gain a more material sense of the real presence of divine face amongst us in the contemporary world.

Constructing the Face of God: Seeing/Enfacement as Relational, Communal and Embodied

One theme that emerges not only from Blake, but from several voices in the theological traditions considered, is that of humans and God together being involved in the work of enfacement and mutual redemption. In Blake's treatment of Job, 'the divine in the human means that the redemptive narrative of Job must also include the redemption of divinity' (Rowland 2011, 58). We have come across similar thinking elsewhere. The relationship between God and Israel depicted in the OT was one of covenantal partnership, albeit that the partnership was unequal (Brueggemann 2009, 60ff.). The cult of the Temple seems to have relied upon a mutual meeting between God and God's people which led to the mutual shining of faces in which divine glory shone forth (Barker 2004, 2011). While the idea of humans having any part in the creation or recognition of the image of God was lost after Aquinas, this theme is picked up by modern process theologians. They argue that humans contribute something towards God, albeit as junior partners (Robinson 2011; Poling 2011, 21). Those influenced by the *Shekinah* tradition of Jewish thought also maintain that human redemption is bound up with divine redemption, and that humans therefore have work to do in healing and making visible the face of the divine (Moltmann 2010; Raphael 2003).

In more prosaic, sociological mode, it could be argued that without a human community that makes real and sees the face of God, God has no face on earth. It is only as God is seen, recognised and embodied in human communities that God has a face or presence (Stoller 1997). And it is in those same communities that humans find their own faces and see the face of God reflected in the faces of others.

So there is a real sense in which God and humans can be regarded as making each other's faces and presence real. Drawing on Martin Buber's thought, Raphael writes:

> For Buber, it is basic to Judaism that, "true human life is conceived to be a life lived in the presence of God". The radiance of divine glory or presence "glows dimly in all human beings, every one of them; but it does not shine in its full brightness within them – only between them". Divine presence may be revealed within the individual, "but it attains to its earthly fullness only where ... individual being open themselves to one another, disclose themselves to one another, help one another; where immediacy is established between one human being and another". Where this occurs ... "the eternal rises in the Between". It is in "this seemingly empty space" that God and the community are realised. (Raphael 2003, 100–101; Buber 1967, 108–13)

This perspective produces several prompts for contemporary Christian theologies of enfacement.

First, it suggests that enfacement, discovering and saving the faces of the divine and the human, is a mutually shared activity between God and humans, and between humans and their fellows.

Secondly, mutual enfacement is a relational, dynamic matter. The faces of God and of humans are not static; they are continually being created, sustained or violated. There is no fixed endpoint at which face is realised. The quest for mutual mirroring and enfacement in ongoing, not final: and it depends on partners and others being willing to be act together to bring faces into being. If all are mirrors to each other, if humans in some way mirror the image of God, and *vice versa*, then enfacement is an eternal dance or *perichoresis*, requiring relational movement and continual engagement (Winnicott 1974, 138).

Thirdly, this quest for mutual enfacement and seeing faces fully is a communal matter. We do not find our faces, or the face of God, by looking at our own faces in solitude. Rather, we find all faces, including the divine face and our own, in the community where faces are recognised and found, or disregarded and lost.

Finally, the journey to find mutual enfacement and recognition is not a metaphorical or narrowly spiritual matter. As the women of Auschwitz witnessed with caring, cleansing acts towards the besmirched, shamed faces of their sisters, finding the place where divine and human faces can be seen clearly is a physical thing. God's face and image are not abstractions. They can only be seen in an embodied community where human faces are looked at, recognised, tended and valued. There are no mirrors to the divine face that are not enfleshed with human skin. So theological thinking and consideration must support real physical seeing and attention to actual human faces if it is to help in seeing what we can of the divine face dispersed among us. It is human faces, then, that are basically 'the face of God for now', and for us (Wilken 2003, 76). And it is by attending to these faces that we can discover the face of God distributed through and between the human race, past, present and to come. By discovering embodied mutuality with others in community, we can discern all that is available to us of the face of God. And in doing that, we witness to, and create, the face of God, even if we can never see it fully as it draws us into the future.

Imago dei as Dynamic and Social Work in Progress

There are many dimensions to the *imago dei* tradition in Christianity. While there is universal agreement that Jesus Christ is the true and visible image of God, some of the early Fathers, for example, believed that the image of God was only to be found in the human soul or faculty of reason, not, for example, in the body of a defecating beggar. There was also disagreement about what the image of God bestowed in the human (rationality, freewill, sovereignty) and about whether image and likeness are the same thing (Young 2011). Here I just want to pick up two strands of thought relating to the *imago dei*. These might provide some inspiration for the work of making faces, human and divine, more consciously visible.

The first element is the idea that the *imago dei* is not a settled essence or stamp that is fixed, once and for all. The tradition of seeing the likeness of God as being a work in progress, so that there is a process of becoming in humans, suggests that creating and seeing the *imago dei*, the face of God, has an eschatological and future-oriented nature. Just as Gregory of Nyssa suggests that we never see the face of God, only God's back, so the Christian path is one of endless desire and discipleship. Thus the business of creating humans in the image of God is a process of desire, creation and discovery (Gregory of Nyssa 1978, 119; Young 2007, 18).

Humans, then, are by the grace of God, called to disclose, recognise and create the *imago dei* in themselves and others so they can see the divine in each other and perhaps so that God can recognise the divine in them. This suggests an endless process of creative seeing of other humans and of God so that the image and face of God becomes visible in the present world. While this remains an unfinished process, the idea of the continual creation of God's image in, and between, people gives humans an important role in helping to bring the divine image and face to visibility. There is no reason to assume that this has nothing to do with individual, physical faces. If the defecating beggar embodies the *imago dei* and can be physically engaged in the quest for gaining the likeness of God, how much more the face of that beggar – or that of any other human? If we desire to see the face of God, we must seek to find, create and recognise God's image in others and in ourselves.

The second element that I want to pick up is that of the corporate nature of the *imago dei*. Gregory of Nyssa and some others believed that the image of God was not fundamentally to be found in individuals, but rather that it was dispersed amongst all members of the human race corporately (Schaff and Wallace 2007, 406; Buber 1967, 109). The implication of this is that finding the face of God is not simply a matter of individual discipleship or of cultivating some kind of unique inner essence that lies within oneself like a genetic code. Rather, people cannot find the image of God within themselves or others on their own. The image can only be constructed and seen with others through corporate effort and communion. Thus the image or face of God can only be grasped if there is a willingness to recognise it in the entire human race. And one might dare to say, it is only when it is recognised and seen as existing within and between all people that God will be able to see the image in its totality. For God to see God's image in humanity, all of humanity must act as a corporate mirror.

The imperative to a developmental notion of the face and image of God that involves humans, all humans that have and ever will be, imaging and mirroring God, is difficult to imagine. Perhaps the clearest way of illustrating what might be figured here in relation to face is to point to the famous and expensive face advertisement for British Airways (BA) filmed in the late 1980s.

BA hired thousands of people to go out into the Utah salt flats in the USA. Differently dressed in black, white, blue and red, the people formed a huge face with eyes, mouth and nose. At a particular moment, some of the people moved in a particular direction so that the face appeared to wink broadly. Clearly, God is greater than BA, and the human race is more than a few thousand people strong. But in this advertisement it is perhaps possible to see something of what Gregory and other theologians are pointing to. It is when people come together and work to create and recognise an unfinished and continually recreating image of God that, together, and as part of the process of creating the image, they corporately become the image, the smiling face of God. It is as if seeing and recognising all of the human faces on earth in their individuality also then creates a much larger total, corporate face that is the face of humanity, mirroring and perhaps to some extent creating and completing the image and face of God. This kind of thinking about the *imago dei* as corporate, unfinished, eschatologically enticing, humanly demanding and universal might then inspire us to take seeing faces human and divine more seriously.

Presence and Absence in Divine-human Relations – Living with Veils

An important theme in the Christian theological tradition about seeing the face of God has been that of the absence or hiddenness of God. In the narrative of the OT, God seems, from time to time, to remove the divine presence from Israel, sometimes because Israel seems to have sinned, sometimes just arbitrarily and inexplicably (Balentine 1983; Breuggemann 2009b; Miles 1995).

It can be argued that this ambiguity of absence and presence helped to create the faith of the Hebrews. Commenting on Ps. 27, Terrien (1978, 311) writes:

> Ambiguity remains attached to the metaphor of the divine face. Presence is an absence and even abandonment when it is hidden, but this absence has the power to bring forth the most peculiar ingredient of Hebraic theology: faith as an instrument of knowledge as well as a *modus vivendi*.

Thus it is no longer the presence, but the absence of God that adduces the vision of faith and reassures humans. This fits in with the general Hegelian commonplace that if something is familiar and omnipresent, it is not easily possible to perceive it: 'Like is not known by like, for what is not different is a matter of indifference' (Moltmann 2010, 173).

The theological tradition of seeing the face of God bears witness to the belief that God's presence is often only indirectly and occasionally glimpsed, so there is no clear comprehension of God's being as an object in the world. Paul captures this sense of God's partially withheld presence using the 'veil scale' in his letters (Mitchell 2010). And the tradition that God's face is both present and absent, known, in fact, partly in its very absence, is taken up by Luther and later theologians who make much of the idea of *deus absconditus*, the God who is both hidden in his revelation in Christ crucified, and hidden behind this revelation (Dillenberger 1953). For theologians like Luther, God remains perpetually veiled and only ever partially apprehensible in any kind of revelation. Indeed, revelation defines God as a God who is hidden (Dillenberger 1953, 119).

There are very good reasons for this. If God is taken to be like an object in the world, then God becomes no more than an idol, a human projection that is useful to us:

> The idol reflects back to us, in the face of a god, our own experience of the divine. The idol does not resemble us, but it resembles the divinity that we experience, and it gathers it in a god in order that we might see it. The idol does not deceive; it apprehends the divinity. (Marion 2001, 6)

Furthermore, if God is wholly available and visible to humans, then God is objectified, so the mystery of God's otherness and being is lost. Thus seeing by means of revelation in faith involves simultaneously veiling and unveiling as the way in which God is made known to humans. God reveals Godself as being for humans, knowable to them, but also as ungraspable in Godself. Thus Marion (2001, 36): 'The withdrawal of the divine would perhaps constitute its ultimate form of revelation. This is what we attempt to delineate under the name of distance.'

This kind of thought is designed to ensure that humans do not become arrogant in identifying and knowing the divine, mistaking their own apprehensions and beliefs for the reality of God. It constitutes an important theological move to preserve divine mystery and transcendence. However, it might be argued that if we do not confuse the totality of any human with their visible face – perhaps one cautionary note that this kind of theological thinking might alert us to – then there is no reason why we would make the mistake of confusing our ideas and understandings of God's face with the totality of the divine being. Perhaps fears of idolatry, which have haunted the Protestant imagination in particular since the Reformation, have been exaggerated here. Idolatry and objectification are not necessary correlates of imaging and experiencing God; 'idolaters' are generally aware that they should not mistake a part for the whole of person-like reality (Koerner 2002; Pattison 2007b, 241–3).

The main point that I want to take from this tradition here is that God's face cannot ever be fully seen. It will always be veiled and only partially available to humans in the physical world. This then reinforces the idea that finding the face of God is a quest, a process, an end, not a finally achievable reality. In looking for the divine face, we are faced with an endless, uncertain journey, not with a clear endpoint. Seeking the face of God is a gradual process which involves glimpses and glances rather than steady gaze that fixes and objectifies.

More positively, veiling, hiddenness, partial sight and concealment can be the means of arousing intrigue, curiosity, desire and attraction in religion, as in other parts of life (Meyer and Pels 2003). Absence, loss and partial knowledge can create the motivation to know more (Leader 2002). It is the known, perceived absence of the face of God that creates desire and lures people on to seek the fullness of divine face and presence (Alves 1986, 1990). The invisible, or partially visible, fuels the quest for knowledge and understanding. The truth and full presence of God, like the truth and full presence of a loved human face of another, is always hidden from us under a kind of mask (Lemma 2010). Ultimately, it lies both within and beyond the visible face: 'truth abides in darkness: those who see are blind, and only the blind can see' (Alves 1990, 28).

This kind of thinking relativises the human capacity and quest for the visible face of God and the venture more fully to see the faces of humans. It also validates the desire to see and to understand better. The partial indicates and beckons on to the whole, both sensually and intellectually. While we must live in a world of partial perspectives and shadows, the desire to see, to know, and to be known face-to-face, can draw us on. The theological tradition of the hiddenness and veiling of God highlights the partial, limited nature of the quest for full knowledge and sight.

For some theologians like Ford (1999), the hiddenness or absence of God also denotes the space of freedom in which humans take responsibility for the world and develop their potential. And I have myself argued that the motif of God's hidden or averted face allows humans room not to feel ashamed before what might be felt as the persecutory gaze of an omniscient, 'eye in the sky' surveilling deity (McFague 1993, 193; Pattison 2000, 303–6;). However, as we have noted, womanists like Melissa Raphael (2003, 44–50) vigorously oppose the notion of divine absence or withdrawal from the world. God is not visible because the divine is concealed by the defilement wrought by human beings so that God cannot face humans or be seen by them.

In any thinking about the presence/absence hiddenness/visibility of God, it is, then, very important to be aware that we do not envisage God in the image of human ideologies like patriarchy which prize disembodiment, absence, abstraction and theory rather than compassionate, embodied engagement with real contemporary people. But having said this, it should be remembered that the Lutheran tradition of the beauty and truth of God being hidden within the revelation of God in the ugly sight of the suffering, crucified Christ allows the possibility of finding the reality of God's presence and face in places and people which seem far from God (de Gruchy 2001; Koerner 2004). This affirmation of incarnational presence in distress and suffering, as well as in beauty and serenity, is a very important theological insight. It may well be helpful in thinking about how we might deal with the problems and difficulties of seeing human faces, especially shamed and alienated human faces.

The Missing and Polymorphic Face of Christ

One of the intriguing things noted in looking at NT and historical evidence is that, although Jesus Christ is deemed to be the incarnate image of God, there is no record of what his face actually looked like. Jesus' face is, in a sense, missing, blank, featureless. Furthermore, the absence of a definitive, controlling image of Jesus then allowed his face to be portrayed in many different ways, as it continues to be, so that his face could be described as polymorphic. Jesus' face, then, could be nothing or anything, nobody's face, anybody's face, everybody's face. Once again, this seems implicitly to signal a theological devaluing of real, physical human faces, a dis-identification with a vital part of the physical human condition. The divine might then be seen to be faceless, expressionless, abstract and difficult to relate to in intimate, real ways. What kind of theological inspiration might be derived from these apparently very unhelpful, contradictory perceptions?

In fact, a number of critical, creative points can be made here. First, the absence of a tangible physiognomy for Jesus can denote the fact that God's face is not fixed or graspable as an object. It is a temptation to make Jesus as we would like to see him, as would best suit us, to create a timeless and authoritative essential face that would allow humans to pin down exactly who and what Jesus might be and become. The witness to his facelessness forces the recognition that physical and mental representations of Jesus' face are only guesses at something that is ultimately elusive, however attractive it may appear in depictions like icons.

This implicitly iconoclastic move pushes us away from the search to find and cleave to one historical physical image from the past and into finding the faces of Jesus and God in the present and among our contemporaries. If there is no one face of God or Jesus upon which we can gaze, we must try to glimpse aspects of the face of Jesus in those around us now. The face of Jesus remains an intriguing enigma that draws us on to look harder and wider amongst our fellow human beings. The fact that it is not fixed in a single physical form for all time means that it has to be created, found and recognised now. This allows much scope for humans to image and imagine the possibilities inherent in the face of God.

Jesus' face is then an eschatological possibility that embodies all sorts of possible representations and manifestations, rather like one of Picasso's cubist portraits of faces. Many angles and aspects have to be included to make a complete representation, and these cannot and will not be attained within the present world, though we must strive to see them precisely here.

In this context, it is to be expected that many actual human faces will contain aspects of the face of God and Jesus as this is constructed and recognised by humans eschatologically attracted by the hope of the ultimate realisation and recognition of the face of God. The full knowledge and vision of our individual and corporate faces, like our lives, is hidden with Christ in God (Col. 3:3). Jesus' face will thus be found fragmentarily amongst the faces around us now. His face, being specifically unrecognisable, like his name, becomes the face of every person on earth. This theologically warrants the quest to take all human physical faces with absolute seriousness and respect (Altizer 1997, 185–204).

There is a particular value here for those who have physical and other problems with faces, who have been defaced and alienated in one way or another. The lack of a particular countenance for Jesus together with the polymorphy with which his face has been represented validates the experience of those for whom face is a particular problem. Non-specificity and pluriformity mean that there is a space for all faces as representations of the incarnate Christ. Those who find faces problematic cannot be discriminated against in the light of some kind of seen ideal, divinely inhabited face. All of us can and must seek to find our own faces mirrored in Christ, but only by looking for Jesus' face in the faces of the others who can, in turn, help us to see our own faces. Once again, the elements of elusiveness, corporate image and searching for incomplete, partial awareness, and engaging in unending concrete quest is affirmed by the tradition of Jesus' face being unknown and represented in many different ways.

Conclusion: Shining Up the Face of God for Mutual Enfacement

The end of the Christian life is to see the face of God. However, in Western Christianity since the thirteenth century, and particularly since the Reformation, the aspiration to see the face of God in anything but a figurative way has largely disappeared from Christian thinking. God has become invisible, and belief in human *theosis* and agency in relation to seeing the face of God has largely disappeared. Emphasis has been put on the distance and difference between God and humanity and the essential passivity of humans in relation to trying to create, realise or recognise the image of God in the material world. Correlatively, the notion of the face of God has often become no more than a metaphor for a vague, general sense of divine presence, while the quest to seek the face of God is thought to be merely figurative and abstract. This may well have contributed to the marginalisation of the quest to seek God in the faces of the human beings who together might be seen to provide real glimpses of the face of God 'for now'.

In this chapter, I have not constructed a systematic theology that supports the quest to find or save the face of God and the faces of human beings. However, by ranging through a variety of insights and motifs contained within the Christian tradition, I have attempted to indicate that the notion that the theology of the face of God is worth attending to in the contemporary world.

At the very least, the concept of the face of God, however understood, needs to be seriously thought about, and its implications for theology and practice explored. This theological tradition raises critical questions for contemporary Christian beliefs and practices: what do we understand by the face of God? Where is it to be seen and how? How does the quest for the vision of God's face affect ways of seeing human faces?

But more than that, this exploration raises questions about whether there really is some kind of physical and this-worldly reality to the quest to see God face-to-face. Perhaps we have construed sight too thinly and too abstractly. We may thus be tempted too quickly to dismiss the importance of actual faces, both human and divine, within the abstracted, logocentric world of Christian theology. Our journey through motifs and concepts relating to seeing the face suggests that there is much to think about in retrieving a tradition of seeing God and finding God's face.

Specifically, the theological tradition has suggested the following ideas as matters for concern and exploration. First, we need to consider whether our ways of seeing are appropriate; a thicker, more material and creative understanding of sight and what might be seen that reverses the spiritualising of vision might be appropriate if we are to take divine engagement with the world seriously. Like Blake, perhaps we need to develop a wider vision of what it might mean to see the world theologically that encompasses divine and human faces. Secondly, we need to recognise that humans and God together create, discover and mirror each other's images in partnership, thus bringing each other to presence. Seeing the face of God is a matter of some mutuality, so humans have an active role to play in making the face of God visible. This is a communal, material and embodied matter, involving real faces, not just a nice idea. Thus, one of the main ways in which the face or image of God is likely to be glimpsed and made known is, like the Jewish women of Auschwitz, by attending to the faces of other humans who become for us 'the face of God for now'. The business of helping to create, discover and recognise the face of God involves recognising that the image of God is found in the faces and persons of all members of the human race; in realising their own potential, they all help to realise God's image and face in the world.

This is a quest, a continuing process that has no end. Indeed, there is a sense in which God's face can never fully be seen and grasped in the present order of things; God's face remains in some sense veiled, only partially graspable. However, in trying to recognise it in the faces of others, those who are God's face to us for now, we are drawn on into a future fuelled by desire to know God and other enfaced beings more fully. We may see through a glass darkly, but at least we can make the effort to see and recognise God in all the faces that surround us. Sign, symbol and lure of this quest for faces – God's, our own, those of others – is the missing and polymorphic representation of the face of Jesus Christ which prompts us to find the face of God in all human faces and refuses to be fixed in any one face. If we cannot see God directly, then the quest to see Jesus requires us to take all human faces seriously, particularly those that are in any way shamed or alienated.

To conclude with one final metaphor, I would like to suggest that the mutual business of seeking and finding the face of God for us for now can be figured as 'shining up the face of God'. In the Jerusalem Temple, God and God's people beheld each other in mutual joy. God smiled upon Israel, 'the people which sees God', and Israel smiled back. This was a joint project and a tangible realisation of the rule of God; it was not just as metaphor but a lived reality. If we have an invisible God who we cannot see and who cannot smile upon us in our embodied form, then we will not be able to believe that we are seen, and so at a fundamental, embodied level we will remain alienated and unhealed. Discovering how to shine up the face of God through shining up the faces of those around us is then a vital concern and essential to the elimination of shame, sin and sorrow.

What this might mean in all its fullness is well beyond the scope of this book. But in the next chapter, I will begin to consider some more practical ways of engaging with human faces and seeing what might help to make the necessarily speculative thoughts of the present chapter slightly more concrete.

Chapter 9
Just Looking: Seeing Faces More Clearly

God does not see as human beings see; they look at appearances but Yahweh looks at the heart.

(1 Sam. 6:7 NJB)

Whoever sees Jesus Christ does indeed see God and the world in one. [They] can henceforward no longer see God without the world or the world without God.

(Bonhoeffer 1964, 70)

We want to be more spiritual than God. Where Jesus Christ speaks to us of life, of the body, of the world, we would have preferred that he talked to us of the secrets that lie beyond the tomb.

(Alves 1983, 32)

Real life is the bodiliness that I am, unlived life is the alienated bodiliness that I have.

(Moltmann 2010, 61)

Our brief, partial examination of the theological tradition suggests that seeing the face of God and seeing the faces of other people may be in some ways integrally linked. Faces, both human and divine, have been largely ignored in Western Christian thought and practice for the last few centuries. If we want to glimpse 'the face of God for now', then we need to take the visible faces of other humans seriously. In particular, we need to take very seriously the faces of those who are marginalised, shamed and stigmatised, those who are deemed to have problems with living in a facially oriented world that excludes them, either because they do not have 'acceptable' or 'normally functioning' faces, or because they are perceived to have problems with facial interaction in some way. These include people with facial disfigurements mild or serious (acne, burns, birthmarks, blemishes, injuries, missing or distorted features), paralysed or non-functioning faces (people with dementia, Bell's palsy, strokes, Parkinson's disease), and those with problems of facial engagement, for example, people with Asperger's syndrome and various mental health problems.

As we noted earlier, 'face' is a very complex phenomenon. Physical face quickly gives way to metaphor and symbol. In that context, it also becomes the site of social and cultural judgement involving issues of politics, power and acceptability. In this complex, ambivalent situation, face can become a metonym for social position and belonging. Face is a mercurial phenomenon that will not remain still, physically or conceptually; it is endlessly moving and recursive.

Much of the experience of face is pre-verbal and momentary, as expressions and viewing positions change and shift. Ways of understanding and of describing face, along with the vocabulary and analytic tools for providing a full, accurate and useful phenomenology of face, are at an early stage of development.

It is not feasible here to provide a complete guide to dealing sensitively and proactively with face in all its meanings and dimensions. While it would be unacceptable in a work of practical theology to leave face in the realm of abstract appreciation and concern, I cannot do more here than suggest a few directions for response and exploration with regard to the theoretical, theological and practical issues raised heretofore. Practical theology rightly poses the question to theological and theoretical understanding, so what? (Pattison and Woodward 2000). What might be the significance of all this for everyday practice and living? In what follows, I can provide only broad and fragmentary clues as to what might constitute more adequate practical approaches and responses to face.

To include the widest view of concepts of face and responses to the various possible understandings and interpretations of it, I have characterised my overall approach as one of 'Just Looking'. In Deut. 10:17–18 God is described as one 'who is not partial and takes no bribe'. The direct Hebrew meaning of 'not partial' refers to a metaphor emanating from slave markets. The slaves (in chains) were not allowed to look up directly at prospective buyers. When interested buyers came along, the slave was hit with a stick under the chin and required then to look into the face of the prospective purchaser. The value of a slave depended on his/her face value and the quality of their teeth. The translation of the biblical passage might therefore be, 'The God who does not lift up faces' (in order to objectify, evaluate and exploit them). As verse 18 makes clear, God is just and compassionate in his seeing: 'He executes justice for the fatherless and widow, and loves the sojourner ...' (RSV). A similar kind of meaning is found in Acts 10:34. Here Peter claims that God is impartial, not valuing people by their faces. The passage uses a word that literally means, 'taking someone by their face', maybe 'valuing them at face value'. Here Peter is claiming that people of every nation are acceptable to God if they fear God and do God's will – their appearances and cultural identities are irrelevant otherwise.[1]

It is this biblical metaphor of God's not taking faces at face value and so objectifying people, integrally linked with justice, compassion, inclusion and, by implication, the dissolution of shame and alienation, that I will use to frame my consideration of seeing faces differently. By seeing, I primarily want to highlight the physical act of beholding and being beheld physically. But I also want my discussion to extend to practices of relating that affect the metaphorical and social consequences of taking face seriously, dealing with issues of shame, loss of face and exclusion that are often connected with physical face and visual perception.

I want to keep this discussion in the realm of the social and political, as the texts from Deuteronomy and Acts imply, because seeing or not seeing the faces of others,

---

[1]   I am grateful to Daniel Louw for this translation and the critical point made here.

whether physical, or metaphorical/imagistic, is a socially and culturally inflected phenomenon involving issues of power. In trying to learn a more appreciative, inclusive attitude to faces and persons, our own and others, we must continue to be aware that we are in a process of creation, construction and recognition that is not just about individual physiognomy and identity, but rather about creating a certain kind of society. The Christian community, like Israel, should see differently. It is called to catch glimpses of God in the faces of others within a context of justice that reflects the reign of God inaugurated in the ministry of Jesus, the image of the invisible God.

Having framed my practical intent within a general aim of promoting 'just looking', I now go on to develop some ideas that might contribute to more appropriate ways of seeing faces.

First, I will discuss aspects of oblivion, objectification and appearing as they relate to shame and exclusion, and consider how this relates to facial interactions. Physical face is a main site for people to orient and present themselves to others; it is also the source and locus of shame. I want to explore the relationship of face to shame with a view, secondly, to discussing developing more conscious and subtle ways of looking and engaging with faces so that we begin to gain more awareness of what the significance of our own and others' faces might be. I have entitled this second section, Developing Ways of Looking and the Practical Hermeneutics of Face. Here, I want to look at types of seeing with a view to raising consciousness about what we do and do not do with our eyes in relation to faces. Wherever I can, I will try to refer to cases and examples of seeing in practice, but ultimately this can only be a suggestive introduction to just looking at faces.

Shame, Oblivion and Objectification

The author of the Epistle of James has some harsh things to say about a particular human organ, the tongue. He describes it as a 'fire', 'an unrighteous world among our members, staining the whole body, setting on fire the cycle of nature, and set on fire by hell'. He goes on to argue that 'no human being can tame the tongue', 'With it we bless the Lord and Father, and with it we curse men, who are made in the likeness of God' (Jas. 3:4–9 RSV).

Many of these observations could have been extended and, indeed, intensified had he chosen to consider the face. People mostly cannot consciously control all the expressions on their faces and the ways in which they look at the faces of others. And in looking at others in some ways, for example with horror, disgust, contempt, it is possible to consign or confine them to shame, alienation, oblivion, even to hell. By the same token, the ways in which people look at each other can build others up, including them, making them feel attractive, lovable and wanted.

Shame is often visually and facially focused and mediated, conferred and confirmed. It polices and disciplines the boundaries of human relations and communities, affirming what is taken to be good, acceptable and desirable and excluding the ugly, the deviant and the unwanted. This is all accomplished in an instant; an exchanged or avoided look or glance conveys more effectively and faster than words what the state of relations is (Casey 2007).

Unfortunately, this kind of movement flourishes on stereotyping, and rapid, pre-conscious, non-verbal judgements based on initial, often physical impressions and features. It is heavily influenced by social norms and assumptions, so that it is as if the look of the physical eye and face is really a matter of being seen through some kind of socially inflected inner eye (Ellison 2001, 3). The faces of those who shame and are shamed may be individual, like the consciousness within them, but the judgements made, and the phenomena experienced, are socially shaped and shared. While they feel like instant, visceral, instinctive reactions in the moment, they are often highly socially patterned, and, to some extent, predictable. We are taught to see and not to see and respond to certain conditions and sights in different contexts (Morgan 2012).

Here is an example of instant stereotyping and judgement based on facial impression in action. It concerns two well-known people, the one a cleric who later became a bishop, Mervyn Stockwood, the other, the writer, a psychoanalyst, Patrick Casement, who attended Stockwood's sermons as a student:

> Whenever Mervyn Stockwood was addressing the congregation he used to speak out of the side of his mouth and I quickly developed an intense dislike of him because of this, as I was assuming this to be an affectation ... However, I later learned that he had suffered a serious stroke. ... He could only make himself heard if he worked the muscles on one side of the face to compensate for the other side. I was shocked. I had totally misjudged this man through seeing him only in terms of my assumptions about him. (Casement 2006, 34–5)

Casement does not record his own facial response to Stockwood, but it is not difficult to imagine that he might have averted his gaze, stared, or in some other way signalled his dislike. Stockwood was not severely facially impaired and enjoyed very high individual social status. So Casement's aversion to, and stigmatisation of him probably did not do him much damage. But those who are poor, from ethnic minorities, from other low status groups, and those who are more severely impaired might not be so fortunate. The unwarranted, stereotyping vision of the appearance of others might damage them quite considerably, particularly if it builds on poor internal self-image (Gilbert 2002). Ugliness (and by implication, beauty) 'is a designation infused with power dynamics which helps to police wider categories of gender, social class, race and subjectivity itself' (Baker 2010, 188). I will return to the social, systematic aspect of this in a moment.

But before going on to discuss systematic social shaming and exclusion further, it is worth acknowledging that we all make casual judgements about the faces and the value of others on a daily basis. While God may not judge people according to their faces, humans do this all the time, mostly without a second thought. How we judge and respond to the faces of others may radically affect how much time, money or opportunity they access, for example in health care, employment, social life. It is common to hear someone say that they have dismissed or avoided dealing with another because 'they did not like their face'. And not liking or relating to the face of a particular person may have nothing to do with any kind of blemish or disfigurement. As we noted earlier, people tend to privilege facially average and attractive people with symmetrical features (Hamermesh 2011; Perrett 2010). So many individuals in all classes of society may find that they are unwittingly discriminated for, or against, simply because of the way their faces look. Beyond this kind of casual, apparently individualistic acceptance or rejection of the 'beautiful' and the 'ugly' in all our everyday lives, there lies the possibility for more widespread discrimination and shaming that attaches to particular kinds of faces or faces which are thought to represent certain groups and values.

It is systemic social exclusion and shaming mediated to a large extent through vision and facial relations that is captured in the concept of 'oblivion' developed by political philosopher Hannah Arendt (Curtis 1999). Many groups and individuals or groups in society, including those with problems with face and seeing face, are in danger of suffering 'the insult of oblivion' (Curtis 1999, 67). They are systematically overlooked, seen round, or seen through.

Obliviation, the practice of consigning people to oblivion or obscurity by seeing round or through them, is a reflexive, rather than an intentional, strategy. It is founded in visceral responses of attraction and aversion/disgust (Fulkerson 2007; Kelly 2011; Korsmeyer 2011; Nussbaum 2004). This means that it is not easily available to rational criticism or will; it is simply unthinkingly operant. Its effects are devastating.

Here is John Adams, the early American reformer, talking about the condition of obscurity and shame felt by poor people:

> The poor man's conscience is clear; yet he is ashamed ... He feels himself out of the sight of others, groping in the dark. Mankind takes no notice of him: he rambles and wanders unheeded. In the midst of a crowd, at church, in the market ... he is in as much obscurity as he would be in a garret or a cellar. He is not disapproved, censured or reproached: he is only not seen ... To be wholly overlooked, and to know it, are intolerable. (Arendt 2006, 59)

This sense of visible invisibility, often mediated and reinforced by facial visuality, is familiar to many kinds of people with impairments and other problems with faces, as well as to those who belong to other dis-preferred social groups.

Not seeing people, as in the case of oblivious seeing, is a primary form of injustice. If we do not see and recognise people as subjects, we cannot act justly towards them. But there are other kinds of looking involved with shaming and exclusion. These might loosely be grouped under the heading of objectification.

One of the problems with faces in the present age is that they have become no more than objects and commodities, detached from persons and their value (Scruton 2012). They are thus objectified. Objectification, and the shame that often accompanies it, is a complex phenomenon. On the one hand, it can be expressed by people being looked at in a fixing or hostile way. This occurs when people stare at a blemish or injury without apparently seeing or acknowledging the person who they are looking at. Thus people can feel themselves to be fixed objects of spectacle. On the other hand, paradoxically, people can be objectified by people failing to see them at all, so that their faces and bodies are excluded from things like public photographs and advertisements.[2] Objectifying spectacular staring is often experienced by disabled people, but so, too, is the objectifying and ignoring of their subjectivity which is conveyed by making them invisible. Disabled academic Sharon Betcher bears witness to this paradoxical situation:

> I am on public display: always seen, always overlooked. The toxicity of the social staring wearies and wears down the psyche … Eli Clare … observes, "I store the gawking in my bone". Not infrequently I swallow the social abjection and refuse myself. (Betcher 2007 26)

It is not just disabled people who can find themselves objectified. The exclusion of the dead faces of soldiers and civilians killed in conflict from newspapers and other media is a way of excluding them and objectifying their significance. It prevents them from having lives and deaths that are of value and significance. To realise that enfaced young men or civilians die in war might be for society to have to acknowledge its own shame and guilt. Thus their existence has to be hidden as, to a large extent, does the existence of soldiers who have been mutilated, particularly facially (Butler 2006; Nussbaum 2004).

This is not a clear-cut issue. Depending on the circumstances and context, not showing dead faces can be either respectful or disrespectful, objectifying or subjectifying. And it should be recalled that here again, while the worst effects of objectification and obliviation may be felt by members of poor, marginalised groups, these factors can come into play even with wealthy and attractive people who may find that they are not really seen for what they feel they are.

Stereotyping, occluding and objectifying people's faces are powerful, mostly unremarked ways of abnegating their existence, subjectivity and value. The antidote to this obscuring of subjects and groups is to move 'away from oblivion toward the presence of others'. Persons need to appear to others, to move towards display. This will not happen by magic or by determination to be 'kind' to people. It requires a 'mutual responsiveness, provocation, and eliciting self-display' (Curtis 1999, 15). This emerges in an agonistic, conflictual kind of situation where

---

[2]   Kilborne (2002) notes that shamed people have a very ambivalent relationship with wanting to be seen and recognised and simultaneously not wanting to be seen, to be invisible. This psychologically-based observation seems also relevant in the case of groups. In social and individual cases alike, the common denominator is that the shamed subject loses control and influence over the way they are perceived and present themselves. See also Velleman (2006), Wurmser (1995).

people are mutually and sensually provoked into existence and recognise each other's presence and reality, however uncomfortable and inconvenient that may be.

In this context, 'our sense of reality is engendered through our eliciting self-presentation, whereby we seek to countenance and be countenanced by others' (Curtis 1999, 49). By presencing and countenancing others, recognising their bodily and subjective reality, however difficult that may be, we engage with reality within an 'ontology of display'; this involves 'difficult seeing' (Curtis 1999, 74, 127). Changing one's response to the world and others to recognise their appearance and visibility in a world of mutual provocation cannot be a comfortable process; it may involve pain and conflict. But the alternative is to live in a kind of unreality in which people, including the powerful, are trapped in worlds of retreat and obscurity characterised by passivity.

Christians have much to learn from these ideas. That Christian communities should be places where people and groups are able to 'appear' in all their diversity and difference seems vital. The idea of actively encouraging the emergence of presence and difference to enrich and adjust concepts of reality is valuable; I particularly value the idea of 'responsive countenancing', what might be translated here as 'conferring and enjoying mutual face and presence' (Curtis 1999, 144). The ideal of recognising and being recognised as different is compatible with Christian traditions of creating, recognising and confirming the image of God in all people. This will often be a stretching, difficult process involving conflict and 'difficult seeing' that moves all parties from passivity to activity. So this is not just about learning how to better contemplate and accept the appearances and being of others. It is about growing and changing to incorporate difference, including physical difference of all kinds, on the part of all concerned.

An example of responsive countenancing cited by one of Arendt's commentators is that of a race rights activist recognising and bringing into the political world a Ku Klux Klan activist in the USA (Curtis 1999, 146ff.). This countenancing began with the latter abusing the former and then being changed by being recognised by them. In whatever way countenancing happens, it is likely to involve stretching, change and conflict, not always welcome experiences in quietistic Christian communities, despite their mission to reach out and love even 'enemies'. To be recognised as an enemy might be nearer to the possibility of mutual countenancing than quiescent, but blind 'acceptance' in which people know their place and are kept there.

Christians, Appearing, and 'Difficult Seeing'

A Christian community that wishes to move from obliviating and obscuring practices with regard to faces and the people who have them must change and develop in fundamental ways. The nature of the challenge to engage in 'difficult seeing' might perhaps more adequately be seen by briefly considering the work of Sharon Betcher, a radical Canadian theologian of disablement.

Betcher (2007, 194) suggests that Christianity has been complicit in, and perhaps causative of, the denial of corporeality and transient life represented in disablement. Adopting a kind of normative Platonic idealism and perfectionism, Christianity has fallen into a dualistic way of thinking that relegates embodied life, particularly that perceived as 'defective', to subaltern, colonised status. Believing in a kind of 'technological sublime', and committed to compulsory holism requiring all to be changed to conform to the ideal, so all that is defective is fixed, Christianity promotes ideas of healing and wholeness that subjugate disabled bodies. These are then used to bolster the quest for the ideal and the normal:

> In an economy in which image sells and looking good is everything, the disabled body may not be at all irrelevant, but may rather be a needed, if abject, other – a silenced body of evidence serving the ideal. (Betcher 2007, 51)

Failing to bless multiple corporeal flourishings, including the bodies of disabled people, questing for wholeness rather than wholesomeness, Christianity uses the normalising optic of modernism to promote 'decency theologies'. These 'become conflated with middle-class morality and, consequently, begin to discipline bodies into the status quo' (Betcher 2007, 52). Decency theologies and attitudes civilise and subjugate simultaneously. Disablement becomes 'a politically and religiously deployed metaphor of boundaries and their trespass' which actually helps to define and reinforce ideals of bodily normality as a kind of Other. This kind of shaming 'thinking with the body of persons with disabilities … presumes physiological disablement to be a lack, then leaps over the testimony of persons with disabilities to repair and rescue' (Betcher 2007, 53, 60). Non-disabled, powerful people can then think of the silenced disabled as weak and needy, needing help and rescue. This inadvertently demonstrates their own power and confirms their own worldview and identity as powerful and non-disabled. In doing this, even from a standpoint of liberation and justice, Christians have often assumed representational responsibility for serving as voice of voiceless, taking upon themselves a role of 'prosthetic ventriloquism', as if disabled persons lack capacity to speak for themselves (Betcher 2007, 69). This well-meant, idealising, colonialising and essentially demeaning perspective has very unfortunate, shame-deepening effects. The 'politics of piety and rescue' that strives to save or fix disabled people results in aggressive pity and a sort of 'theological violence' against them (Betcher 2007, 106, 119). Another disablement academic, Nancy Eisland (1994, 116), notes that 'Our bodies have too often been touched by hands that have forgotten our humanity and attend only to curing us'.

Christians therefore need to develop a new optics that recognises the bodily reality, vulnerability and pain represented in disablement. Rejecting notions of the 'fitter' and so implicitly 'superior' self, curing, helping or rescuing, a new kind of compassion has to be developed based on a desire for a larger sense of being, purpose and community. Here respons-ability rather than duty is key, and hospitality to difference needs to be paramount. Central to this kind of community is the need for non-idealising, 'open seeing', 'seeing with the innocence of a baby' that might be equated with being born again in the Spirit (Betcher 2007, 119, 157).

In this renewed and, I would suggest, often 'difficult' seeing, imperfection, suffering, pain and disablement can be recognised as part of human life and existence and included as part of vibrant living, with a trust in life that is faithful to its corporeality and transience. Thus all are enriched by the recognition of non-idealised vulnerability, and disabled people are objects no longer. They can 'appear', stare back or perhaps share warm mutual sight, looking in the eye those who have hitherto looked down on, or through, them (Razak 1998). Thus disabled people, and others who are deemed to have 'problems with faces', those who are in some way 'all body' and 'no body', can become 'some body' alongside all the other bodies and faces filling churches and other communities (Betcher 2007, 197).

All the faces that comprise Christian communities need to be seen and loved as equally and differently valuable if the face of God is to be glimpsed. The task for all Christians is, therefore, to create a space in which the faces of people and of the divine can appear to one another. Paradoxically, if the example of Jesus is to be followed, creating this luminous space requires the absolute acceptance of people experiencing all kinds of alienation and apparently bodily based 'pollution', whatever its nature. Thus sexuality, bodily appearance, gender and many other things, as well as faces as such, need to be included, or the space will not allow mutual appearing. So much, then, for the attempts of many churches to create polluted and polluting 'out groups' on the basis of perceived or fantasised bodily 'purity' (Pattison 2007a, 155–63).

Faces need to be valued, but people should not taken at face value. And those whose faces do not fit for one reason or another can be the catalyst for the kind of transformed but 'difficult' seeing that may give all a place, all a face. Embodied difference can then be welcomed as a path to corporate growth and transformation, in which the glory and face of God may be seen.

But what of the actual act of seeing or beholding others? It is one thing to set up a general framework for thinking about seeing, but what about seeing itself? If we possess the sense of vision, can we become a bit more aware and knowledgeable about practices of seeing and using our eyes if we possess the sense of vision? This is what I will explore in the remainder of this chapter.

Developing Ways of Looking and the Practical Hermeneutics of Face

Although sight is often regarded as the most powerful and important of the senses, we mostly do not have nuanced and sophisticated ways for understanding and analysing it (Elkins 1997; Pattison 2007b). Many of us do not think about different ways of seeing, or their practical and theoretical implications at all. This is unsurprising; sight is a non-verbal, pre-verbal matter. There is, then, plenty of scope to develop a detailed and sensitive phenomenology of social seeing generally, and then perhaps a more nuanced typology of ways and types of seeing faces specifically. Here, all I can do is to point up some broad issues and concepts in the interests of increasing awareness of the ways in which faces can or should be looked at.

A rough, but useful, primary distinction that can be made is that between gaze and glance as different ways of looking. Gaze is variously defined (Bryson 1983, chapter 5; Elkins 1997, 200–212). It is mainly differentiated by the fact that it is slower, more lingering and more focused than the kind of looking that is found in the glance:

> When I gaze at something, I allow my look to linger – to caress the surface of what I'm looking at, or else to plumb its depths patiently. Gazing is taking the world at one's own pace; it is open-eyed, literally unblinking, as if I were swimming in the ocean of the world with my eyes open. (Casey 2007, 132)

There are different modes of gazing (Casey 2007, 133–4). Contemplation is a kind of gazing with a soft focus. It can give way to scrutinising, which is more a kind of focused looking to find something specifically. This may then give way to scanning to examine the details of a visual object. At the far end of this mode of gaze lies staring, fixed looking in a very specific way. And this may give way to glaring, a more intense form of staring which can be perceived as invasive and attract hostility if it is directed towards another person.

It is the staring end of gaze that is explored by Sartre and others who characterise this kind of looking as objectifying, dominating and fixing, so that it may create a sense of shame (Sartre 1969, 221–302). It can be perceived as disembodied and detached, as the look of surveillance, sovereignty and control, of heaviness. This kind of gaze is often associated with God the Pantocrator, who sees all, and from whom no secrets are hidden (Pattison 2000, 190–98, 303). Not only can it fix and objectify those who fall into it, unwavering, unblinking looking can also produce a kind of narrowing blindness and paralysis for both those who gaze and those who are stared at: 'A really piercing stare is its own kind of blindness, and it even causes blindness in those who receive it' (Elkins 1997, 210).

Glance contrasts with gaze in that it is a quicker, more mobile and more inclusive kind of looking. If gaze lingers, glance takes note of what is going in and takes in the surfaces of the visual world very swiftly. This sense is captured in common phrases such as 'stealing' or 'catching' a glance. Glancing is composed of looking around, glimpsing and peeking, or peeping.

Looking around is a kind of comprehensive looking. To glimpse something is to briefly see something that is only momentarily visible. To peek is to gain partial view of something where full gaze is impossible. And peeping is an intense kind of looking which can develop into the more fixed seeing of gazing. While looking around is comprehensive, the other modes of glimpse are more partial. People often assume that glancing is trivial and superficial looking, but it can be regarded as a very connective way of looking at the world that reveals depths even as it passes quickly on and back to the eye of the viewer (Casey 2007). A glance at someone else's face or into their eyes can quickly reveal their depths and can then be the beginning of a sensitive, ethical response. We glance at others all the time; in our glances we affirm or disconfirm their being and presence, albeit very rapidly. Everyday life is threaded with swift, often unattended glancing that allows people to be 'seen' or be 'seen to be unseen'. Even 'a meagre look assures us of our being human: we are upheld in the look of the other', even if that look may be unnoticed or quickly forgotten (Casey 2007, 351).

Clearly, glance and gaze are not completely separable; gaze is made up of glances, and glance can act as a kind of advance guard for gaze. But they are in some ways distinguishable, and have different effects for both seers and seen. Both these modes of vision weave between seers and seen, web like, full of desire, meaning and communication: 'Every field of vision is clotted with sexuality, desire, convention, anxiety, and boredom' (Elkins 1997, 21, 69, 95). Thus there are very different qualities of gazing and glancing. Gaze can be appreciative as well as shaming, desirous, glassy, avaricious, amorous, far away and so on. Glances can be curious, interested, shared, exchanged, abstracted, sideways, withdrawn, distant, admonitory, averted, passing, downward, away or fleeting (Casey 2007, 31ff.). We can glance after, at, through or into things in the visual world.

Seeing and visually responding to being seen is a complex, subtle matter that changes momentarily. Recognising the variety and complexity of seeing and being seen, Morgan (2012, 67–80) outlines a morphology of visual fields within religion; this further elaborates the nature of seeing and can be applied to human relations generally. In unilateral gaze, seeing is asymmetrical, so that the seer is powerful while the seen is placed in a subordinate, submissive position. Occlusive gaze allows the seen to deflect the gaze of the seer – in everyday life, this might be the responsive, aggressive stare that stops others staring at one. Aversive or circumspect gaze occurs when the seer casts their gaze around the seen so as not to look it full on; it represents perhaps casting the eyes down, out of respect, or perhaps out of fear. In reciprocal gaze, however, seers and seen return each other's looks in an attentive, respectful, equal way. In devotional or loving gaze, people long to look at the beloved; this can again be an asymmetric, one-way kind of seeing. Liminal gaze, on the other hand, is a kind of stereotyping looking that establishes the limits of community, what is worth looking at and what can be seen. It is not closely attentive. Contemplative or aesthetic gaze can also have a distant, objective quality to it.

The point of discussing these different ways of seeing is to raise awareness of the subtle complexity of looking and beholding in human relations, within and outwith religious communities. To see the faces of humans fully and aright, it is necessary to become aware of the ways that we see and do not see others and the how vision and sight are constantly involved in mediating relations, mostly automatically and in an unconscious way. Recognising how everyday facial looking is full of different types of seeing and non-seeing, with different modes and meanings that are involved in the creation, recognition and exclusion of others does not necessarily lead to immediate behavioural change. Expressions of love and disgust are likely to continue to appear on our faces and those of others in spontaneous, 'instinctive' and unbidden ways, despite our conscious intentions and wishes. But recognising that they are significant may gradually allow us to begin to take responsibility for them and their reception in new ways. If possible, we need to begin to take custody of our eyes and faces in a more mindful, considered way if we can.

Seeing More Clearly and More Justly

I will conclude this book by making some practical suggestions about looking at and taking in faces and persons. Here, then, are some practically related, if fragmentary and unsystematic, desiderata on how the seeing of faces might be taken more seriously.

The first consideration is that faces are important and deserve full attention, visual and other. It seems that faces have not received the intentional interest and attention they deserve in Western Christianity. This needs to be amended. Faces and bodies are integral to persons, not adjuncts to be seen through and past.

Secondly, and apparently paradoxically, it is important not to overrate the significance of faces. Faces and facial relations are very important, but they are not all-important. People are not just their faces; it is vital not to confuse the reality and fullness of persons with their faces. Blind people and others with problems with face live full lives without the benefit of facial relations. We make a fundamental mistake in thinking visual knowledge of the face tells us all or even most of what we need to know about the person who possesses it. Faces tell us a lot; we rely on them for much of our knowledge of others. However, knowledge gained this way is at best partial, and it may be misleading, stereotyped and unhelpful. In this sense, it may be helpful to resort to the Protestant theological insight that our sense of vision is fallible, imperfect and 'fallen'. If we rely on the evidence of our eyes to understand and evaluate others, we are likely to fall into sin, disordered and erroneous perception and judgement.

Having acknowledged both the importance and relative unimportance of faces in social life, how might we enhance our appreciation of them, become better at seeing them, more just in our vision, and also work to overcome our prejudices and difficulties with the faces of people deemed ugly, disfigured or in other ways problematic?

The first thing here is to try to become aware of how we look at the faces of others and of the expressions on our own faces. It is impossible to have a moment-by-moment knowledge of how we see, look and are seen. However, it may be possible to think more carefully about how we are looking, to become more conscious of how our facial muscles are behaving and of the messages that are being conveyed. Other people, particularly intimates, can give valuable feedback here. It is also possible to observe carefully how others look at us and to consciously consider what this might reveal about them – and about us.

As an extension of this practice of trying to gain a fuller and more responsible sense of seeing and being seen as facial beings, it might be helpful to look more carefully and attentively at the faces around us. In this connection, drawing or photographing faces (with the permission of others, and in the right context) might be one way of becoming more aware of what faces are, mean and do. Looking at photographs and portraits in a careful, contemplative way might also increase this kind of awareness and sensitivity. A very powerful way of increasing awareness of the power, vulnerability and importance of faces is to gaze directly into someone else's face and eyes for a prolonged period. This can be unnerving, but also very moving. The performance artist Marina Abramovic spent several months in 2010 gazing all day silently into the faces of others sitting opposite her at the Museum of Modern Art in New York in an exhibition entitled The Artist is Present. Many of her sitters, and she herself, had tears in their eyes as strangers encountered one another in a facially very direct manner, as did the viewers in the gallery – and as did I, as I watched some of the sitters on video (Abramovic 2012). It is difficult to understand why this should be so powerful a means of connecting and communicating because it is pre-verbal in nature. But as to the power of facial encounter of this kind, there can be no doubt.

As a matter of course, it might be helpful to try to notice one's instant reactions to the faces of others, whether positive or negative. Whatever the reaction, it might be useful to reflect on why it has been as it has been. And then it might be appropriate, particularly if the reaction is a strong one, to think about whether to accept and act upon it, or whether it might be better to suspend judgement until further evidence such as speech or longer acquaintance has been allowed to enter in. It is likely that many first reactions to people's faces are wrong and misleading. To allow time for these reactions to be modified might be very important.

This brings us to reactions to faces which seem damaged, ugly, unattractive or difficult for some reason, for example because they do not move, respond or react like those of 'normals'. This reaction can be very misleading and also hurtful, excluding and shame-inducing. I have noted a number of times that such reactions are often socially shaped and formed, so they seem instinctive and visceral, but it is here that it is most important to try and take responsibility and to change behaviour.

Instant reactions can perhaps be modified by taking time to both react and note how one has reacted. James Partridge, a facially disfigured person, argues that if he can talk to people for ten seconds, they stop seeing him only as his damaged face. Superficial reactions to the faces of others are at their most intense in the first few seconds of encounter: so one way of ensuring that we do not allow reactions to prejudice relations is to ensure that we get into conversation with people. After a while, the face will not matter nearly so much; it may become familiar and lovable.

Even professionals can find it difficult to cope with faceless and facially disfigured people (Elkins 1997, 166). Here is a ward orderly writing about working with severely wounded, defaced soldiers, designated 'hideous', in the Masks for

Facial Disfigurements Department run by a sculptor in a First World War military hospital in London:

> I had not known before how usual and necessary a thing it is ... to gaze straight at anyone to whom one is speaking, and to gaze with no embarrassment ... He is aware of just what he looks like, therefore you feel intensely that he is aware you are aware, and that some unguarded glance of yours might cause him hurt. This, then, is the patient at whom you are afraid to gaze unflinchingly ... (Muir 1918, 143–4)

This quote sharply underlines the danger of difficult, shame-filled seeing. Shame is a highly contagious, 'sticky' or miasmic condition. It easily spreads between seers and seen in an unregulated, spontaneous way, creating anxiety and shame in those who witness it, or who sense the threat of its attaching to them (Nussbaum 2004; Pattison 2000). When we see others shamed, in a place where they are seen to be needy, weak or out of control of their situation, or even in a position where they might become so, an instinct might be to avert the gaze to avoid both shaming them and being shamed ourselves. Perhaps this accounts for my turning away from, or seeing through, the faces of beggars on the street. I neither want to be reminded of their vulnerability and powerlessness, my vulnerability and powerlessness, or of the relationship between us. So I simply fail to acknowledge their existence, obliviating them.

But over time it may be possible to relate to the people with their faces and no longer to stare, look through or look away from them. And if we do find ourselves engaged in these aversive responses, we can at least acknowledge that this is occurring. It is possible to think about why we have reacted thus, rather than pretending that we have not done so which can only perpetuate alienation and shame, probably in both seers and seen. Willingness to confront our own ways of looking and reacting might, then, help to enable the kind of 'difficult' but creative mutual seeing that might create the kind of 'responsive countenancing' discussed above.

The charity Changing Faces issues the following helpful guidance for those who want to feel more confident in meeting and appreciating people with facial disfigurements. It is very obvious really, and some of it would be generally useful for any kind of difficult facial encounter, for example with a person with a very beautiful or famous face. I reproduce the advice to seers, here, but there is also advice for how people can deal with discomfited starers. This emphasises the point that seeing faces needs to be seen as a mutual experience:

Don't know where to look?
Look them in the eye, just as you would anyone else – or if it's hard to look – look at the bridge of the nose – it has the same effect.

Worried you might be staring?

It's okay to be interested in someone's face but imagine what it feels like to be stared at every day. Just be sure you're not too interested.

Don't know what to say?

Say "hello". Talk about the weather, what's happening in the news – engage in normal casual conversation.

Express interest in something about them, for example, "You're my first customer today. Would you like some more coffee?"

Don't make "what happened to you?" be the first question you ask – wait until you know someone better or they bring it up in the conversation.

If you are still curious, ask "do you mind if I ask what happened?" – but be prepared for the fact that they may not choose to answer.

Don't know what to do?

Shake hands, if appropriate. Nod your head in acknowledgment. (Changing Faces, Face to Face Interaction. http://admin.changingfaces.org.uk/downloads/ Disfigurement%20Confident%20Leaflet%202010.pdf. Accessed 8th November 2012)

Shamed people and people with difficulties with face may find it very difficult to look others in the face for any length of time or, indeed, at all. Another practical thing to think about, then, is how to arrange spaces and activities so people feel comfortable to be with others and get used to them. Doing things with other people, driving side by side and other ways of avoiding and deflecting direct face-to-face gaze may be very helpful in facilitating non-shaming encounters that allow personal contact to emerge over time. It is interesting to speculate whether perhaps St Paul, as a tent-maker, had many of his important conversations working side by side with people rather than confronting them directly face-to-face.[3] And some modern Christian ministers have found engagement in common tasks a better way of coming alongside the shamed and alienated than by trying to talk to them directly and full on, for example in the Liverpool bread-making project in which people come together to make bread as a way of being and becoming a community (Glasson 2006).

Specifically in public church contexts, there are a number of ways in which people might try to become more facially aware and appreciative. Often when people engage in formal worship and prayer, they close their eyes to draw close to a God within. Perhaps it would be more appropriate if people opened their eyes more to take in the faces of those around them and if they thought about their expressions and significance. It is these people, with these faces, who are the body of Christ. It is in their faces, individually and corporately, that God's face and glory might be glimpsed. So learning to see, appreciate and enjoy those faces on a routine basis is important.

---

[3]   I owe this thought to Robert Jewett.

I know one priest who looks very carefully at all the people who have assembled in the church as the service starts. This, and other kinds of looking, can, if insensitively and too insistently done, be intrusive and shaming. But to see and to be seen and acknowledged in a mutual gaze can be affirming and countenancing. To this extent, the introduction of services in the round where everyone can see the faces of their fellow worshippers is helpful, as is the moment of the giving of the peace where people can look into (or perhaps sensitively away from) the faces and eyes of others to affirm their human being and their simultaneous being in God.

But there is a stage of awareness that must go beyond particular communities. I have consistently argued that seeing is socially inflected. The ways in which individuals see, what they can see and the way in which they look at and interpret the faces of others therefore varies according to context, time, place and community. To have a wider, more inclusive, less stereotyping, more appreciative approach to faces it is therefore necessary to learn from other communities and cultures what they understand and see. This, then, is a kind of ecumenical dimension. The aim of Christian living is to see the faces of other humans and of God to the maximum extent so that all find themselves included in God's own loving gaze. There is much to be gained from 'ecumenical' dialogue with groups of people that see very differently or do not see at all, for example people with Asperger's syndrome, blind people, to widen understanding of the nature and bounds of sight.

The pointers given here to better recognising, appreciating and including human faces within everyday practice are somewhat vague and inadequate. I hope they are better than nothing. But their thinness and paucity merely underlines the huge task that lies before Christians, alongside other members of Western society and culture, if we are to develop better and more just ways of seeing and appreciating human faces, and by doing that, to recognise, construct and realise the vision of the face of God witnessed to in important parts of Christian tradition.

Conclusion

In the Gospel of John, perhaps the most visually imaged and conceptualised of the NT writings, seeing is a basic metaphor for knowing and being close to God. Arguably, it is a gospel about the reconstruction and reorientation of sight, itself a powerful analogy to faith.

In Chapter 1, the gospel writer suggests that in the past humans did not see God correctly – the creator Word was there, but was not recognised. In Jesus, God becomes physically visible and known. But even then, most people did not see him in the correct light; they continued to dwell in darkness and did not recognise the light. Jesus is the source of light and correct seeing, but his light simply reveals how badly humans see; for some, the light itself is a kind of darkness. Thus, we cannot see aright, and when we do see, we misunderstand and misinterpret. The light coming into the world reveals just how inadequately humans see; it casts a blinding shadow that confuses things further. The overall message seems to be that we did not see correctly, we do not see correctly, and when we think we see aright, we are deluded. In the light of Christ, seeing and sight are not what we think. Our vision was, and is, porous and faulty. In Jesus we do not get what we see, so our very ideas of seeing need to be changed. He comes to reform and transform our ways of looking at reality completely. We see and we don't see, we did not see before and, in some ways, we do not even see properly now. We do not know what appropriate seeing would be.[4]

This is perhaps a good theological context within which to conclude this book. I have argued that, in an era of faciality, somehow human and divine faces have been largely lost from conscious Christian theological and practical attention. I have tried to show that there are elements of Christian tradition that strongly support the quest to find the vision of God, the face of God, not just in the world to come, but in the present, material world. Part of the Christian quest can, then, be seen as helping to create, discover and attend to the face of God as glimpsed in and between human faces and bodies. Arguably, the faces of our fellow humans are 'the face and glory of God for us now'. It is, therefore, important for us to learn better how to recognise, interpret and appreciate the human faces around us. Bearing in mind the inclusive, shame-dissolving nature of the Kingdom of God, it is particularly important to gain competence in including the faces, bodies and persons of people who, in one way or another, are shamed and excluded by the kind of unthinking physical normativity identified by disability theorists and mediated by socialisation into particular ways of exclusive seeing. I have made some tentative, provisional suggestions as to how this might be done and how we might become involved in creative, potentially mutual 'responsive countenancing' and 'difficult seeing'. This work of seeing differently is potentially radical, individually and socially; as Ruskin observes, 'to see clearly is poetry, prophecy and religion, all in one' (Rowland 2012, 234).

The Gospel of John suggests that the matter of looking or beholding is not simple or straightforward. The image and essence of God and of our fellow humans is always elusive and represents an active search, not a final destination. The quest to see God face-to-face involves more adequate ways of seeing other humans face-to-face. This work is an endless calling to go out, to go beyond present ways of sensing and understanding. That it is important cannot be in doubt. It is the vision of God that is promised to Christians and constitutes their purpose and call. It seems that, as far as we are concerned, this vision really cannot be realised without all people seeing and being seen, face-to-face, materially and physically, not just metaphorically.

We live before the face of God, and the face of God lives within and between us. Helping to realise, create, discover and honour faces, human and divine, is one of the main things that Christians are called to do, and one of the promises that

---

4   This paragraph is based on insights purloined from an unpublished talk on John 1 given by Lewis Ayres in Durham in September 2011. I am grateful to Professor Ayres; I only hope I have interpreted his remarks reasonably accurately.

they are called to realise. It is our vocation to create spaces where we can appear to one another and to God so that God's face can appear to us. Blessed, then, are the pure in heart and the broad in vision, for with and by the grace of God, they will see God:

> Restore thine Image, so much, by thy grace,
> That thou may'st know mee, and I'll turne my face.
> (John Donne, Good Friday 1613. Riding westwards)

Bibliography

Abe, Kobe. 2006. *The Face of Another*. London: Penguin Books.

Abramovic, Marina. 2012. *The Artist is Present*. DVD. Directed by Matthew Akers. London: Dogwoof.

Altizer, Thomas. 1997. *The Contemporary Jesus*. New York: State University of New York Press.

Alves, Rubem. 1986. *I Believe in the Resurrection of the Body*. Philadelphia: Fortress Press.

Alves, Rubem. 1990. *The Poet, the Warrior, the Prophet*. London: SCM Press.

Appearance Research Collaboration. n.d. *Identifying the Psychosocial Factors and Processes Contributing to Successful Adjustment to Disfiguring Conditions*. London: The Healing Foundation.

Arendt, Hannah. 2006. *On Revolution*. London: Penguin Books.

Argyle, Michael and Mark Cook. 1976. *Gaze and Mutual Gaze*. Cambridge: Cambridge University Press.

Ashton, John. 2000. *The Religion of Paul the Apostle*. New Haven, NJ: Yale University Press.

Athanasius, St. 2011. *The Incarnation of the Word of God*. Palm Desert, CA: GrievingTeensPublishing.

Assmann, Jan and Albert Baumgarten (eds) 2001. *Representation in Religion*. Leiden: Brill.

Atkinson, Janette. 1995. Through the Eyes of an Infant. In Gregory et al. 1995, 141–56.

Attwood, Tony. 2006 *The Complete Guide to Asperger's Syndrome*. London: Jessica Kingsley.

Auge, Marc. 1999. *The War of Dreams: Studies in Ethno Fiction*. London: Pluto Press.

Augustine, St. 1972. *City of God*. Harmondsworth: Penguin Books.

Augustine, St. 1982. *The Literal Meaning of Genesis*. 2 vols. New York: The Newman Press.

Augustine, St. 1991. *Confessions*. Oxford: Oxford University Press.

Augustine, St. 2002. *On the Trinity*. Cambridge: Cambridge University Press.

Augustine, St. 2003. *Letters 100–155*. Hyde Park, NY: New City Press.

Ayers, Mary. 2003. *Mother-infant Attachment and Psychoanalysis: The Eyes of Shame*. Hove: Brunner Routledge.

Baker, Naomi. 2010. *Plain Ugly: The Unattractive Body in Early Modern Culture*. Manchester: Manchester University Press.

Balentine, Samuel. 1983. *The Hidden God: The Hiding of the Face of God in the Old Testament*. Oxford: Oxford University Press.

Barasch, Moshe. 1995. *Icon: Studies in the History of an Idea*. New York: New York University Press.

Barker, Margaret. 2004. *Temple Theology: An Introduction*. London: SPCK.

Barker, Margaret. 2011. *Temple Mysticism: An Introduction*. London: SPCK.

Barthes, Roland. 2000. *Camera Lucida: Reflections on Photography*. London: Vintage.

Batchen, Geoffrey. 1997. *Burning with Desire*. Cambridge, MA: MIT Press.

Batchen, Geoffrey. 2004. Ere the substance fade: photography and hair jewellery. In Edwards, Elizabeth and Janice Hart (eds) 2004. *Photographs Objects Histories: On the Materiality of Objects*. London: Routledge, 32–46.

Bates, Brian with John Cleese. 2001. *The Human Face*. London: BBC.

Belting, Hans. 1994. *Likeness and Presence: A History of the Image Before the Era of Art*. Chicago: Chicago University Press.

Belting, Hans. 2005. Image, medium, body: a new approach to iconology. *Critical Inquiry* 31, 302–19.

Benthien, Claudia. 2002. *Skin: On the Cultural Border Between Skin and the World*. New York: Columbia University Press.

Bentley, G.E. 2001. *The Stranger from Paradise: A Biography of William Blake*. New Haven, NJ: Yale University Press.

Berger, John. 1972. *Ways of Seeing*. Harmondsworth: Penguin Books.

Berger, Peter, Brigitte Berger and Hansfried Kellner. 1974. *The Homeless Mind*. Harmondsworth: Penguin.

Besancon, Alain. 2000. *The Forbidden Image: An Intellectual History of Iconoclasm*. Chicago: University of Chicago Press.

Betcher, Sharon. 2007. *Spirit and the Politics of Disablement*. Minneapolis: Fortress Press.

Bland, Kalman. 2000. *The Artless Jew: Medieval and Modern Affirmations and Denials of the Visual*. Princeton, NJ: Princeton University Press.

Bonhoeffer, Dietrich. 1964. *Ethics*. London: Fontana.

Bowden, John. 1988. *Jesus: The Unanswered Questions*. London: SCM Press.

Brilliant, Richard. 1991. *Portraiture*. London: Reaktion Books.

Brown, Richard. 1989. *A Poetic for Sociology: Towards a Logic of Discovery for the Human Sciences*. Chicago: University of Chicago Press.

Bruce, Vicky and Andy Young. 1998. *In the Eye of the Beholder: The Science of Face Perception*. Oxford: Oxford University Press.

Brueggemann, Walter. 1993. *The Bible and Postmodern Imagination*. London: SCM Press.

Brueggemann, Walter. 2009a. *Redescribing Reality: What We Do when We Read the Bible*. London: SCM Press.

Brueggemann, Walter. 2009b. *An Unsettling God: The Heart of the Hebrew Bible*. Minneapolis, MN: Fortress Press.

Bryson, Norman. 1983. *Vision and Painting: The Logic of the Gaze*. Basingstoke: Palgrave.

Buber, Martin. 1967. *On Judaism*. New York: Schocken Books.

Buckley, Michael. 1987. *At the Origins of Modern Atheism*. New Haven, NJ: Yale University Press.

Bull, Malcolm.1999. *Seeing Things Hidden: Apocalypse, Vision, and Totality*. London: Verso.

Burrus, Virginia. 2008. *Saving Shame: Martyrs, Saints, and Other Abject Subjects*. Philadelphia, PA: University of Pennsylvania Press.

Burt, Anne, and Christina Baker Kline (eds) 2008. *About Face: Women Write About What They See When They Look in the Mirror*. Berkeley, CA: Seal Press.

Butler, Judith. 2006. *Precarious Life: The Powers of Mourning and Violence*. London: Verso.

Bynum, W.F. and Roy Porter. 1993. *Medicine and the Five Senses*. Cambridge: Cambridge University Press.

Campbell, Colin. 1987. *The Romantic Ethic and the Spirit of Capitalism*. Oxford: Blackwell.

Carroll, Lewis. 1970. *The Annotated Alice*. Harmondsworth: Penguin Books.

Casement, Patrick. 2006. *Learning from Life: Becoming a Psychoanalyst*. Hove: Routledge.

Casey, Edward. 2007. *The World at a Glance*. Indianapolis, IN: Indiana University Press.

Chidester, David. 1992. *Word and Light: Seeing, Hearing, and Religious Discourse*. Urbana, IL: University of Illinois Press.

Christian, William. 1992. *Moving Crucifixes in Modern Spain*. Princeton, NJ: Princeton University Press.

Christian, William. 1999. *Visionaries: The Spanish Republic and the Reign of Christ*. Berkeley, CA: University of California Press.

Christian, William. 2012. *Divine Presence in Spain and Western Europe 1500–1960*. Budapest: Central European University Press.

Coakley, Sarah. 2002. *Powers and Submissions: Spirituality, Philosophy and Gender*. Oxford: Blackwell.

Cole, Jonathan. 1998. *About Face*. Cambridge, MA: MIT Press.

Cole, Jonathan, with Henrietta Spalding. 2009. *The Invisible Smile: Living Without Facial Expression*. Oxford: Oxford University Press.

Collins, John and Michael Fishbane (eds) 1995. *Death, Ecstasy, and Other Worldly Journeys*. New York: State University of New York Press.

Connor, Steven. 2004. *The Book of Skin*. London: Reaktion Books.

Coughlan, Geraldine and Alex Clarke. 2002. Shame and burns. In Gilbert and Miles, 2002, 155–70.

Cumming, Laura. 2009. *A Face to the World: On Self-portraits*. London: Harper Press.

Curtis, Kimberley. 1999. *Our Sense of the Real: Aesthetic Experience and Arendtian Politics*. Ithaca, NY: Cornell University Press.

Dalrymple, William. 1998. *From the Holy Mountain*. London: Flamingo.

Danchev, Alex. 2011. *On Art and War and Terror*. Edinburgh: Edinburgh University Press.

Danziger, Kurt. 1997. *Naming the Mind*. London: Sage.

Darwin, Chales. 1998. *The Expression of Emotions in Man and Animals*. Third edn. London: Harper Collins.

Davies, Paul. 1993. The face and the caress: Levinas's ethical alterations of sensibility. In Levin, 1993, 252–72.

de Gruchy, John. 2001. *Christianity, Art and Transformation*. Cambridge: Cambridge University Press.

Deleuze, Gilles and Felix Guattari. 2004. *A Thousand Plateaus*. London: Continuum.

Denery, Dallas. 2005. *Seeing and Being Seen in the Late Medieval World*. Cambridge: Cambridge University Press.

deSilva, David. 1999. *The Hope of Glory: Honour Discourse and New Testament Interpretation*. Collegeville, MN: Liturgical Press.

deSilva, David. 2010. Turning shame into honour: The pastoral strategy of 1 Peter. In Jewett, 2010, 159–86.

Dillenberger, John. 1953. *God Hidden and Revealed: The Interpretation of Luther's* deus absconditus *and its Significance for Religious Thought*. Philadelphia, PA: Muhlenberg Press.

Douglas, Mary. 1973. *Natural Symbols*. Harmondsworth: Pelican Books.

Duchenne de Boulogne, G.-B. 1990. *The Mechanism of Human Facial Expression*. Cambridge: Cambridge University Press.

du Gay, Paul, Jessica Evans and Peter Redman (eds) 2000. *Identity: A Reader*. London: Sage.

Dyrness, William. 2004. *Reformed Theology and Visual Culture: The Protestant Imagination from Calvin to Edwards*. Cambridge: Cambridge University Press.

Eck, Diana. 1998. *Darshan: Seeing the Divine Image in India*. New York: Columbia University Press.

Eco, Umberto (ed.) 2007. *On Ugliness*. London: Harvill Secker.

Edelman, Diana. 1996. *The Triumph of the Elohim: From Yahwisms to Judaisms*. Grand Rapids, MI: Eerdmans.

Edwards, Elizabeth and Janice Hart (eds) 2004. *Photographs Objects Histories: On the Materiality of Objects*. London: Routledge.

Eisland, Nancy. 1994. *The Disabled God: Towards a Liberatory Theology of Disability*. Nashville, TN: Abingdon Press.

Ekman, Paul. 2004. *Emotions Revealed: Understanding Faces and Feelings*. London: Phoenix.

Ekstromer, Ann-Sophie. 2002. Body Shame in Children with Bowel Disorders. In Gilbert and Miles, 2002, 171–85.

El Guindi, Fadwa. 1999. *Veil: Modesty, Privacy and Resistance*. Oxford: Berg.

Elkins, James. 1997. *The Object Stares Back: On the Nature of Seeing*. San Diego, CA: Harcourt, Brace and Co.

Elliott, John. 1992. Matthew 20:1–15: A parable of invidious comparison and evil eye accusation. *Biblical Theology Bulletin* 22, 53–65.

Elliott, John. 1994. The evil eye and the sermon on the mount. *Biblical Interpretation* 2:1, 51–84

Elliott, John. 1995. Disgraced yet graced. The gospel according to 1 Peter in the key of honour and shame. *Biblical Theology Bulletin* 25, 166–78

Ellison, Ralph. 2001. *Invisible Man*. London: Penguin Books.

Ellul, Jacques. 1985. *The Humiliation of the Word*. Grand Rapids, MI: Eeerdmans.

Etcoff, Nancy. 1999. *Survival of the Prettiest*. New York: Anchor Books.

Fanon, Frantz. 2008. *Black Skin, White Masks*. London: Pluto Press.

Finney, Paul. 1994. *The Invisible God: The Earliest Christians on Art*. Oxford: Oxford University Press.

Flannery-Dailey, Frances. 2004. *Dreamers, Scribes and Priests: Jewish Dreams in the Hellenistic and Roman Eras*. Leiden: Brill.

Ford, David. 1999. *Self and Salvation: Being Transformed*. Cambridge: Cambridge University Press.

Fossum, Merle and Marilyn Mason. 1986. *Facing Shame*. New York: W.W. Norton.

Foster, Hal (ed.) 1988. *Vision and Visuality*. Seattle, WA: Bay Press.

Frank, Georgia. 2000a. *The Memory of the Eyes: Pilgrims to Living Saints in Christian Late Antiquity*. Berkeley, CA: California University Press.

Frank, Georgia. 2000b. The pilgrim's gaze in the age before icons. In Nelson, Robert (ed.) 2000. *Visuality Before and Beyond the Renaissance: Seeing as Others Saw*. Cambridge: Cambridge University Press, 98–115.

Freedberg, David. 1989. *The Power of Images: Studies in the History and Theory of Response*. Chicago: University of Chicago Press.

Freeland, Cynthia. 2010. *Portraits and Persons*. Oxford: Oxford University Press.

Freud, Sigmund. 1985. *Art and Literature*. London: Penguin Books.

Frith, Uta. 2008. *Autism: A Very Short Introduction*. Oxford: Oxford University Press.

Fulkerson, Mary McClintock. 2007. *Places of Redemption: Theology for a Worldly Church*. New York: Oxford University Press.

Gavrilyuk, Paul and Sarah Coakley (eds) 2012. *The Spiritual Senses: Perceiving God in Western Christianity*. Cambridge: Cambridge University Press.

Gell, Alfred. 1998. *Art and Agency*. Oxford: Oxford University Press.

Gerhardt, Sue. 2004. *Why Love Matters: How Affection Shapes a Baby's Brain*. London: Routledge.

Giddens, Anthony. 1991. *Modernity and Self-identity*. Cambridge: Polity Press.

Giddens, Anthony. 1992. *The Transformation of Intimacy*. Cambridge: Polity Press.

Gilbert, Paul. 2002. Body shame: A biopsychosocial conceptualistaion and overview, with treatment implications. In Gilbert and Miles, 2002, 3–54.

Gilbert, Paul and Jeremy Miles (eds) 2002. *Body Shame: Conceptualisation, Research and Treatment*. London: Routledge.

Gilman, Sander. 1988. *Disease and Representation: Images of Illness from Madness to AIDS*. New York: Cornell University Press.

Gilman, Sander. 1993. Touch, sexuality and disease. In Bynum and Porter, 1993, 198–244.

Gilman, Sander. 1995. *Health and Illness: Images of Difference*. London: Reaktion Books.

Gilman, Sander. 1998. *Creating Beauty to Cure the Soul: Race and Psychology in the Shaping of Aesthetic Surgery*. Durham, NC: Duke University Press.

Gilman, Sander. 1999. *Making the Body Beautiful: A Cultural History of Aesthetic Surgery*. Princeton, NJ: Princeton University Press.

Glancy, Jennifer. 2006. *Slavery in Early Christianity*. Minneapolis, MN: Fortress Press.

Glasson, Barbara. 2006. *Mixed Up Blessing: A New Encounter with Being Church*. London: Inspire.

Goffman, Erving. 1968. *Stigma*. Harmondsworth: Penguin Books.

Goffman, Erving. 1971. *The Presentation of Self in Everyday Life*. Harmondsworth: Penguin Books.

Goffman. Erving. 2005. *Interaction Ritual: Essays in Face to Face Behaviour*. New Brunswick, NY: Aldine Transaction.

Gombrich, E.H. 1972. The mask and the face: the perception of physiognomic likeness in life and in art. In Gombrich, Hochberg and Porter, 1972, 1–46.

Gombrich, E.H., Julian Hochberg and Max Black. 1972. *Art, Perception, and Reality*. Baltimore, MD: Johns Hopkins University Press.

Gombrich, Ernst. 1977. *Art and Illusion: A Study in the Psychology of Pictorial Representation*. London: Phaidon.

Grealy, Lucy. 2003. *Autobiography of a Face*. New York: Harper Perennial.

Gregory of Nyssa, St. 1954. *The Lord's Prayer, the Beatitudes*. New York: Paulist Press.

Gregory of Nyssa, St. 1978. *The Life of Moses*. New York: Paulist Press.

Gregory, Richard. 1997. *Mirrors in Mind*. London: Penguin Books.

Gregory, Richard, John Harris, Priscilla Heard and David Rose. 1995. *The Artful Eye*. Oxford: Oxford University Press.

Gruzinski, Serge. 2001. *Images at War: Mexico from Columbus to Blade Runner (1492–2019)*. Durham, NC: Duke University Press.

Gurtner, Daniel. 2007. *The Torn Veil. Matthew's Exposition of the Death of Jesus*. Cambridge: Cambridge University Press.

Haberman, David. 1994. *Journey Through the Twelve Forests: An Encounter with Krishna*. New York: Oxford University. Press.

Hahn, Cynthia. 2000. *Visio Dei:* changes in medieval visuality. In Nelson 2000, 169–96.

Haiken, Elizabeth. 1999. *Venus Envy: A History of Cosmetic Surgery*. Baltimore, MA: Johns Hopkins University Press.

Hamburger, Jeffrey. 1998. *The Visual and the Visionary: Art and Female Spirituality in Late Medieval Germany*. New York: Zone Books.

Hamburger, Jeffrey. 2002. *St John the Divine: The Deified Evangelist in Medieval Art and Theology*. Berkeley, CA: California University Press.

Hamermesh, Daniel. 2011. *Beauty Pays: Why Attractive People Are More Successful*. Princeton, NJ: Princeton University. Press.

Hamilton, Peter and Roger Hargreaves. 2001. *The Beautiful and the Damned: The Creation of Identity in Nineteenth-century Photography*. London: Lund Humphries.

Hand, Sean (ed.) 1989. *The Levinas Reader*. Oxford: Blackwell.

Harrison, Nonna. 2010. *God's Many-splendored Image: Theological Anthropology for Christian Formation*. Grand Rapids, MI: Baker Academic.

Harrison, Peter. 1998. *The Bible, Protestantism and the Rise of Natural Science*. Cambridge: Cambridge University Press.

Hartley, Lucy. 2001. *Physiognomy and the Meaning of Expression in Nineteenth-century Culture*. Cambridge: Cambridge University Press.

Harvey, John. 1995. *Visual Piety: The Visual Culture of Welsh Nonconformity*. Cardiff: University of Wales Press.

Harvey, John. 1999. *Image of the Invisible: The Visualization of Religion in the Welsh Nonconformist Tradition*. Cardiff: University of Wales Press.

Harvey, Susan Ashbrook. 2006. *Scenting Salvation: Ancient Christianity and the Olfactory Imagination*. Berkeley, CA: California University Press.

Heathcote-James, Emma. 2009. *Seeing Angels*. London: John Blake Publishing.

Himmelfarb, Martha. 1993. *Ascent to Heaven in Jewish and Christian Apocalypses*. New York: Oxford University Press.

Hole, Graham and Victoria Bourne. 2010. *Face Processing: Psychological, Neurophysiological, and Applied Perspectives*. Oxford: Oxford University Press.

Hollander, Martha. 2003. Losses of face: Rembrandt, Masaccio, and the drama of shame. *Social Research* 79:4, 1327–50.

Hull, John.1991. *Touching the Rock: An Experience of Blindness*. London: Arrow.

Hull, John. 2000. Blindness and the face of God: Toward a theology of disability. In Ziebertz, Schweitzer, Haring and Browning, 2000, 215–29.

Hull, John. 2001. *In the Beginning There Was Darkness*. London: SCM Press.

James, William. 1981. *The Principles of Psychology*. Cambridge, MA: Harvard University Press.

Jantzen, Grace. 1984. *God's World, God's Body*. London: Darton, Longman and Todd.

Jantzen, Grace. 1995. *Power, Gender, and Christian Mysticism*. Cambridge: Cambridge University Press.

Jantzen, Grace. 1999. *Becoming Divine: Towards a Feminist Philosophy of Religion*. Manchester: Manchester University Press.

Jay, Martin. 1988. Scopic regimes of modernity. In Foster, 1988, 3–23.

Jensen, Robin. 2000. *Understanding Early Christian Art*. London: Routledge.

Jewett, Robert. 1999. *St Paul Returns to the Movies: Triumph Over Shame*. Grand Rapids, MI: Eerdmans.

Jewett, Robert. 2007. *Romans: A Commentary*. Minneapolis, MN: Fortress Press.

Jewett, Robert (ed.) 2010. *The Shame Factor: How Shame Shapes Society*. Eugene, OR: Cascade Books.

John of Damascus, St. 1980. *On the Divine Images*. Crestwood, NY: St Vladimir's Seminary Press.

Johnson, James. 2011. *Venice Incognito: Masks in the Serene Republic*. Berkeley, CA: University of California Press.

Johnson, Mark. 1990. *The Body in the Mind*. Chicago: University of Chicago Press.

Joppke, Christian. 2009. *Veil: Mirror of Identity*. Cambridge: Polity.

Jordanova, Ludmilla. 1993. The art and science of seeing in medicine. Physiognomy 1780–1820. In Bynum and Porter, 1993, 122–33.

Joyce, Paul. 2007. *Ezekiel: A Commentary*. London: T & T Clark.

Jungel, Eberhard. 1983. *God as the Mystery of the World: On the Foundation of the Theology of the Crucified One in the Dispute Between Theism and Atheism*. Grand Rapids, MI: Eerdmans.

Kellett, Stephen. 2002. Shame-fused acne: A biopsychosocial conceptualistation and treatment rationale. In Gilbert, Paul and Jeremy Miles (eds) 2002. *Body Shame: Conceptualisation, Research and Treatment*. London: Routledge, 135–54.

Kelly, Daniel. 2011.*Yuck! The Nature and Moral Significance of Disgust*. Cambridge, MA: The MIT Press.

Kemp, Martin (ed.) 2001. *Leonardo on Painting*. New Haven, NJ: Yale University Press.

Kemp, Martin. 2011. *Christ to Coke: How Image Becomes Icon*. Oxford: Oxford University Press.

Kemp, Sandra. 2004. *Future Face: Image, Identity, Innovation*. London: Profile Books.

Kent, Gerry and Andrew Thompson. 2002. The Development and Maintenance of Shame in Disfigurement. In Gilbert and Miles, 2002, 103–16.

Kilborne, Benjamin. 2002. *Disappearing Persons: Shame and Appearance*. New York: State University of New York Press.

Kirk, Kenneth. 1932. *The Vision of God: The Christian Doctrine of the* summum bonum. London: Longmans, Green and Co.

Kleege, Georgina. 1999. *Sight Unseen*. New Haven, CT: Yale University Press.

Koerner, Joseph. 2002. Icon as iconoclash. In Latour and Weibel (eds), 2002, 164–213.

Koerner, Joseph. 2004. *The Reformation of the Image*. London: Reaktion Books.

Korsmeyer, Carolyn. 2011. *Savoring Disgust: The Foul and the Fair in Aesthetics*. Oxford: Oxford University Press.

Kristeva, Julia. 1991. *Strangers to Ourselves*. New York: Columbia University Press.

Kuhnel, Bianca. 2001. Jewish art and iconoclasm: the case of Sepphoris. In Assmann, Jan and Albert Baumgarten (eds) 2001. *Representation in Religion*. Leiden: Brill, 161–80.

Kundera, Milan. 1991. *Immortality*. London: Faber and Faber.

Kunzl, Hannelore. 2001. Jewish artists and the representation of God. In Assmann and Baumgarten, (eds) 2001, 149–60.

Lakoff, George and Mark Johnson. 1980. *Metaphors We Live By.* Chicago: Chicago Univ. Press.

Lasch, Christopher. 1991. *The Culture of Narcissism.* New York: W.W. Norton.

Lash, Nicholas. 1996. *The Beginning and the End of 'Religion'.* Cambridge: Cambridge University Press.

Latour, Bruno and Peter Weibel (eds) 2002. *Iconoclash: Beyond the Image Wars in Science, Religion and Art.* Cambridge, MA: MIT Press.

Lavater, John Caspar. 1878. *Essays on Physiognomy.* London: William Tegg and Co.

Leader, Darian. 2002. *Stealing the Mona Lisa: What Art Stops Us from Seeing.* London: Faber and Faber.

Lemma, Alessandra. 2010. *Under the Skin: A Psychoanalytic Study of Body Modification.* Hove: Routledge.

Levin, David (ed.) 1993. *Modernity and the Hegemony of Vision.* Berkeley, CA: University of California Press.

Levinas, Emmanuel. 1969. *Totality and Infinity: An Essay on Interiority.* Pittsburgh, PA: Duquesne University Press.

Levinas, Emmanuel. 2006. *Entre Nous.* London: Continuum.

Lewis, C.S. 1956. *Till We Have Faces: A Myth Retold.* San Diego, CA: Harcourt Books.

Lewis, Helen Block. 1971. *Shame and Guilt in Neurosis.* New York: International Universities Press.

Lieb, Michael. 1991. *The Visionary Mode: Biblical Prophecy, Hermeneutics, and Cultural Change.* Ithaca, NY: Cornell University Press.

Lieb, Michael. 1998. *Children of Ezekiel: Aliens, UFOs, the Crisis of Race, and the End of Time.* Durham, NC: Duke University Press.

Lossky, Vladimir. 1983. *The Vision of God.* Crestwood, NY: St Vladimir's Seminary Press.

Louth, Andrew. 1989. *Denys the Areopagite.* London: Continuum.

Lynch, Gordon. 2012. *The Sacred in the Modern World.* Oxford: Oxford University Press.

Lynd, Helen Merrell.1958. *On Shame and the Search for Identity.* New York: Harcourt Brace.

MacGregor, Neil. 2000. *Seeing Salvation: Images of Christ in Art.* London: BBC.

Mack, John (ed.) 1996. *Masks: The Art of Expression.* London: The British Museum Press.

Magee, Brian and Martin Milligan. 1998. *Sight Unseen.* London: Phoenix.

Malina, Bruce. 1983. *The New Testament World: Insights from Cultural Anthropology.* London: SCM Press.

Malina, Bruce. 1996. *The Social World of Jesus and the Gospels.* London: Routledge.

Malina, Bruce. 2010. Anachronism, ethnocentrism and shame: The envy of the chief priests. In Jewett, 2010, 143–58.

Malina, Bruce and Jerome Neyrev. 1996. *Portraits of Paul: An Archaeology of Ancient Personality*. Louisville, KN: Westminster John Knox Press.

Malina, Bruce, and John Pilch. 2008. *Social-science Commentary on the Book of Acts*. Minneapolis, MN: Fortress Press.

Malina, Bruce and Richard Rohrbaugh. 1998. *Social-science Commentary on the Gospel of John*. Minneapolis, MN: Fortress Press.

Marion, Jean-Luc. 2001. *The Idol and Distance: Five Studies*. New York: Fordham University Press.

Mathews, Thomas. 1999. *The Clash of Gods*. Princeton, NJ: Princeton University Press.

Mauss, Marcel. 1990. *The Gift*. London: Routledge.

Maxwell, Meg and Verena Tschudin (eds) 1990. *Seeing the Invisible: Modern Religious and other Transcendent Experiences*. London: Arkana.

McCabe, Herbert. 2010. *God Matters*. London: Continuum.

McDannell, Colleen. 1995. *Material Christianity: Religion and Popular Culture*. New Haven, CT: Yale University Press

McFague, Sallie. 1987. *Models of God: Theology for an Ecological, Nuclear Age*. London: SCM Press.

McFague, Sallie. 1993. *The Body of God: An Ecological Theology*. London: SCM Press.

McFague, Sallie. 1997. *Super, Natural Christians*. London: SCM Press.

McGinn, Bernard. 1991. *The Foundations of Mysticism*. London: SCM Press.

McGinn, Bernard. 2005. Visions and visualisations in the here and hereafter. *Harvard Theological Review* 98:3, 227–46.

McNeill, Daniel. 1998. *The Face*. London: Penguin Books.

Mead, George. 1934. *Mind, Self, and Society*. Chicago: University of Chicago Press.

Melchior-Bonnet, Sabine. 2002. *The Mirror: A History*. London: Routledge.

Merleau-Ponty, Maurice. 1964. *The Primacy of Perception*. Evanston, IL: Northwestern University Press.

Merleau-Ponty, Maurice. 1983. *The Structure of Behaviour*. Pittsburgh, PA: Duquesne University Press.

Mettinger, Tryggve. 1995. *No Graven Image? Israelite Aniconism in the Ancient Near Eastern Context*. Stockholm: Almqvist and Wiksell.

Meyer, Birgit and Peter Pels (eds) 2003. *Magic and Modernity: Interfaces of Revelation and Concealment*. Stanford, CA: Stanford University Press.

Miles, Jack. 1995. *God: A Biography*. New York: Alfred Knopf Inc.

Miles, Margaret. 1983. 'Vision: the eye of the body and the eye of the mind in St Augustine's *De Trinitate* and *Confessions*. *Journal of Religion* 63:125–42.

Miles, Margaret. 1985. *Image as Insight*. Boston: Beacon Press.

Miller, William. 1997. *The Anatomy of Disgust*. Cambridge, MA: Harvard University Press.

Mitchell, Margaret. 2010. *Paul, the Corinthians and the Birth of Christian Hermeneutics*. Cambridge: Cambridge University Press.

Mitchell, W.J.T. 1986. *Iconology: Image, Text, Ideology*. Chicago: Chicago University Press.

Mollon, Phil. 1993. *The Fragile Self*. London: Whurr Publishers.

Mollon, Phil. 2002. *Shame and Jealousy: The Hidden Turmoils*. London: Karnac Books.

Moltmann, Jürgen. 2010. *Sun of Righteousness, Arise! God's Future for Humanity and the Earth*. London: SCM Press.

Morawetz, Thomas. 2001. *Making Faces, Playing God*. Austin, TX: University. of Texas Press.

Morgan, David. 1998. *Visual Piety: A History and Theory of Popular Religious Images*. Berkeley, CA: University of California Press.

Morgan, David. 1999. *Protestants and Pictures: Religion, Visual Culture, and the Age of American Mass Production*. Oxford: Oxford University Press.

Morgan, David. 2005. *The Sacred Gaze: Religious Visual Culture in Theory and Practice*. Berkeley, CA: University of California Press.

Morgan, David and Sally Promey (eds) 2001. *The Visual Culture of American Religions*. Berkeley, CA: University of California Press.

Morgan, David. 2012. *The Embodied Eye: Religious Visual Culture and the Social Life of Feeling*. Berkeley, CA: University of California Press.

Morris, Wayne. 2008. *Theology Without Words: Theology in the Deaf Community*. Aldershot: Ashgate.

Moser, Paul. 2008. *The Elusive God: Reorienting Religious Epistemology*. Cambridge: Cambridge University Press.

Moxnes, Halvor. 1988. Honour, shame and the outside world in Romans. In Neusner, Borgen, Frerichs and Horsley (eds), 1988, 207–18.

Muir, Ward. 1918. *The Happy Hospital*. London: Simpkin, Marshall, Hamilton, Kent and Co. Ltd.

Murdoch, Iris. 1985. *The Sovereignty of Good*. London: ARK.

Murray, Stuart. 2008. *Representing Autism: Culture, Narrative, Fascination*. Liverpool: Liverpool University Press.

Napier, David. 1986. *Masks, Transformation, and Paradox*. Berkeley, CA: University of California Press.

Nathanson, Donald. 1992. *Shame and Pride*. New York: W.W. Norton.

Nelson, Robert (ed.) 2000. *Visuality Before and Beyond the Renaissance: Seeing as Others Saw*. Cambridge: Cambridge University Press.

Neusner, Jacob, Peder Borgen, Ernest Frerichs and Richard Horsley (eds) 1988. *The Social and Formative World of Christianity*. Philadelphia, PA: Fortress Press.

Nicholas of Cusa. 1997. *Selected Spiritual Writings*. New York: Paulist Press.

Niehr, Herbert. 1997. In search of YHWH's cult statue in the first temple. In van der Toorn, 1997, 73–95.

Nightingale, Andrea. 2005. *Spectacles of Truth in Classical Greek Philosophy: Theoria in its Cultural Context*. Cambridge: Cambridge University Press.

Nunley, John and Cara McCarty. 1999. *Masks: Faces of Culture*. New York: Harry N. Abrams, Inc.

Nussbaum, Martha. 2004. *Hiding from Humanity: Disgust, Shame, and the Law*. Princeton, NJ: Princeton University Press.

Orsi, Robert. 1985. *The Madonna of 115th Street: Faith and Community in Italian Harlem*. New Haven, CT: Yale University Press.

Orsi, Robert. 1996. *Thank you, Saint Jude: Women's Devotion to the Patron Saint of Lost Causes*. New Haven, CT: Yale University Press.

Orsi, Robert. 2005. *Between Heaven and Earth: The Religious Worlds People Make and the Scholars Who Study Them*. Princeton, NJ: Princeton University Press.

Ortony, Andrew (ed.) 1993. *Metaphor and Thought*. Second edn. Camnbridge Univ. Press.

Orwell, George. 1983. *The Penguin Complete Novels of George Orwell*. Harmondsworth: Penguin Books.

Otter, Chris. 2008. *The Victorian Eye: A Political History of Light and Vision in Britain 1800–1910*. Chicago: University of Chicago Press.

Ouspensky, Leonid. 1992. *Theology of the Icon*. Two vols. Crestwood, NY: St Vladimir's Seminary Press.

Pagels, Elaine. 1982. *The Gnostic Gospels*. London: Penguin Books.

Partridge, James. 1990. *Changing Faces: The Challenge of Facial Disfigurement*. London: Penguin Books.

Pascal, Blaise. 1995. *Pensées*. London: Penguin Books.

Pattison, Stephen. 1997. *Pastoral Care and Liberation Theology*. London: SPCK.

Pattison, Stephen. 2000. *Shame: Theory, Therapy, Theology*. Cambridge: Cambridge University Press.

Pattison, Stephen. 2007a. *The Challenge of Practical Theology: Selected Essays*. London: Jessica Kingsley.

Pattison, Stephen. 2007b. *Seeing Things: Deepening Relations with Visual Artefacts*. London: SCM Press.

Pattison, Stephen. 2010. Shame and the unwanted self. In Jewett (ed.), 2010, 9–29.

Pattison, Stephen and James Woodward. 2000. Introduction. In Woodward and Pattison (eds), 2000, 1–9.

Pearl, Sharrona. 2010. *About Faces: Physiognomy in Nineteenth-century Britain*. Cambridge, MA: Harvard University Press.

Pelikan, Jaroslav. 1997. *The Illustrated Jesus Through the Centuries: His Place in the History of Culture*. New Haven, CT: Yale University Press.

Pegis, Anton. 1997. *Basic Writings of Saint Thomas Aquinas*. 2 vols. Indianapolis: Hackett Publishing Co.

Peperzak, Adrian, Simon Critchley and Robert Bernasconi (eds) *Emmanuel Levinas: Basic Philosophical Writings*. Bloomington, IN: Indiana University Press.

Perkins, Judith. 1995. *The Suffering Self: Pain and Narrative Representation in the Early Christian Era*. London: Routledge.

Perrett, David. 2010. *In Your Face: The New Science of Human Attraction*. Basingstoke: Palgrave MacMillan.

Perrin, Nicholas. 2010. *Jesus the Temple*. London: SPCK.

Pilch, John. 1984. *Visions and Healings in the Acts of the Apostles: How the Early Believers Experienced God*. Collegeville, MN: Liturgical Press.

Pilch, John. 1998. Appearances of the risen Jesus in cultural context: Experiences of alternate reality. *Biblical Theology Bulletin* 28, 52–60.

Pilch, John. 2005. Holy men and their sky journeys: A cross-cultural model. *Biblical Theology Bulletin* 35, 106–11.

Poling, James Newton. 2011. *Rethinking Faith: A Constructive Practical Theology*. Minneapolis, MN: Fortress Press.

Pollak, Seth, Dante Cicchetti, Karen Hornung and Alex Reed. 2000. Recognising emotion in faces: developmental effects of child abuse and neglect. *Developmental Psychology* 36:5, 679–88.

Porter, Martin. 2005. *Windows of the Soul: The Art of Physiognomy in European Culture 1470–1780*. Oxford: Oxford University Press.

Pseudo-Dionysius. 1987. *The Complete Works*. New York: Paulist Press.

Pylyshyn, Zenon. 2003. *Seeing and Visualizing: It's Not What You Think*. Cambridge, MA: MIT Press.

Rahner, Karl. 1979. *Theological Investigations Volume 16: Experience of the Spirit: Source of Theology*. New York: Seabury Press.

Ramachandran, V.S. and Sandra Blakeslee. 1999. *Phantoms in the Brain*. London: Fourth Estate.

Raphael, Melissa. 2003. *The Female Face of God in Auschwitz: A Jewish Feminist Theology of the Holocaust*. Abingdon: Routledge.

Ravitz, Jessiva. 2012. Saving Aesha. CNN.com. http://edition.cnn.com/interactive/2012/05/world/saving.aesha/index.html. Accessed 21 November 2012

Razack, Sherene. 1998. *Looking White People in the Eye: Gender, Race, and Culture in Courtrooms and Classrooms*. Toronto: University of Toronto Press.

Rivers, Christopher. 1994. *Face Value: Physiognomical Thought and the Legible Body in Marivaux, Lavater, Balzac, Gautier, and Zola*. Madison, WI: University of Wisconsin Press.

Rizzuto, Ana-Maria. 1979. *The Birth of the Living God*. Chicago: University of Chicago Press.

Robinson, Dominic. 2011. *Understanding the* Imago Dei. Farnham: Ashgate.

Rowland, Christopher. 1982. *The Open Heaven*. London: SPCK.

Rowland, Christopher. 2011. *Blake and the Bible*. New Haven, CT: Yale University Press.

Royal College of Surgeons of England. 2003. *Facial Transplantation: Working Party Report*. London: Royal College of Surgeons of England.

Rumsey, Nichola and Diana Harcourt. 2005. *The Psychology of Appearance*. Maidenhead: Open University Press.

Russell, James. 1994. Is there universal recognition of emotion from facial expression? A review of the cross-cultural studies. *Psychological Bulletin* 114:1, 102–41.

Russell, James. 2003. Core affect and the psychological construction of emotion. *Psychological Review* 110:1, 145–72.

Sacks, Oliver. 1985. *The Man Who Mistook His Wife for a Hat*. London: Picador.

Sanders, E.P. 1991. *Paul*. Oxford: Oxford University Press.

Sanders, E.P. 1995. *The Historical Figure of Jesus*. London: Penguin Books.

Sartre, Jean-Paul. 1969. *Being and Nothingness: An Essay on Phenomenological Ontology*. London: Routledge.

Sawicki, Marianne. 2000. Crossing Galilee: Architectures of contact in the occupied land of Jesus. Harrisburg, PA: Trinity Press International.

Schaff, Philip and Henry Wallace (eds) 2007. *Nicene and Post-Nicene Fathers: Second Series, Volume 5*. New York: Cosimo Classics.

Schaap-Jonker, Hanneke. 2008. *Before the Face of God*. Zurich: LIT Verlag.

Scheff, 1997. *Emotions, the Social Bond, and Human Reality*. Cambridge: Cambridge University Press.

Scholem, Gershon. 1991. *On the Mystical Shape of the Godhead: Basic Concepts in the Kabbalah*. New York: Schocken Books.

Scholem, Gershon. 1996. *Major Trends in Jewish Mysticism*. New York: Schocken Books.

Schore, Allan. 2009. *Affect Regulation and the Origin of the Self: The Neurobiology of Emotional Development*. Hove: Psychology Press.

Schussler Fiorenza, Elisabeth.1983. *In Memory of Her*. New York: Crossroad.

Scruton, Roger. 2012. *The Face of God*. London: Continuum.

Searles, Harold. 1984. The role of the analyst's facial expressions in psychoanalysis and psychoanalytic therapy. *International Journal of Psychoanalytic Psychotherapy* 10:47–73.

Segal, Alan. 1990. *Paul the Convert: The Apostolate and Apostasy of Saul the Pharisee*. New Haven, CT: Yale University Press.

Sennett, Richard. 1986. *The Fall of Public Man*. London: Faber and Faber.

Sennett, Richard. 1992. *The Conscience of the Eye: The Design and Social Life of Cities*. New York: W.W. Norton.

Shults, LeRon and Steven Sandage. 2003. *The Faces of Forgiveness: Searching for Wholeness and Salvation*. Grand Rapids, MI: Baker Academic.

Sobieszek, Robert. 1999. *Ghost in the Shell: Photography and the Human Soul 1850–2000*. Cambridge, MA: MIT Press.

Soussloff, Catherine. 2006. *The Subject in Art: Portraiture and the Birth of the Modern*. Durham, NC: Duke University Press.

Stephens, Mitchell. 1998. *The Rise of the Image and the Fall of the Word*. New York: Oxford University Press.

Strathern, Marilyn. 1988. *The Gender of the Gift*. Berkeley, CA: University of California Press.

Stern, Daniel. 1985. *The Interpersonal World of the Infant*. Np: Basic Books.

Stern, Daniel. 1998. *Diary of a Baby: What Your Child Sees, Feels, and Experiences*. New York: Basic Books.

Stern, Daniel. 2002. *The First Relationship: Infant and Mother*. Cambridge, MA: Harvard University Press.

Stoller, Paul. 1997. *Sensuous Scholarship*. Philadelphia, PA: University of Pennsylvania Press.

Strathern, Marilyn. 1988. *The Gender of the Gift*. Berkeley, CA: University of California Press.

Sturken, Marita and Lisa Cartwright. 2001. *Practices of Looking: An Introduction to Visual Culture*. Oxford: Oxford University Press.

Swinton, John. 2012. *Dementia: Living in the Memories of God*. Grand Rapids, MI: Eerdmans.

Synnott, Anthony. 1989. Truth and goodness, mirrors and masks – Part 1: A sociology of beauty and the face. *British Journal of Sociology* 40:4, 607–36.

Synnott, Anthony. 1990. Truth and goodness, mirrors and masks – Part 2: A sociology of beauty and the face. *British Journal of Sociology* 41:1, 55–76.

Synnott, Anthony. 1993. *The Body Social: Symbolism, Self and Society*. London: Routledge.

Taussig, Michael. 1999. *Defacement: Public Secrecy and the Labour of the Negative*. Stanford, CA: Stanford University Press.

Taylor, Charles. 1989. *Sources of the Self*. Cambridge: Cambridge University Press.

Taylor, Charles. 1991. *The Ethics of Authenticity*. Cambridge, MA: Harvard University Press.

Taylor, Charles. 2004. *Modern Social Imaginaries*. Durham, NC: Duke University Press.

Terrien, Samuel. 1978. *The Elusive Presence: Toward a New Biblical Theology*. New York: Harper and Row.

Tomasello, Michael. 2000. *The Cultural Origins of Human Cognition*. Cambridge, MA: Harvard University Press.

Trevarthen, Colwyn. 1995. Mother and baby – seeing artfully eye to eye. In Gregory et al., 1995, 157–200.

Trumble, Angus. 2004. *A Brief History of the Smile*. New York: Basic Books.

Tugwell, Simon (ed.) (1988). *Albert and Thomas: Selected Writings*. New York: Paulist Press.

Turner, Denys. 1995. *The Darkness of God: Negativity in Christian Mysticism*. Cambridge: Cambridge University Press.

van der Toorn, Karel (ed.) 1997. *The Image and the Book*. Leuven: Peeters.

Velleman, David. 2006. *Self to Self: Selected Essays*. Cambridge: Cambridge University Press.

Walker Bynum, Caroline. 1995. *The Resurrection of the Body*. New York: Columbia University Press.

Wandel, Lee. 1994. *Voracious Idols and Violent Hands: Iconoclasm in Reformation Zurich, Strasbourg, and Basel*. Cambridge: Cambridge University Press.

Watson, David. 2010. *Honour Among Christians: The Cultural Key to the Messianic Secret*. Minneapolis, MN: Fortress Press.

Wawrykow, Joseph. 2005. *The SCM A-Z of Thomas Aquinas*. London: SCM Press.

West, Shearer. 2004. *Portraiture*. Oxford: Oxford University Press.

Wiebe, Phillip. 1997. *Visions of Jesus: Direct Encounters from the New Testament to Today*. New York: Oxford University Press.

Wilde, Oscar. 2003. *The Picture of Dorian Gray*. London: Penguin Books.

Williams, Donna. 1999. *Nobody Nowhere: The Remarkable Autobiography of an Autistic Girl*. London: Jessica Kingsley.

Wilken, Robert. 2003. *The Spirit of Early Christian Thought: Seeking the Face of God*. New Haven, CT: Yale University Press.

Winnicott, D.W. 1974. *Playing and Reality*. Harmondsworth: Penguin.

Wittgenstein, Ludwig. 1998. *Culture and Value*. Oxford: Blackwell.

Wittgenstein, Ludwig. 2009. *Philosophical Investigations*. Chichester: Wiley-Blackwell.

Wolfson, Elliot. 1994. *Through a Speculum that Shines: Vision and Imagination in Medieval Jewish Mysticism*. Princeton, NJ: Princeton University Press.

Woodall, Joanna (ed.) 1997. *Portraiture: Facing the Subject*. Manchester: Manchester University Press.

Woodward, James and Stephen Pattison (eds) 2000. *The Blackwell Reader in Pastoral and Practical Theology*. Oxford: Blackwell.

Wright, Kenneth. 1991. *Vision and Separation: Between Mother and Baby*. London: Free Association Books.

Wright, Kenneth. 2009. *Mirroring and Attunement: Self-realisation in Psychoanalysis and Art*. Hove: Routledge.

Wurmser, Leon. 1995. *The Mask of Shame*. Northvale, NJ: Jason Aronson.

Young, Frances. 2007. *Brokenness and Blessing: Towards a Biblical Spirituality*. London: Darton, Longman and Todd.

Young, Frances. 2011. From image to likeness. Bampton Lecture delivered in Oxford March 8.

Young, Frances and David Ford. 1987. *Meaning and Truth in 2 Corinthians*. London: SPCK.

Zaleski, Carol. 1987. *Otherworld Journeys: Accounts of Near-death Experiences in Medieval and Modern Times*. Oxford: Oxford University Press.

Ziebertz, Hans-Georg, Friedrich Schweitzer, Herman Haring and Don Browning (eds) 2000. *The Human Image of God*. Leiden: Brill.

Index